AN
AMERICAN
JOURNEY

CAMPAGNA BOOKS
by JAMES ERNEST SHAW

AN ITALIAN JOURNEY
Celebrating the Sweet Life of Tuscany

AN ITALIAN JOURNEY
A Harvest of Revelations in the Olive Groves of Tuscany

AN
AMERICAN
JOURNEY

Travels with Friday
in Search of America
and Americans

JAMES ERNEST SHAW

CAMPANILE

First Edition

ISBN 978-0-9846585-2-7

The text in this book is composed in Giovanni

Cover by Roger Morgan
Cover design by George Foster
Interior design by Susan Knopf
Cover of the Colorado State Capitol by James Ernest Shaw

Publisher's Cataloging-in-Publication Data
Shaw, James Ernest, 1946 – An American Journey: Travels with Friday in Search of America
and Americans / James Ernest Shaw 1. United State (Midwest) – Description and travel.
2. United States – Traditions, social life, and customs. 3. Farming – United States.
4. Local Food – United States. 5. Farmers – United States. 6. Christianity – Current and
History. 7. Political Science – Current and History.

Campagna Books
http://www.facebook.com/Campagna

Printed in the United States of America

10 9 8 7 6 5 4 3 2 1

This book is dedicated to my family—
generations past, present, and future.
JAMES ERNEST SHAW

I want to acknowledge all the kind
and spirited people I met on
my American journeys.
This country is vast and beautiful,
but the fine character of the people
is what makes this great land
unique in the world.
JAMES ERNEST SHAW

Contents

Introduction   Summer of '62   1

One   Too Old at Sixty-five?   9

Two   Too Far Down the Road   29

Three   A Rhythm to the Days   43

Four   Getting on the Road Early   57

Five   One of My Own   71

Six   For Such As These   91

Seven   A Day Unlike Any Other   121

Eight   Probably Never Heard of Our Country   135

Nine   Main Street USA   149

Ten   Why Did I Not Know?   169

Eleven   Looking Back   181

Twelve   In Time of Trouble   293

Thirteen   Another View of Life   213

Fourteen   The Roots Still Run Deep   229

Fifteen   With No Frustration, Apology, or Embarrassment 255

Sixteen   A Giant Blue Bear   259

Seventeen   The Eyes of the World   267

Eighteen   Reflection   277

Epilogue   The Responsibilities of Freedom and Free Will   281

Afterword   A Broken Heart—A Battle Cry   301

AN
AMERICAN
JOURNEY

Introduction

A journey is a person in itself; no two are alike.
And all plans, safeguards, policing, and coercion are fruitless.
We find that after years of struggle that we do not take a trip;
a trip takes us.
JOHN STEINBECK

Summer of '62

The summer of '62 I was fifteen years old and feeling adventurous. John Steinbeck's *Travels With Charley: In Search of America* had captured my imagination, and I wanted to follow as best I could in his footsteps. He had traveled in a pickup truck and camper with his dog Charley as a companion. I planned to travel alone on a 3-speed bicycle carrying only a sleeping bag.

John Steinbeck began his trip in the shadows of New York City, on a ferry pulling out of Long Island Sound. My journey would begin from a small town in the middle of America—Hayes Center, Nebraska, population 248. Despite all the differences—in age (he was fifty-eight), in accomplishment (he was the author of some of America's most beloved and admired books, *The Grapes of Wrath, East of Eden, Of Mice and Men*), in wealth (I assumed he had plenty of money; I had next to none), I still felt connected to John Steinbeck, in temperament, drive, and ambition. I also noticed that our initials were the same, and had an "e" been added to Steinbeck's "Ernst," we would have shared the same middle name, Ernest.

John Steinbeck felt that he had lost touch with America. He felt that fame and big-city living had insulated him from the "real America" and the hard-working people he had grown up working with in the fertile fields near Salinas, California. He wrote about these people in books like *The Red Pony, Cannery Row,* and *The Grapes of Wrath.* I knew hard-working people, and therefore more about America than I realized. But back then, America was *out there,* somewhere beyond my small hometown, and I wanted to discover as much about it as I could.

In looking back, I now see that 1962 America was more like Mayberry R.F.D. than Woodstock. The Cuban Missile Crisis had not yet spilled onto the front pages of America's newspapers. The assassination of President John F. Kennedy which would sear everyone's mind into a still frame of horror, was still a little over a year away. That summer I was going to movies like *Dr. No* (the first James Bond film), *Lawrence of Arabia, The Miracle Worker, How the West Was Won,* and *To Kill a Mockingbird* and looking forward to putting my arm around my girlfriend, Lynda, at the next Elvis Presley movie. We did not yet know how much change was bearing down on us.

My hometown was similar to Mayberry, North Carolina, except we didn't have even one stoplight. We did have a sheriff, though, and enough colorful characters to populate our own *Andy Griffith Show.* One of those characters was my best friend, Rossy. Even though he was only sixteen, most of Hayes Center saw the other characters of our hometown through his eyes. He was like a cartoonist who could capture the essence of a person in just a few well-chosen pencil strokes. But Rossy's medium was nicknames. He had a pet name for just about everyone in town. He was especially good at choosing a moniker based upon some peculiar characteristic of the new teachers who would come to town every year to get experience in our little school before moving on to jobs in bigger towns. He also had nicknames for his friends. Ross gave me a couple of names but neither of them was ever mentioned in front of adults, so I won't mention them here either. I would have loved having Rossy join me, to get his perspective on my American journey, but he already had his driver's license and a car as well. In those days, you quit riding a bicycle when you turned sixteen.

The choice of where to go on my grand adventure was easy. The mountains west of Denver had become my family's vacation of choice. Each August my father's sister offered her cabin near Conifer to us. Late summer, just before we planted wheat, was the only time when the demands of our farm consistently gave us any time off. I finished up what was known in western Nebraska as *summerfallowing*, the preparation of the seed bed, knowing that even if it rained the very next day, I'd have ten days to two weeks before the weeds grew enough that I'd have to *rodweed* the fields again. And if it didn't rain at all, come September we could begin planting wheat right in that seedbed I had prepared in early August.

I enjoyed rodweeding. I knew I was getting something done. By the time I had circled the field, the weeds uprooted on the previous pass were already withered and dying. I also liked it because it was a field operation peculiar to our region. The chisel plow with a rod attached that cut the weeds off at the roots was invented and manufactured in nearby Stratton. It was also one of Dad's best-selling implements and one that I loved to put together when they arrived on the semis completely disassembled.

Dad agreed about the timing of my adventure, but he was dubious about my plans. No one from Hayes Center had ever done such a thing. He wanted to know how long it would take to ride my bike to Brighton,

Colorado where my aunt lived. I had no idea. The farthest I had ridden was to my married sister's place, nine and a half miles northeast of town, and back—a total of less than twenty miles. All I could tell him was that I thought I was up to it. If he was concerned about my safety, he didn't mention it.

We settled on a plan that put me on the road on Sunday, August 19th. The rest of the family would depart on Wednesday, giving me a three-day head start. If I found out that I couldn't ride that far, all I had to do was get word to Dad, and he would come along and pick me up. Coordinating such a rescue back then would not have been easy, but still it gave me a sense of security knowing that I had an option just in case the adventure was more than I could handle. Thinking back over that trip, I marvel at the lack of contingency plans I made. I had a tube repair kit and a tire pump—but that's about all. I had no spare tire. I don't even remember having a water bottle attached to the bike. But I do remember bringing along a transistor radio.

For my 2012 cross-country trip to Colorado, a fifty-year commemoration of my youthful enthusiasm and Steinbeck's inspiration, I was better prepared, especially for emergencies. For one thing, I would be traveling with a cell phone—my wife was a lot more worried about the adventure than my dad had been. America has changed a lot in the past fifty years—at least that was the presumption with which I began my journey—and I wanted to experience firsthand those differences. But if I hadn't promised to keep that phone with me, turned on, and volume up, twenty-four/seven, I don't think my wife would have let me go.

The phone gave her the comfort of knowing that if I had trouble I could call for help. She was also comforted knowing that if she, or one of our children or grandchildren, had an emergency, she could get in touch with me immediately, and if necessary I could pack up my bike and fly home. But the phone was comfort, not necessarily protection. Any time a cyclist leaves home, he knows he can be hurt—just a few weeks earlier, my twenty-five year old son had suffered a horrendous biking accident. I said good-bye to my wife with that realization firmly planted in my mind.

But the desire to once again take the pulse of America outweighed my fears. Steinbeck too was concerned about safety as he set out to get to know America again. He carried a rack in his truck loaded with "a shotgun, two rifles and a couple fishing rods" so as to attract as little attention to himself as possible—"for it is my experience that if a man is going hunting or fishing his purpose is understood and even applauded." I hoped to lessen the dangers of the open road by following rails-to-trails routes and choosing low-traffic-count roads with wide shoulders, even if following them increased both travel time and distance. My interest was not in speeding across America but in meeting and talking with as many people as possible.

The timing of Steinbeck's travels was not random. He wanted to discover what Americans were thinking in the months leading up to the presidential election of 1960, between Richard Milhous Nixon and John Fitzgerald Kennedy. And I wanted to find out what Americans were thinking in the months leading up to what many were calling the most important election of their lifetime, between Governor Mitt Romney and President Barack Obama. Steinbeck was often disappointed by the unwillingness of people to share their views about themselves and America, especially regarding politics.

I, on the other hand, had been surprised by how much the people I had met on my youthful trip were willing to share with me—and how hospitable they were. I attributed it to the fact that I was traveling by bike, not cut off from the world around me by the steel and glass of a car. I felt that people saw me as vulnerable and they were willing to allow some vulnerability for themselves as well.

Steinbeck considered himself an old man, and so did his wife. He had suffered a stroke a few years earlier and she was worried about him being able to handle such an arduous journey. But for Steinbeck the trip was a way to push back against time. And maybe the same was true for me. Steinbeck was fifty-eight when he drove away from his home on Long Island. I was sixty-five when I set out from our rented house in West Salem, Wisconsin. I was feeling the significance of the age of retirement and the supposed onset of old age. This journey may have been my way of saying I was ready for neither.

Steinbeck's route could be described as a quixotic counter-clockwise swing around the outer ring of the country—he headed first toward the far reaches of Northern Maine—into the heart of taciturnity. My route, although not cast in stone, would take me through four states where people were more open to casual conversation—three "swing" states (according to political pundits) and one state said to be firmly in the camp of Governor Romney. Wisconsin, where I was beginning my ride, had just witnessed a very contentious battle to recall its governor, Scott Walker. The national media had been focused on the recall election because of the importance of the vote to unions and its implications for the upcoming presidential election.

Steinbeck had planned to leave on Labor Day 1960, but Hurricane Donna delayed his departure three weeks as he dealt with the destruction wreaked upon his home and the community of Sag Harbor, Long Island. Unsettled weather was threatening the upper Midwest on Labor Day 2012, but nothing strong enough to warrant delaying my adventure. I was eager to get going—to see if Americans would still welcome strangers into their lives who travel about the country by bicycle, just as they had done fifty years ago.

I knew that Italians still welcomed strangers. In 2009 I had biked around Tuscany picking grapes and olives and the Italian people took me in wholeheartedly. If my experience in Italy can serve as a barometer, I can report that an old man riding a bicycle intrigues people. My bike flies an Italian flag, which helps people see me—and piques their curiosity. I love talking to everyone, but I have a special fondness for visiting with folks of Italian descent. Even though I'm Irish, and have no known Italian blood, I feel a strong affinity for Italians and their love of the land, conversation, and hospitality.

But of all the conversation starters traveling with me as I set out on my grand adventure, the most effective were the small tires of my Bike Friday. People young and old wondered why a man six foot three inches tall was riding a bike that looked like it should be outfitted with training wheels. That weird-looking little bike introduced me to most of the people you are about to meet.

I knew I wouldn't be traveling nearly as many miles as Steinbeck, but I allowed myself just as much time. He left in late September and got home seven weeks later in November. I was leaving in early September and was willing to stay on the road until cold weather overtook me, unless I too found myself succumbing to Steinbeck's malady toward the end of his journey. *"John got awfully lonely on that trip,"* his wife Elaine *recalled in a book she edited of Steinbeck's letters. "That was the main problem, I think, though it doesn't really come out in the book much. He was homesick most of the time."*

Loneliness led Steinbeck to let Rocinante, his truck, race back to Long Island like a horse heading for its barn. *My own journey started long before I left, and was over before I returned. The miles rolled underneath me unacknowledged* Steinbeck wrote in the final chapters as he bypassed America at five hundred-plus miles a day in his sprint from New Orleans to New York.

Steinbeck traveled more than ten thousand miles. I traveled a tenth of that distance. Steinbeck knew the results of the 1960 election before he finished writing *Travels with Charley.* I knew the results of the 2012 election before I finished writing *An American Journey.*

I wanted to know what Americans were worried about in 2012, and I didn't want their concerns passed through the sieve of the media. I wanted to talk to Americans in their hometowns and on their main streets. I wanted to listen to Americans in ways I had not done for many years and use that information to take what I hoped would be a fresh and discerning look at our country today by comparing it to the America of my youth. And I wanted to do it before Americans had chosen which fork in the road they were going to take. This book is a reflection of what I remember and journaled about the America of 1962, and what Steinbeck wrote of his 1960 journey, juxtaposed against my assessment of America as voiced to me by the people I met on my own American journey in the fall of 2012.

Join me on my odyssey as I introduce you to the people who introduced themselves to me as I rode across America's heartland at just a few miles an hour. My hope is that their stories are your stories and that they are America's stories. The older I get, the more strongly I believe that stories are more useful than statistics or polls in discovering the true character of a country. I believe that the stories Italians told me helped me to better understand Italians, and I was betting, as I set out on my adventure, that the stories that Americans would tell me would help me to better understand my own country as well.

James Ernest Shaw
Phantom Lake
July 4, 2013

Chapter One

One of the most important days of my life
was the day I learned to ride a bicycle.
MICHAEL PALIN

Too Old at Sixty-five?

John Steinbeck began *Travels with Charley* wondering whether he would ever outgrow his *urge to be someplace else.* Those words resonated with the fifteen-year-old farm boy I was in 1962. I too wanted to be someplace else. I felt John Steinbeck was speaking to me when he wrote of setting off in his heavy-duty pickup truck with a custom-made camper on a journey *in search of America.* I liked that phrase—it stoked the fires of adventure burning in my soul.

And so late that summer, a few weeks after reading Steinbeck's book, I set out on my own grand adventure—riding my bike from my hometown of Hayes Center, Nebraska across the plains of southwestern Nebraska and eastern Colorado to my aunt and uncle's home in the foothills of the Rockies. That ride didn't end up satisfying my thirst for adventure;

it only whetted it—I spent my adult years producing adventure films all over the world.

I have a lifetime of wonderful memories from those years, but my appetite for adventure still has not been satisfied. As I started this new adventure, however, my wife was worried that, at sixty-five, I was too old to be hopping on a bike and riding five times farther than I had ridden when I was fifteen. She also knew that people can get hurt riding a bike. A few weeks earlier she had said good-bye to me and our son Jonathan as we left for a day's ride through the Ocooch Mountains of Wisconsin. The next time she saw us was in surgery at the Hillsboro hospital. Normally a cyclist only suffers a skinned elbow and some embarrassment when he can't free his bike shoe from his pedal and topples over. But during his slow-motion fall Jon suffered the worst gash I have ever seen—a cut so deep and so long in his calf that even the emergency room personnel were stunned and looked away. But thanks to a skillful surgeon Jonathan's muscles and tendons and flesh were sewn back together and within a few days Jon was hobbling around on crutches.

When I saw the gash in Jon's leg, I impulsively reached for the technology of 2012—my cell phone. But as I was punching in the numbers I asked, *WHY? An ambulance will take at least a half hour to get here. Jon doesn't need to lie here bleeding that long.* I shut off the phone and turned to the technology of 1962. I flagged down the first vehicle I saw, which happened to be a pickup driven by two cowboys—two wise young men who had been hurt themselves and had seen others hurt—and that's how Jon and I got to the hospital quickly and efficiently and calmly. Those strangers told us stories of other injuries they had seen, cuts and gashes that didn't remain cuts and gashes, but had turned into scars—scars that chicks dig Jon was told. And that put a smile on Jon's face—and his dad's too. And those smiles made it possible for us to look past that awful moment and get a glance of a better future.

Even though the cell phone played no part in getting Jonathan to the hospital, it did play a part in getting word to my wife that Jon had been hurt—she was able to arrive at the hospital almost as quickly as we did. And that contact with the world was what gave her the peace of mind to let me take off on my quixotic adventure.

That technological advance, more than any other, represents to me the most significant difference between my bike ride of 1962 and my bike ride of 2012. But in going *in search of America* as John Steinbeck did on his epic journey I wanted to discover what else had changed in the intervening fifty years and what, if anything, was still essentially the same about America. In 1962 I had learned that a person traveling by bike was welcomed by strangers and I hoped that was still true today. America, I think it is safe to say, is now more susceptible to violence. However, one of the most vivid memories of my childhood is the terror that gripped my home state during the five-week murder spree of Charles Starkweather of Lincoln who, accompanied by his fourteen-year old girlfriend, killed eleven people on their five hundred mile rampage across Nebraska before they were captured just across the border in Wyoming in January 1958. Those terror-filled days were so memorable because they were so rare. Sadly today, killing sprees are not rare. And I feared that Americans might no longer be as friendly or hospitable as I had found them to be when I was a teenager.

On the day after Labor Day, with America in the midst of the presidential campaign, I pulled out of West Salem, Wisconsin bound for the mountains of Colorado. Between Wisconsin and Colorado lie the states of Iowa and Nebraska. Of those four states, only Nebraska seemed decidedly for Governor Romney. Wisconsin, Iowa, and Colorado were all listed as "swing states." I mention this to place in context the many conversations I overhead in the mom-and-pop cafés as I worked my way across the heartland. Americans were engaged, not only about the election, but also about the future of America because of concerns about the nation's debt and our sluggish economy.

My concerns though, the morning of my departure, were on the immediate future. I was focused on ensuring that I wasn't carrying anything I wouldn't need. Cyclists hate carrying extra weight. With memories of all my previous mistakes in mind, I tried to pack only the essentials in the Samsonite suitcase that holds my bike when flying and doubles as a trailer when biking. I did, however, finally decide to pack a sleeping bag, an insulated inflatable mattress, and a small tent. I knew I wouldn't need them often but I wanted the insurance of having a place to sleep if necessary—for those times when I wasn't staying with a friend, or renting a motel room, or on those nights when nothing better presented itself.

I zeroed my trip meter, made note of the mileage, (1918 miles—half of which I had ridden in Italy three years earlier), and pushed off on my 21-gear Bike Friday just before nine o'clock in the morning. I had decided to ride a rails-to-trails route for at least the first day and possibly longer. A thick fog hung over the valley that morning. Riding on the trail meant I wouldn't have to worry that a driver of a car or a truck wouldn't see me. Trails are less interesting than roads because the grade is moderate, and in Wisconsin the route is often through a tunnel of trees, but on this morning safety was my most pressing concern. I had also decided not to leave Wisconsin immediately—I love the state and wanted to experience more of it. The Mississippi River was less than an hour's ride west of my home, but when I reached the trail I turned east. My itinerary was very loose. I planned to let circumstances, weather, and the general flow of the day tell me what to do and where to go, and most importantly, who to spend time talking with.

I have found over the years that when you set out in the morning with a specific agenda—such as how many miles you expect to ride—or you have made a decision about what town you plan to sleep in that night, spontaneity is lost and your adventure suffers. Letting each day unfold naturally would be my *modus operandi*—at least that was what I began the trip telling myself.

Focusing on miles biked also prevents a rider from stopping to take photos, and I vowed as well to not let that happen. I wanted pictures of this trip. On my ride through Tuscany three years earlier I had carried a camera, but on this trip I carried only a phone—a phone that takes pictures as good as those taken by any camera I have owned in my life—and as a professional cinematographer and photographer I have owned some good cameras. But my recently purchased Galaxy III, which slipped easily into the side pocket of my handlebar bag, gave me the capability to bring back as many photos as I could find time to stop and take, and to do it without the additional expense of film and processing. As a professional filmmaker, I find this technological advance simply incredible—almost on par with the fact that I would be able to be in constant contact with my wife.

As I kissed Mardi good-bye and biked away from our early twentieth-century-era Victorian home on the wide boulevard that is Leonard Street, I was pulling over three hundred pounds—three hundred thirty-four to be exact, two-thirds of which was me. I was about fifteen pounds heavier than I expected to be at the end of my trip—and a full thirty pounds heavier than I was when I had biked around Tuscany three years earlier. Contributing to my fitness then was a summer of training and competitive road racing getting ready for my ride around Italy. By the time that summer was over I had ridden more than six thousand miles. I wasn't in that good a shape for my American journey, having ridden less than two thousand miles for the year, but I felt I was fit enough to begin my journey.

Despite a slight headwind I was clipping along at thirteen or fourteen miles per hour on the trail's gravel surface. If I had been on my Orbea road bike I would have been riding much faster, but this was a respectable pace that if maintained for eight hours would easily net me one hundred-plus miles for the day. But miles were not my goal— people and memorable experiences were. Five miles from town, near Bangor, I met my first jogger on the trail, and heard my first rooster crow. A few miles later I noticed a sign designating the area as "natural grassland." I hit the brakes, parked Bike Friday, grabbed my phone, and walked back to take the first photograph of my journey. I discovered that the trail I was riding on was part of the Aldo Leopold Legacy Trail System, which would carry me to Sparta, Wisconsin and the beginning of the Elroy-Sparta State Trail. Wisconsin has an interesting history of naturalists who have been instrumental in preserving America's heritage. Two of America's most famous, Aldo Leopold and John Muir, have deep connections to the part of Wisconsin I was biking through, and I planned to travel at a pace that would allow me to absorb that heritage and that beauty.

John Steinbeck and Charley traveled through Wisconsin. In fact, he was traveling through the Wisconsin Dells region, the part of the state toward which I was riding, when he was moved to declare that Wisconsin is "the prettiest state I ever saw." Since he had heard about Wisconsin all his life and had seen photographs of the state, he wondered, "Why then was I unprepared for the beauty of this region, for its variety of field and hill, forest, and lake?" He went on to talk about the light he experienced the morning he drove though the Dells area: "I've seen that kind of light elsewhere only in Greece."

The first time I saw Wisconsin, my reaction was similar to Steinbeck's. I was a young cinematographer just a few months out of the U.S. Army working for a producer in Omaha, Nebraska, who needed shots of gorgeous farmland for a movie he was making about farming. He had a big budget and could have sent me anywhere in the country to get the footage. He chose Wisconsin. The company pilot and I flew right over Wisconsin Dells in the Beech Baron and landed in Stevens Point to rent a car so that we could go back to film all the gorgeous farms we had scouted from the air. At the time I had no idea that I would ever live in the state, but I did know without a doubt that this part of America possessed a unique beauty.

I'm still enchanted. Even though I've lived in Wisconsin over twenty-five years, I was in no rush to leave the state. By mile seven, my mind had settled into a relaxed groove. I was enjoying the quiet loveliness of the morning, my body was working comfortably, my heart was pumping at one hundred twenty beats a minute, pushing my *train* along the old railroad grade at an average speed of thirteen and a half miles an hour. My mind was flowing unfettered and took me back fifty years to that moment when I pulled out of my hometown on my big adventure. I was riding a 3-speed Raleigh Sports with a perfectly conformed Brooks leather saddle—every ball bearing and component on that bike cleaned, tuned, and aligned. I was not pulling a trailer; I carried only a sleeping bag, and a few extra clothes. I had very little money, no credit card, and zero experience riding cross-country. Except for having a well-maintained bike, I was ill prepared. But back then life was less threatening and I knew not how little I knew.

The fifteen miles to the first town, Palisade, Nebraska, flew by quickly with no incidents. I don't think I saw even one car on the road to Palisade that early Sunday morning. By the time I hit Wauneta, the second town on my route, I realized that my early morning estimates were way off. I was going to get to Imperial just after lunch instead of late evening. The fifty-mile ride went by so fast that I decided to go swimming. But after an hour in the pool I got bored and wanted to get back on the road.

Similarly, on my first day of riding across Wisconsin, I thought I might eat an early lunch in Sparta, but I got there so early that after filling my water bottles and chatting with Barb and Pete at the Sparta Tourist Center, I decided to go on. As I biked up and over I-90 and took up a southeasterly course, I began thinking about our conversation. I think it's fair to say that Pete was surprised that a man my age would bike to Colorado. He was a few years younger than me, in his early to mid-fifties I would guess, and it seemed as if he was trying to imagine himself taking off on such a trip. Barb, on the other hand, was a writer and was surprised that an author lived nearby. She was interested in my book, *An Italian Journey*, especially its journey to an agent and eventual publication. I'm always happy to share my experience—the barriers to publication are many and I love to offer whatever encouragement I can. Barb and Pete offered me a Danish left over from a morning board meeting and sent me down the trail with their good wishes and the recommendation that I would find a good place to eat in Norwalk, one tunnel and a dozen miles down the trail.

Between Sparta and the good lunch they promised, was my first encounter with rising terrain. It slowed my pace from thirteen miles per hour to just over ten miles an hour. I was enjoying following a trail and not having to think about traffic or even whether I'd be turning at the next intersection. I had no idea where I would sleep that night, who I was going to meet, or even whether I might get to Norwalk so early that

I'd ride on without eating. So far I was doing a good job of taking the day as it came.

The day was getting hotter. Sweat was beginning to drip from my chin. I had stripped to just riding shorts and my favorite short-sleeve biking jersey—a bright patriotic shirt from the U.S. Air Force proclaiming the benefits of staying fit. Suddenly the temperature dropped—a cool, moist wind smelling of freshly plowed earth was blowing straight down the trail at me. My first thought was that a cold front had overtaken me. The temperature continued to drop and the speed of the wind increased. The earthy smell finally made me realize what had caused the temperature to drop—that wind was coming from deep in the middle of a mountain.

I kept riding, and I kept enjoying the cool breeze, and I kept looking for the entrance to a tunnel that I was certain I would see any minute. But around every curve was another bend in the trail. I must have ridden over half a mile before the arched opening appeared. The wind had become so cold and so wet that I stopped at the entrance to pull on my windbreaker despite the fact that drops of sweat were still falling from my face.

I peered into the darkness and saw nothing but a speck of light at the other end—at least I thought I was seeing the other end of the tunnel. Signs warned that bikes must be walked through the tunnel. I couldn't imagine doing otherwise. By the time I had walked fifteen yards into the tunnel I couldn't see my hand just inches in front of my nose. The trail was pockmarked with small craters caused by dripping water. Even walking was unsteady.

A third of the way through the tunnel I began hearing voices, but could see no one. Finally, what I had thought was the other end of the tunnel became a faint glimmer from a flashlight. As I looked into the dark, taking soundings like a bat, I began thinking that within two or three minutes I'd meet up with the voices of the people I couldn't see.

I never did see the people. I just knew that I had passed them when the slight Doppler effect of their passing voices hit my ear, and the pinprick of light from their headlamp became larger, then passed by. I said hello to the darkness, and kept walking, kept feeling my way. Within a few moments I could no longer hear the people; their voices had been drowned out by the sound of water cascading from the ceiling. I had apparently passed the midpoint of the tunnel, if not in distance then certainly in elevation. The sound of the water flowing beside my feet had reversed direction and was now heading toward Elroy, just as I was.

During the long walk through the middle of the mountain my body cooled off completely. Emerging from the mouth of the tunnel and feeling again the warmth of the sunshine was the best part of the experience. It also felt good to be walking again on level ground and enjoying the feeling of being able to see. The experience made me realize that walking though a long, dark, cold, wet tunnel is a good way to combat complacency. It made me realize how many essential senses and gifts we take for granted.

After a half hour of stumbling along in the dark at just a mile or two an hour, that tunnel made me appreciate the speed of a bike. In less than the time it had taken to walk through the tunnel, I arrived in Norwalk. I had forgotten whether Barb and Pete had recommended a specific restaurant, so I rode up and down the main street looking for a large concentration of either bikes or cars. I found a half-dozen bikes parked behind Lil's, so I added Friday to the collection. Inside I found a bunch of brightly clad diners, a roast beef special and an all-you-can-eat salad/soup/dessert bar for $7.95.

I was looking forward to the chance to chat with other bikers and to get more recommendations on where to eat down the line, and what to do and see. An enthusiastic middle-aged couple greeted me when I walked through the door. Within moments I learned that they had recently picked up two bikes at a garage sale for fifty dollars for the pair. They were out enjoying the incredibly good deal given to them by someone who just wanted a garage with less clutter and didn't mind selling the bikes at five cents on the dollar. They weren't new to biking, but it had been a long time, and they were regretting the good times they had missed. Another brightly clad couple was eating lunch, but they weren't engaging anyone else in the restaurant, so I just said hello and left it at that. They soon left without saying good-bye to anyone. My approach to this journey is that I will share information about myself and/or my ride if asked, but my preference is to allow the focus to remain on the people I'm meeting, if they are interested in sharing.

The food was good. The place was a popular choice with locals too, but the buffet was geared toward cyclists. However, an all-you-can-eat meal poses a danger for a biker. The tendency is to focus on the calories burned and tank up. And I almost succumbed, because I wanted to "get my money's worth." Even though I ate slowly, I still felt a bit heavier in the stomach than I would have liked to as I left the café. However, within a few minutes the slight discomfort in my side was gone and I was biking comfortably along enjoying the day. The temperature was hot, topping out at ninety-three degrees. Sweat was again dripping from my chin and nose. I still had no idea where I would sleep that night, but bedding down without a shower was an option I didn't want to consider.

Early in his trip, Steinbeck also came to the realization that even though he was carrying his home with him, he occasionally wanted a shower at a *mom-and-pop motel* to get cleaned up. For my journey I had not budgeted enough to spend every night in a motel, not even close to it, but I had no doubt as the sweat continued to drip from my chin that my first night on the road I would not be camping if I could avoid it.

To get away from thoughts about the budget I might soon be blowing, I turned instead to thinking about the countryside. I was climbing again. The grade was gradual but steady, and I began realizing that the tops of barns were appearing below me. I was even looking down at the tops of silos. I was on fill dirt piled so high that I was riding through the upper branches of the massive oak trees that lined the old railroad grade. No longer was I in the fat-burning zone—my heart rate was up into the one hundred forty-some beats a minute range and the pedal cadence was near one hundred—I was now in the cardiovascular zone, but well below my red zone.

My mind was drifting through a wide range of thoughts when an explosion of wind spiked the hairs on the back of my neck. I looked up just in time to see the talons of a massive vulture swooping low over the trail, just a few feet above my head. The sight of that creature so close to me sent chills surging all the way down my spine. The vulture pulled up sharply to cut airspeed, then settled gently and gracefully onto a high branch of an overhanging oak. I stopped the bike and stared at him. He stared back before turning to look out into an adjoining field. I, too, looked but could not see what had captured his attention. I was thankful, though, that he was no longer looking at me. His stare was unnerving.

The humbling feeling reminded me of an encounter with a fox thirty years ago that still makes my back tingle when I think about it. I was biking from Aspen to my home in Emma, Colorado. I had just passed Woody Creek Tavern a few miles back. A slight tailwind was pushing me downvalley at speeds approaching forty miles an hour. I was a silent missile on that lonely curving road. About fifty yards ahead a lone red fox stepped nonchalantly out of the tall grass and onto the road. His relaxed gait told me that he thought he was alone in the world. The sudden sight of me bearing down on him made him panic. Instead of ducking back into the three-foot-tall grass and disappearing from sight, he began running down the road, darting from side to side—unable to make up his mind which ditch to duck into.

With each change of direction I got closer to him and the chills coursing along my spine shot all the way through my body. The whole scene began playing out in my mind in super slow motion. I was aware of our speed, but I was also aware of having a heightened sense of perception. For some thirty glorious seconds, as we sped down River Road with my front wheel only inches from his flickering tail, the whole world had been reduced to just me and that fox. Whenever I want to feel humble, I conjure up that moment and revel in the glorious feeling that passed between that animal and me. I don't know what that fox felt, but I felt a connection between us that I can describe only as otherworldly. *Peaceful* seems to be an odd word to use to describe something so full of energy, but it gets close to describing what I felt. Words fail the feeling of being so intimately connected to a wild animal—and it was only because I was on a bike that I could experience, ever so briefly, his incredible world of raw speed and agility.

A human can't run as fast as a fox, but by being so close to him, I felt I too was running that fast—and it was thrilling. Chasing a fox in a car would not have been the same. A similar situation might occur between a snowmobile driver and a fox, but the glory of the moment would be broken by the noise of the engine. But my silent pedaling action was keeping me only inches from that fox. As I looked down at the glistening hairs on his tail I felt closer to that wild animal than I imagined it was possible for a human being to feel.

Moments like these turned me onto biking when I was first old enough to venture out by myself and I was delighted that on my first day on the road I was once again experiencing the joy of encountering creatures so close that they were sending chills surging down my spine. Being close enough to a wild animal to gaze into its eyes is an unforgettable experience. I love the feeling of being overwhelmed with admiration for things that are beyond human understanding.

Another thing I love about biking is the frame of mind that traveling slowly puts you in. Part of the reason is that stops are necessary for water, for snacks, for "natural breaks." Those pauses become opportunities to visit with people. I stopped to fill my water bottle at the Kendall Chamber of Commerce Information Center and met Rose, who works there a few days each week. The conversation began with a throwaway comment about the weather and didn't end until we'd discussed most of the twentieth century and some of the twenty-first.

Rose told me stories of riding the trail I was following—when the rails were still in place. Back then the charge was seven cents to ride the seven miles to Elroy and the movie theater. A penny a mile, she always figured, but often she got to keep her pennies because the conductor got so used to seeing her on her Saturday excursions that he passed right on by her, but to her delight he never failed to ask her older brothers for their money. Those seven pennies that the conductor let her keep would buy a bag of popcorn and have two cents left over for candy, which she shared with her jealous brothers.

They saved none of their pennies for the return trip because the train would get them home too late at night, so their dad drove each Saturday night to Elroy to pick them up. Rose was revealing her age by the prices she was mentioning; I knew she was in a generation slightly older than mine. Popcorn was ten cents when I first started going to movies and the tickets were a quarter; Rose told me she paid only twelve cents. But Rose spoke of nickels, dimes, and quarters just as I did when I was a kid. Those coins liberated us. We were mesmerized by the big world out there that we only got to see by going to the movies.

Conversation, as it often does, made a big leap from childhood to the present. Rose had mentioned in passing a lifelong friend who had died. I'm always intrigued when people mention their friends. I sensed a story. I asked about their friendship. Rose began by telling me about a promise she had made long ago—a promise to take care of her friend's husband if her friend died before he did. Her beloved friend died in 1995, and Rose has been honoring her word and her friend ever since. As she reminisced about those years, I was struck by the power of love, friendship, and words. Had Rose looked so many years into the future when she made that commitment to her friend? Did she understand that seventeen years later she might still be taking care of her friend's husband?

She accepts no money, she grows and cans much of the food the two of them eat, and she prepares their meals. Her compensation is a room that she maintains in the house of her late friend and her husband. He was in his early sixties when she began caring for him—and now he is eighty.

"Who would take care of him if you weren't?" I asked.

"There's no one. I'm afraid his children would put him in a nursing home," Rose answered quietly.

As she told the story, I felt deep admiration for her. She didn't feel she was doing anything extraordinary, nor did she feel that she should be applauded for keeping her word. She was just doing what she had said she would do. I got the feeling she didn't think anyone should feel sorry for her either. She is of that World War II generation that all of America should be thankful for, not just those of us who are benefiting directly. We all have a great debt of gratitude to the generation that raised people like Rose. I have known some Roses in my life and I don't think it's going too far to say that Rose and the people like her made America great—and it's my hope that there are enough Roses left in America to reclaim America's greatness.

I had gone on the road hoping that stories like Rose's were still out there, but fearing that they might not be—that we were too many years away from the Greatest Generation. But here was Rose and she had crossed my path only six hours into my journey.

She didn't say why, but she told me she was going to break a rule she usually follows. "Normally I'm very politically correct—I don't mention politics or religion," Rose said, almost in a whisper. I looked around, expecting to see that someone had come into the center, but I could see no one.

"I don't mind," I said in an epic understatement. We had been talking for over an hour at that point—I was fascinated by her story and was full of questions. She delved further into the story of the man she was caring for.

"Even though his brother died of prostate cancer, they're denying him treatment for the same cancer that killed his brother," Rose said. "It made me so mad I began reading the Affordable Healthcare Act."

Upon initially meeting Rose I think few would consider her an alarmist or prone to hyperbole. You don't have be in her presence long to focus instead on her saintly qualities. But it quickly became obvious that what she encountered in the thousands of pages detailing Obamacare scared the hell out of her, although she used the word *crap*. She said the words quietly, cautiously, and with much consideration, but she is convinced that rationed care is the ultimate intent of Obamacare. And that the denial of services will be based upon the productivity to society of the insured—as Rose put it, "Care will be provided based upon some bureaucrat's determination of whether the insured has a quality of life worth paying for."

The language that pertained to handicapped children especially troubled Rose. It had now become obvious to me why she was breaking her rule about talking politics. She passionately feared the implementation of Obamacare, which she took great pains to point out, would be fully implemented by 2014 if Obama were elected. I had not given her any indication who I might be inclined to vote for, so I admired her spunk tremendously. Because of what she strongly believed, she was willing to clearly express her opinion—it was obvious that she was not going to be cowed by the *thought police* that George Orwell warned us about in his chillingly prophetic book *1984*.

If I had been more forthcoming, I would have said more than *I don't mind* when she told me she was going to ignore *PC* etiquette. I might have mentioned Steinbeck—I might have told her that I'd love to hear what she thought about what was going on in Washington. Steinbeck had warned me that I should not expect to find any Roses. *I came out on this trip to learn something of America. Am I learning anything? If I am, I don't know what it is.* Just one page later he again voiced his frustration. *I came with the wish to learn what America is like. And I wasn't sure I was learning anything.*

During my Italian journey I grew to admire the willingness of Italians to ignore conventional American wisdom—that neither religion nor politics should be discussed. Italians seemed to have no qualms about discussing either. I loved that Italians could have the most heated debates about either religion or politics, or even both, without allowing what seemed to be heated animosity to affect their general wellbeing or their willingness to be friends. Seldom is that the case today in America. When politics or religion is discussed, animosity often follows. But Rose was concerned enough that she didn't care. She had uncovered something that in her mind was evil, and she had accepted the responsibility of pointing out the dangerous road she felt Americans were traveling.

In a world where the opinions of others weren't demonized and dismissed, the most ardent supporters of Obamacare—no matter how convinced they were that only *they* knew what was best for America—would listen to a woman like Rose. The dialogue would have been helpful. I knew that I was going to pay attention to what she was saying because in hearing her story, and the way she told it, I was convinced that standing before me was one of the most selfless people I had ever met. It was obvious that her concern was not for herself but for others. I had heard enough of her story to know that she had been demonstrating sacrifice most of her life, certainly for the past seventeen years. And for that she deserved to be listened to. In fact I was sorry that I couldn't listen to her longer, but we had talked so long that it was closing time. Our conversation had begun mid-afternoon and it was now almost five o'clock. I had gone *in search of America and Americans,* and already I had learned what one American cared about—and cared deeply about—the preservations of our freedoms and a valuation of life, all life including the sick and the handicapped, and to her the implementation of Obamacare would be an attack on both. I said good-bye to her with regret, but at the same time thankful, that *the well had been primed*—that her willingness to talk boded well for the rest of the trip.

I stepped outside to find a huge black cloud bearing down on the town from the northwest. I had not planned to ride less than fifty miles on my first day, but if I continued on from Kendall it looked certain that I would encounter not only rain but high winds as well. At the edge of town I saw a quaint motel that obviously catered to bicyclists—a short path led from the trail right to the office. But on the door I found a note: "Gone shopping—will return soon," "Soon" was not defined, nor was a time written on the note. I surmised by the handwriting that the writer was a woman, and I also knew from growing up in a small town that by asking a few questions on Main Street I might be able to determine where she was shopping and how soon she'd be back. I might even be able to find her.

I rode back into town and stopped at the convenience mart. I quickly discovered that "gone shopping" most likely meant she had driven to Baraboo and that "soon" could mean an hour or two, but still I had no idea what time she had left. I checked the radar with my smartphone—it told me that I didn't have any options—the storm was bearing down on Kendall. It looked just as fierce electronically as it did in person, and it was only a few miles away.

So I rode back to the motel, pulled my bike and trailer onto the covered wraparound porch, and prepared to wait out the return of the manager or the arrival of the storm, or both. I had no idea whether any rooms were available, but only a couple of cars were parked outside of the rooms, so I settled myself into a comfortable rocking chair on the lee side of the building to write notes about what had been a memorable and promising start to my American journey.

I first began journaling in the fourth grade with daily *Dear Diary* entries in a little green journal I received for Christmas. But what had been a sporadic practice in grade school, high school, and college became a daily routine in the months leading up to my college graduation in 1970. During my years at the University of Nebraska I had written on eight-by-five note cards, but once I had my degree, I turned to a more permanent record and now have filled seventy-seven hardbound journals. When I began writing those notes I didn't know why I was doing it so faithfully. The thought of being a writer didn't occur to me until late in life, although I had written extensively of my childhood while stationed in Vietnam. Our small army unit didn't have an assigned office manager, so on a rotating basis we were required to staff an office that hardly anyone ever called, and no one ever came to, so we had little to do. When it was my turn, I wrote to pass the time.

And that's exactly what I did while watching the storm clouds approach. I've followed this practice no matter where I've traveled, and I am very grateful. My memory is fallible. When rereading my journals years later, I have discovered details and even whole episodes that are so unfamiliar that it is as though they had happened to another person. I have found this to be especially true when traveling. The sheer volume of new experiences coupled with the lack of restful sleep, often makes it impossible for my brain, and maybe the brains of others, to remember all the great stories that come our way.

For the next hour and a half as the sky turned black and winds battered the trees surrounding the motel, I sat next to the ice machine writing. I filled almost a dozen pages with anecdotes. I was enjoying recounting the day, but I was getting a bit nervous. As people came and went they confirmed that the owner wasn't shopping in Kendall, but in a nearby town. I also discovered that despite seeing few cars, the motel was quite full. I was beginning to feel that I might have to ask permission to pitch my tent on the lawn—and the only shower I would get would be the one I was going to have to sleep through.

But all my concerns slipped to the back of my mind as an energetic man from Iowa stopped by to get ice. He noticed my bike and he began sharing his love of cycling with me. He also told me that he was a frequent guest at the motel, that the owners were great people, and that he thought I had a good chance of getting a room. I relaxed a bit and turned the conversation to my cycling friend's fondness for this motel. I learned that he and his wife, Cheryl, enjoyed *geocaching* and that southwestern Wisconsin was their favorite place to follow clues to the *treasures*. That prompted a question that led to a story of the small company he had founded in his hometown that made it possible for him to take frequent trips to enjoy their hobby now that he was near retirement age.

I would not have guessed from his humble appearance and manner, but as our conversation caromed like a billiard ball from topic to topic, I discovered, even though he didn't directly tell me, that he was a member of the class that some are fond of calling the "one per centers." Jim had only a high school education and started his career at a motor home manufacturing company making $1.80 per hour. But he became convinced that he could "build a better mousetrap," and was now the owner of a manufacturing firm that employs almost fifty people. The number piqued my curiosity.

"Is there a reason you mentioned you have fewer than fifty employees?" I asked.

"You bet, and it's going to have to stay under fifty," he said.

"Why's that? You said business was going very well and that you had more orders than you could handle," I said.

"That's true. I'm going to have to raise my prices to cut down on the demand so we can handle it with the people we have now," he said as the rain and wind began hitting us.

"I don't understand," I said.

"It's Obamacare. My accountants and lawyers have looked at it and they tell me I'd be a fool to hire any more people right now," Jim said.

I was dumbfounded. I didn't see it coming. As the parent of a recent college graduate who has not yet found an adequate job, I was shocked. Here was a man with money to put back into his company, with a product that people obviously liked, and a desire to put people to work, but he was unwilling to take the risk because it would jeopardize his company and the security of his present employees to hire more people.

"Is this one of the unintended consequences of Obamacare?" I asked.

He looked straight at me and said quietly, "I don't think it is unintended."

While we watched the storm rage around us, Jim went on to tell me of all the battles he's been fighting with bureaucrats. He feels the policies as so wrong-headed and shortsighted, so devoid of common sense that he no longer believes that the damage being done to small business is unintended. Jim was so distrustful that he felt it was not outside the realm of possibility that Obama was willing to destroy America's economy to ensure that the federal government would some day be in charge of the nation's health care.

"What has he done that would make you think he really cared about jobs? His solution to just about everything is more government." Jim had answered his own question.

I had heard pundits talk theoretically about businesses sitting on cash, unwilling to expand, but here was a businessman, a soft-spoken man who seemed not at all like the stereotypical ruthless businessman, telling me that were it not for the recently enacted laws and policies of his government, he would be creating jobs for his neighbors in his community. Here was a man who was convinced that his government was at war with him.

On my first day on the road I had already met two people willing to share exactly how they felt about the political landscape in America. Steinbeck would have been envious.

For the second time within a few hours I deeply regretted that a conversation was ending, but Jim was heading out to dinner with his wife. While we were saying good-bye, the last of the storm blew through Kendall, treating us to a spectacular rainbow in its aftermath. Soon afterward the rain ended, and the sky began glowing, and a few minutes after that, the owner of the motel drove in and assured me that yes, just as Jim predicted, she did have a room for me. I snapped it up, and wheeled Friday into the room and began my nightly ritual of washing my biking shorts, jersey, and socks. I followed that with the routine of recording my mileage, adding notes to my maps, topping off my journal, and checking over my bike and trailer to ensure that they would be ready for another day of adventure the following morning.

Normally I would have lingered in the shower, slowly washing the day's grime from my body and soothing my muscles, but I wanted to watch the Democratic National Convention through the prism of what Rose and Jim had shared with me. Those two conversations colored everything I heard that night from the DNC. It is amazing how the perspectives of other people forces us, if we are willing, to take a fresh look at life. I had ridden only 44.4 miles but my journey in search of America was off to a promising—even surprising—start. John Steinbeck was discouraged by the unwillingness of the Americans he met to talk of substantive issues. On this, my first day on the road, the people I had met were showing a readiness to not only share their opinions, but to do it freely, and with great candor.

Chapter Two

A journey is like a marriage.
The certain way to be wrong is to think you control it.
JOHN STEINBECK

Too Far Down the Road

I began day two of my journey even more convinced that my adventure had gotten off to a good start. I discovered on the local morning news that my first day could easily have been a disaster. Tornados and fierce winds had buffeted a large portion of the upper Midwest. I had ridden into the heart of a major storm, but not so far that I had to take cover under a bridge or in a farmer's root cellar. I had allowed the day to have its way with me, and it had turned out just fine. In fact, the long conversation with Rose had protected me. I had let our discussion flow with its own natural rhythm, and that kept me in town rather than out in the open country when the storm hit. The miles for the day were few, but on the other hand, I was neither tired nor sore.

The two-hour wait for the owner of the Sugar Maple Inn to return could have been viewed as a major inconvenience, but it turned out to be icing on the day's cake. Because of that wait, I understood why at least one company in America wasn't hiring. My reasons for traveling by bicycle had already been justified. I most likely would not have met anyone like Jim or Rose were I driving across the country, and I certainly wouldn't have gotten into such a long conversation. I would have been five hundred miles down the road instead of fifty, but I would have known little more than when I began the trip.

I prepared for the second day's ride, just as I did for all my training rides, by eating a concentrated energy bar that converts body fat into fuel. I packed my suitcase/trailer, filled my water bottles, and pushed Friday to the trail. The rain of the previous night had wiped the slate clean. The gravel surface was ready for a new story to be written. Only one biker had hit the trail before me. I suspected it was Jim. He had told me he was an early riser, and the tracks he was leaving, like mine, began at the motel.

I followed that gently weaving tire track through the woods for five miles until it disappeared—a massive tree was blocking the trail. Jim had stopped, picked up his bike and hopped over the trunk of the tree. His track continued on the other side. I took a photo of the downed tree and posted it on Facebook so that my wife would know I had resumed my ride. Getting over the tree wasn't quite as easy for me. I had to unhook the trailer and lift it over the trunk, then clamber back over, grab my bike, and hoist it over the fallen tree. Once clear of the branches I set it down, coupled the trailer to the bike, and resumed following Jim's wandering track.

A few miles down the trail, less than a mile from Elroy, I came upon a tree that had been uprooted, but had not yet crashed to the ground. Its upper branches were hung up in a tree on the opposite side of the trail. I couldn't go around, and I couldn't go over. The only route was under. I got off the bike, leaned it to one side, and guided it under the trunk and through the branches—the whole time keeping a keen ear tuned to the slightest sound of cracking wood. Once clear of the tree, I began breathing again—and hopped back on Friday to resume my ride along the debris-littered trail.

I rode through Elroy and saw no sign of Jim. I did find a couple of apples on a tree overhanging the trail, so I washed them off and ate them while taking a break in Elroy's trailside park. I half expected to see Jim heading back to Kendall, but I saw no other bikers on the trail. I checked the map and concluded that if I kept making good time I would get to La Valle in time for lunch. I had often ridden through that tiny town on my daily rides from my beloved farm near Rockbridge that I'd only recently sold. I could, if I chose to head west out of La Valle, ride right past my farm and add very few miles to my journey.

Even though I had driven at least a dozen times through the low-lying land between Elroy and Union Center since moving to the La Crosse area, I didn't recognize it. The bike path was offset from the highway by only a couple of hundred yards, but the view from the trail presented a totally different picture of the marsh. What I felt not at all in the car I experienced intensely on the bike—the cacophony of sounds, the earthy, pungent smells, the numerous birds taking flight as I pedaled across the bog only inches above the surrounding water level. Regrettably, the trail was straight as an arrow, but it was efficient and pointed right at Union Center.

I rode into town, dismounted in the park to take a drink, and was surprised to see Jim just a few yards off the trail, filling his water bottles. I'd been thinking a lot about what we had discussed, from his love of bicycling in Wisconsin to his dilemma regarding his business. We fell into another easy conversation. I was intrigued to learn that he has nine grandchildren—all in the same school system. He told me he'd been thinking about the southern route I planned to take across Iowa and he wanted to make another suggestion—a northern route. He mentioned that he was a veteran of many crossings of Iowa with RAGBRAI—the annual ride that brings thousands of bicyclists to Iowa to party and ride en masse across the state.

Jim suggested crossing the Mississippi River at Lansing and riding Highway 9 across the state. He sweetened the suggestion by telling me the route went right through his hometown and that I'd be welcome to spend a night or two at his place resting and getting to know his part of Iowa. We parted soon after, but his recommendation began working on me. Each time I took a break that morning I pulled out my Iowa and Wisconsin maps and studied the route I had been considering and the route Jim had suggested. Jim's route, in addition to its other benefits, had the added attraction of being shorter.

Whichever route I chose, the decision was fast approaching. Beyond the town of Wonewoc, which I had never before passed though, lay La Valle, a village that was less than twenty miles from the farm I had hoped would be the one spot on earth where my wife and I would at last settle down and live out the rest of our days—a place where my grandkids could come and experience some of the freedom I had known as a child growing up in a small town. I was a bit envious of people like Jim whose grandkids live nearby. My wife, bless her heart, gave the farm a try, but she never quite came around to the idea of living out her days there, so in 2010 I agreed to put the farm on the market, hoping it wouldn't sell, or at least not quickly—but it did. The good news, at least for me, was that the new owners wondered if we wanted to rent the house back. And we did—until just recently.

Wonewoc turned out to be a delightful throwback to the mid-twentieth century—a great location for a movie set in post–World War II America. Change the highway signs and cue the cars of my childhood, and the director would be ready to shout, "Action." But I wasn't quite ready to eat lunch yet, so after taking a couple of photographs I rode down Main Street, jogged over to rejoin the bike trail, and kept going.

After an hour of delightfully easy riding on a post-rainstorm/ perfect-temperature-and-humidity morning, I pulled into La Valle and headed to what had been an independent gas station until a few years before. The Environmental Protection Agency had shut them down—demanding that the owners spend more money updating their underground storage tanks than they could possibly recoup selling gas in their small community, so they turned to selling sandwiches instead. I was glad that a recommendation had steered me toward the "gas station." I wouldn't have chosen it based on my previous metric of finding "the most popular place"—my bicycle was the only vehicle parked that afternoon in the gas lanes, and I was the only customer besides the owner's mother.

But the mushroom burger and salad combination I enjoyed that day at the Corner Café was absolutely delicious. Selling good food was not likely to replace the owners' lost income from selling gas, but still I admired their spunk—telling the government that if it was going to make it impossible for them to sell gas they'd find another way to support themselves and at the same time give back to their community. Bureaucratic overreach made me the beneficiary of a great sandwich, but such stories are troubling—the federal government dictating solutions for local communities—solutions that benefit big business instead of small towns.

I ate the burger outside on a picnic table set up in what had been the gas lanes and watched the pace of life in that rural community. Neighbors greeted neighbors and came and went from the small grocery store across the street, and a steady stream of customers entered two restaurants a couple of blocks away. I felt the frustration of business owners who felt that their government, instead of helping people make a living in a small town, was making it all but impossible by applying one-size-fits-all, bureaucratic, lacking-in-common-sense solutions. They thought that the EPA should realize that small towns and communities are part of the environment too, and deserve protection as well.

From that picnic bench in La Valle, it was only a dozen miles to the home of the farmer from whom I had bought my beloved farm nine years before. My thoughts went to Bill, a man I'd grown to love. He was a generation older than me, and reminded me very much of my father. He had recently lost his wife to cancer and would probably enjoy a chance to visit. Besides, I could pick up a part for my utility trailer that he'd offered to weld. All good reasons, even if heading to his farm was not the fastest route to the Mississippi River since I would be climbing out of one valley and into another. If I needed more proof that the shortest or fastest route should not be my guiding principle, surely Jim and Rose had given it to me. I made up my mind sitting on Main Street La Valle to abandon my pre-journey plans and head toward Bill's Cozy Nook Farm, which was also bringing me closer to the decision to accept Jim's offer.

Despite the number of times I had ridden that road, one aspect of those miles was unfamiliar. In the unincorporated town of Bunker Hill, a half dozen miles from my farm, is a biker bar (mostly Harleys) in which I had never once set foot. I had biked past it hundreds of times on my daily bike rides, but because I was never in need of a bite to eat so close to home, I had never stopped in. Today I vowed to change that even though Bill's place was only three miles down the road.

I had no need of food or directions, but I rationalized that for the price of a Pepsi and the investment of a bit of time, who knows what I might learn or who I might meet. The moment I stepped into that darkened interior, I regretted that this was the first time I had crossed that threshold. I immediately came face to face with a stereotypical Harley rider sitting at the end of the bar. He was big, bearded, and tattoos covered almost every inch of his massive arms. He introduced himself. He told me that the bar had probably been there long before Bunker Hill became a town. It was pure biker bar—ancient motorcycles hung from the ceiling and paraphernalia from every decade of the twentieth century covered the walls—the place was a quintessential celebration of the American entrepreneurial spirit.

This town, he told me, had humble beginnings. The Bunker Hill Cheese Factory became the Bunker Hill Post Office. Bunker Hill was never very much: a filling station, a blacksmith shop, but not much more. "Yeah, this is the big city of Bunker Hill. This is the original corner store and original bar. But now the population of Bunker Hill is, what, five or six—and I'm one of them."

He introduced me to Nikki, who I assumed was also included in that population. She had the look of having worked many years serving drinks—she stood behind the bar with such a feeling of belonging that once having seen her there, it would be hard to imagine Bunker Hill Bar without her. "What can I get you?"

"I'd love to have a Pepsi."

"You want me to fill your water bottles too? How about some ice?" she suggested with a servant's heart.

"That would be great."

"Hey Nikki, everybody, this guy's riding to Colorado on his bike and it ain't a Harley."

"COLORADO? You're kidding! On a bicycle?" And with that I was introduced to the half dozen folks at the bar. I was a little uncomfortable with all the attention directed at me, so I turned the conversation back to Bunker Hill by asking my biker friend about the gatherings that brought unbroken streams of Harleys past our farm twice a year. I didn't say it quite like that, but he knew what I was getting at.

"Noisy, and a little amazing, isn't it? That began as a group of maybe thirty or so bikers getting together for some music and drinking twenty years ago. And now it's a Woodstock-like extravaganza of bands, music, and beer for two long weekends—the second Saturday after Memorial Day and the second Saturday before Labor Day. Last year we had over ten thousand people here."

"Ten thousand! Did you say ten thousand?" I asked. No wonder the parade of bikes passing by our farm on those weekends seemed unending.

"Yeah, ten thousand—most come on Harleys, maybe sixty percent. But we had over fifteen hundred campers too. Thirty bucks gets you in— bring your bike, your camper, your tent, whatever, and start drinking beer and listening to music all day and all night long—it's just a big party. We have drawings—gave away two Harley-Davidson motorcycles and raised over fifteen thousand dollars for charity. What began as just a bunch of us music-loving, beer-drinking buddies getting together has turned into quite a deal," he said proudly, and I was certain that he played a big part in its success. He was a natural promoter—a born salesman—he could put together a good-sounding string of words, with not an "uh" or a "like" among them.

And with that he led me outside to show me the music stage and the campgrounds that he and others had built to handle the mass of people showing up in the "middle of nowhere to have a great time."

He proudly showed me the huge tumbler from which the names of the lucky Harley winners are drawn. "You can't believe how much we raise for charity every year. I love it." I was touched by how proud he was of his association with the event over the years.

I'm not sure he ever told me his name, but the next time I stop by Bunker Hill I'll remind him of our conversation. When we stepped back into the bar, I was surprised at how busy it had become in the few minutes we'd been touring the campground. As I finished my Pepsi, and gathered my stuff from the bar, a chorus of well-wishers throughout the bar implored me to be careful and be safe. I thanked them, and my hosts, tucked my very cold water bottles into my fanny pack, tipped Nikki, and stepped into the bright sunlight. I was only six miles from my former home, but I'd been introduced in the past hour to a world that for years I had just passed by. As John Steinbeck said in the introduction to *Travels with Charley,* you don't take a journey—a journey takes you. And I had definitely been on a journey from the moment I stepped into the Bunker Hill Bar—so near to my farm, yet so far away that I had somehow never managed to get there.

The ride to Bill's place was quick—just about all of it downhill. Bunker Hill is well named. These days you have little trouble finding the high ground in an area—it will invariably have a cell phone tower nearby, and Bunker Hill is no exception. The bike computer recorded a new maximum for the journey—over thirty-six miles an hour—a speed that felt totally comfortable because I knew the road well—what lay around the curves, the line to take across the bridges to avoid the bumps, even where I might encounter a dog.

I coasted down the long hill, through tunnels of trees, around the bends in the road, up and over the gentle swales in the valley, and pulled into Cozy Nook Farm. I was delighted to find Bill at home. I learn something interesting every time I stop by his place. Even though he is not much older than me, I am reminded when I talk to Bill just how much difference a decade or so can make in a person's attitude about America and about life. Bill's stories remind me how much I wish I had recorded the stories my father told me—both of them experienced a very different America than I did. On this day I learned that Bill's parents had once owned Bunker Hill Bar. His mother ran it for five years in the 1960s after Bill's dad died, until it became too much for her to handle on her own.

Bill and I moved on to farmer talk—the continuing drought, the changes the new owners had made to the farm I'd bought from Bill. I didn't tell him how much I wished I still owned his farm, but I think he knew how much I loved that land—in fact, I think my love for the land may have been a factor in his deciding to sell the farm to me. Bill recognized that love and was kind enough to help me build a cabin so that I had a place to stay each time I came to the farm during the two years before we were able to move into the farmhouse. Bill is known throughout the county for his willingness to work hard. What is not so well known is what a big heart he has. I have come to know a great man of the generation that lies halfway between my father's and mine, whose attitudes were shaped much more strongly by the *Greatest Generation* than mine were. I told Bill about Rose, and as I did I realized that Bill and Rose were probably about the same age.

"My farm," the farm I named Rock Ridge, lies only three miles from Cozy Nook, the farm Bill bought after he sold me his farm. I felt this might be my last bike ride to Rock Ridge. We had moved from the house a few months earlier but were still renting a couple of garage bays to store our stuff. I stopped by to drop off the trailer part Bill had welded. Even though I was feeling nostalgic, I no longer felt like hiking up to the high ridges of the farm. Corn was now being raised on that steep ground, and I no longer felt as close to it as I did when it was providing forage for my goats. It wasn't, I surmised, that I was no longer the owner of the land; it was a deep philosophical difference that troubled me. I felt that land was too steep to be tilled—so steep, in fact, that tractors have overturned on those hills and at least one farmer had been killed. But corn prices were so high that the temptation to grow corn was too great for the new owners.

When I contemplated selling the farm, I thought the day I took leave of the place would be extremely hard on me, but it was not. My attachment to the land had been broken by the changes my farm had undergone since I sold it. As I rode away those hills, I was looking forward and not back. I could not say with certainty where I would be living in twelve months, but it no longer pained me that it would not be on that farm. Considering how much I had loved Rock Ridge only a few years before, I found that remarkable. Whether it was wholly attributable to the fact that the beautiful sod had been broken and roads bulldozed across its hilly woodlands, I couldn't say. Possibly the publication of my first book had permitted me to think that I no longer needed to grow all my own food but could use the money I earned from sales of the book to pay local farmers to raise the healthy food that I had been growing on my land. I can't pin down the reason, but leaving was not the traumatic event I had feared.

As I biked away, an exchange between Isak Dinesen and her lover in the book *Out of Africa* came to mind. I frequently quote it when discussing with my kids their concerns about the future. "Do you know why God made the earth round?"

"No," he said.

She answered, "God made the world round so we would never be able to see too far down the road."

I had tried to see myself on that land for a very long time, but living there had not worked out. Now my future was looking very different—not necessarily worse or better—but demonstrably different. Life is like that box of chocolates Forrest Gump told us about. In fact this bike trip, I was already beginning to see, was very much like a box of chocolates. On this, just my second day on the road, I was already considering crossing the Mississippi River almost one hundred miles north of where I had originally planned.

I briefly considered asking the new owners of "my" farm for permission to stay in the cabin Bill and I had built up on one of the ridges, but I felt that would be looking backward, and that was not my desire for this trip—I was looking toward the future that I and America faced, whatever it turned out to be. My plan now was to ride to Richland Center, the town where we had "traded," where my youngest son went to high school, and where we had gone to church, but I didn't know what I'd do next—whether I would press on and camp along the Wisconsin River or choose a mom-and-pop motel room—the kind where you can pull right up to the room, or in my case, pull my bike and trailer right into the room.

I chose back roads instead of the state highway for the ride to town. It wouldn't be as easy or quick, but it would be prettier, calmer, and safer. While I was taking a photo of Friday in front of Steamboat Rock, a well-known landmark of the Pine River Valley, to let my wife know of my progress, a cycling friend happened by. He didn't recognize me, having never seen me on my fold-up bike, but I recognized him by his sleek steel bike—a yellow beauty that he meticulously maintained. He was surprised and a bit envious. I invited him to come along, but commitments prevented him from accepting my invitation. His life was not yet in the "box of chocolates" stage. He knew what his next few days would look like.

I, on the other hand, didn't even know how far down the road I would travel that day. I continued my ride to town reveling in the beauty of the river valley that I had called home for a half dozen years and the great biking that the paved roads of Wisconsin provide (almost all of the state's roads are paved). I pulled into town passing the hundred-mile mark for the trip with a bit of wind at my back pushing speeds into the twenty-mile-an-hour range. I had not told the local bookseller that I'd be leaving the valley, so I stopped by his shop. He informed me that a local food group had chosen *An Italian Journey* for their book club, but it turned out not to be such good news for him—most of the participants were Kindle users. My sales figures confirm what he was telling me. Electronic sales for some months are as much as five to six times those of print sales; the world is changing, and the publishing industry is confirmation of that change.

I had some daylight left, but before I pulled out of town I decided to stop by a good friend's shop to say good-bye—to tell him that although I would maintain our friendship, for now I wouldn't be seeing him each weekend in church. As I pulled up I noticed a "closed" sign hanging in the window. As I started to leave, I also noticed that a car that had backed out was pulling back in. The driver hopped out and said, "The door's unlocked, and Dean's still in there." Whether he recognized me as a friend or saw me as a customer, I didn't know, but when I later reflected on his action I was once again struck by just how much life is like that box of chocolates. If I'd arrived even fifteen seconds later, I would have experienced a very different ending to day two of my American journey.

The door was indeed unlocked, and Dean was focused on the computer when I walked in, but he quickly switched gears and turned his attention to me and my journey. I had told him in the spring that a long-distance bike trip was in the planning stages, but I hadn't seen him since leaving the farm months earlier. Without missing a beat, and displaying a sincere gift of hospitality, he asked if I would consider staying the night with them. "I'd love to if you'll let me take you and Susie out to dinner."

But when Susie learned of my offer she would have none of it. She had a freezer full of green beans, a refrigerator full of salad fixins, and potatoes in the cellar, and I was treated to a supper that reminded me of the great farm meals of my youth—all I could eat of garden-fresh food. I lost track, but at Susie's urging I may have helped myself to a half dozen helpings of green beans. They were that good and I was that hungry for fresh food.

Enjoying a meal with Dean and Susie reminded me of how much we lost when we, as a nation, quit growing our own food. Dean's garden, which he had proudly showed me before we sat down to eat, reminded me of the gardens that just about every farmer and town-dweller tended when I was a child—big, productive, and overflowing with goodness.

The idea that people couldn't afford the time it takes to grow a garden didn't gain much favor until about the time I went away to college. Farmers began realizing that the debt they were servicing required them to be plowing their fields and not a garden plot. As debt increased on farms, the "time is money" equation prevailed. No longer was there time on farms to milk cows, gather eggs, or butcher hogs. Eating at Dean and Susie's table reminded me of the garden economy of my childhood. It felt good to be among people who honored the simple pleasure of food from the backyard—*the gift of good land* as my favorite author Wendell Berry put it in his book of the same title.

When I began day two of my journey I didn't know how far I'd get or who I would meet. As day two was ending, I was once again marveling at the *chocolates* I had enjoyed. As for day three, I knew only that I was going to seriously consider Jim's offer to stay at his place. It would take me out of Wisconsin sooner, but I was looking forward to getting to know someone who had so many grandkids going to one school.

I checked the map and discovered that the Mississippi River was an easy day's ride from Dean & Susie's place. I had no intention of trying to cast my next day's itinerary in stone, but I did note that Marquette, Iowa, across the Mississippi from Prairie du Chien, was only sixty miles away from Dean's place—the same distance I had ridden since leaving the Sugar Maple Inn where I had met Jim only a little more than twenty-four hours earlier. I was amazed at how, in just two days, my journey had taken on a character and direction that I had not anticipated.

In the first chapter of *Travels with Charley*, John Steinbeck wrote of the need for planning when embarking on a journey, but he quickly added, "Once a journey is designed, equipped, and put in process, a new factor enters and takes over. A trip, a safari, an exploration, is an entity, different from all other journeys. It has personality, temperament, individuality, uniqueness. A journey is a person in itself; no two are alike. And all plans, safeguards, policing, and coercion are fruitless. We find after years of struggle that we do not take a trip; a trip takes us."

What Steinbeck wrote is so true, if we are willing to travel at a pace and in such a way that we allow the character of the journey to shine through. Toward the end of the book he wrote another truism: "In the beginning of this record I tried to explore the nature of journeys, how they are things in themselves, each one individual and no two are alike. My own journey started long before I left, and was over before I returned … the miles rolled underneath me unacknowledged. There was no night, no day, no distance. I must have stopped to fill my gas tank, to walk and feed Charley, to eat, to telephone, but I don't remember any of it."

My goal before I began this journey across America, and one that I reaffirmed at the end of my second day, was to fight hard the tendency to think only of my destination. Of his drive from Louisiana to Long Island, Steinbeck wrote, "I know the countryside must have been beautiful, but I didn't see it." He "bulldozed blindly" through hundreds of miles as he sped toward home. If he talked to anyone, he didn't write about it—except his conversation with a couple of police officers in New York City who helped him negotiate the tunnels and streets of Manhattan to find his way home to Long Island. His journey was over long before he got home.

My vow is to not let that happen on this journey.

Chapter Three

A good writer always works at the impossible.
JOHN STEINBECK

A Rhythm to the Days

I got a great night's sleep, and Susie and Dean treated me to another delicious meal—a breakfast full of stick-to-your-ribs energy from their garden and freezer. They asked about my route. I told them I was thinking about coasting along the Pine River to the Wisconsin River, which would lead me downstream to the Mississippi. To them that sounded like backtracking, and they were right. Following rivers was yesterday's consideration, when I didn't know where I would be spending the night. In getting to their place I had left the valley floor and begun the climb to the high ground south of Richland Center. *Why give up the altitude or the miles?* So I decided to stay with Highway 80 and take a more direct route to Iowa.

The long climb out of Richland Center reminded me why riding the rails-to-trails route had been so easy. On the trail the grade had never been above three percent. A lot of the grades on the routes I trained on near the farm were as high as ten percent, and many jumped to the mid-teens and even higher on the final climb to the ridge tops—pitches so steep that I had rarely encountered them in all my years of biking, even in Colorado. The grades on Highway 80 were more gradual than those on the county roads, but they still rivaled mountains roads. The saving grace of Wisconsin climbs is that they are much shorter than Colorado climbs. I reached the top of the ridge about five or six miles south of Richland Center and crossed from the Pine River Valley watershed to the Wisconsin River Valley.

I was now in "new" country, exploring roads I hadn't ridden before. With the high country behind me, I settled into a comfortable pace as the road snaked along the Wisconsin River, sometimes affording me a great view of the wide, sandy banks, other times cocooning me in a passageway of trees. As I crested a small rise, I glanced down the road and caught sight of an old man half a mile ahead shuffling along the edge of the highway, leaning on a walking stick with each step to steady himself. The man was on my side of the highway, walking against the traffic. Something wasn't quite right, but I couldn't figure out what it was. As I got closer, I was able to see that he wasn't casting a weird shadow—he was being followed by a wild turkey.

I pulled onto the shoulder about fifty yards before I reached him. He looked like a man with a story—a character who had led, judging by his chiseled features, a rather interesting life. I took some extra long swigs of water, hoping that he might want to stop and chat a bit. When he was close enough that it was evident that he was not going to be the first to speak, I greeted him: "Good day, sir! I see you're out taking your turkey for a walk this morning."

He narrowed his eyes, cocked his head slightly, and looked at me, but he didn't stop shuffling along.

With a dip of my head and eyes I indicated that he should look behind him. He turned his head, but not far enough to see the turkey.

He looked back at me, his head now cocked fully sideways, wondering why a stranger was trying to mess with him.

"There's a turkey right behind you," I said.

He twisted his body farther around, caught sight of it, and without breaking stride turned his eyes back to the road and said, "That's not my turkey."

He didn't turn toward me. He didn't smile. He just kept right on walking. The turkey, however, did stop. He cocked his head and eyed me for a second or two before determining that I was not worthy of further consideration and fell back in line behind the man.

I took a nervous drink of water, relieved that the old tom had not attacked, and turned to watch the two of them make their way slowly down the side of the road. I watched them for two or three minutes— long enough for them to pass over the hill. During that whole time, neither of them turned to look back at me.

It hadn't been much of a conversation, but at least I got the turkey to break stride.

However, I had learned nothing about the best bike route to the Mississippi, and my map wasn't helping either. So I rode into the little town of Blue River, hoping to find someone not quite so tight with his words—someone who could tell me whether I should ride along the south shore or the north shore of the Wisconsin River. And I found him under a sign proclaiming that *Broken Arrows* sells *A Little Bit of Everything and A Whole Lot of Nothing.*

But before I asked the man's advice, I introduced myself and asked him about the name of his business. "I just got tired of working for other people. I started out in flea markets and found out I could make a living at it. Did that until I got tired of the traveling, so I opened this shop. Things are going great. Just opened up another shop down the road in Muscoda. Don't have to advertise much—everybody knows we're here," Steve informed me as he led me around the store showing me a little bit of everything.

"I have over a hundred thousand dollars of inventory. I buy up estates, people bring things to me, and if the price is reasonable, I buy it—people are looking for good deals, a way to save some money."

By the time we had circled the store once, he had told me a lot, he had shown me a whole lot of nothing, but he still hadn't told me about the name Broken Arrows, so I asked again.

"Oh yeah, Broken Arrows is my grandfather's name." He noticed the quizzical look on my face. If a stranger were trying to figure out Steve's heritage, it would be a long time before Native American would be guessed. "My mother was Polish," he said.

"How long you had your beard?"

"Ever since I got out of the army. I've cut my hair and beard four times since 1971 for interviews—didn't get the jobs, so I said 'Piss on you—take me the way I am or not at all.' It finally hit me that everybody seemed to be choosing *not at all*, so I started out in flea markets with one little card table and just kept growing. I've had this location now for almost twenty years."

His wife, who had joined us on the stoop at the front door, added, "Nineteen years, eleven months—we opened on Halloween 1992. We're having a big party to celebrate. We'll be closing off the alley, filling it with caskets and 'dead' people, and body parts. Halloween is our favorite time of the year. Steve sets out here in front of the shop on Halloween dressed as a butcher, with a cleaver in his hand."

"It's the only time of year when I can wave a weapon at a cop," Steve chimed in before his wife continued.

"We don't have any normal people in our family. We're all a little off. If any of our girls ever get married, they want to have a Halloween wedding. One daughter wants to be the bride of Frankenstein, the other wants to be a dead whatever as she walks down the aisle. Friday the thirteenth is an awesome day for us."

Steve jumped back in: "When I got married I wanted to have twenty-two children. I only got to six, but I do have five grandchildren, so I'm getting closer." I took a picture of Steve, his wife, and all the children and grandchildren who were around that day. They invited me to come back on Halloween and play a dead man in one of their coffins. Forrest Gump is right. You never know what you're going to get.

Steve began talking again of his grandfather. I asked if he had a picture of him. He didn't, but he proudly showed me a drawing of himself in a headdress. "I'm Ojibwa, what the white man calls *Chippewa.*"

It was a fine drawing. I studied it closely. "That's a treasure," I said as I handed it back.

"If a piece of land was available, I'd head back to the reservation in a heartbeat, back to the red man's law and be done with all of white man's regulations. But there's nothing available. If I took my business up there, it would be a big help to the people. If I wanted to, I could be getting a check from the tribe, but I don't need it, so I tell the tribe to use it where it's needed. If ever I need it, I'll accept it, but for now I don't need it. I'm doing fine."

Talking to Steve that morning, I caught a glimpse of what the American idea makes possible. Here's a man who proudly admits that he and his family don't fit in, but they found a way to make a living and at the same time give back to their community by selling a little bit of everything—including food and produce from local farmers. Steve was showing me that the entrepreneurial spirit was alive and well in America, at least on Main Street, Blue River, Wisconsin. Steve didn't look at all like a businessman, with his scraggly beard, blue work shirt, and short pants revealing his knobby knees, but that's what he was—a hard-working man who wasn't happy about all the regulations his small business had to contend with, but at least for the moment, he had found a way to survive.

As I biked away from Broken Arrows, I realized I had gotten so engrossed in Steve's story that I'd forgotten to ask him on which side of the river I should ride. I had crossed over the Wisconsin to get to Blue River, so I decided to just keep riding on the south side. I noticed how dry the valley was and stopped to take a photo of the parched cornstalks lining the roads, but otherwise I remember little about the ride the rest of that morning. My mind had gotten into a groove, and nothing broke my train of thought. The stunted corn had reminded me of the drought plaguing much of America, and my mind just stayed there as my legs churned and drove me down the road. *Could it ever get as bad as the Dust Bowl of the thirties again?* John Steinbeck's novel *The Grapes of Wrath* came to mind. The movie, starring Henry Fonda, had changed my perception of the Great Depression. I grew up thinking that the stock market crash of 1929 and the depression that followed devastated everyone, but the stark contrast portrayed in the movie between the haves and the have-nots made me realize that lots of people still had money; some people had lots of it, and were getting richer as a result of the crash. And I'm sure that if our economy crashes, it will again be like that.

One of my regrets is that I didn't ask my folks about how the Depression affected them. The stock market crashed in October 1929. My mom and dad got married just over a year later, in December 1930. What must it have been like starting out married life when the country was falling apart around you?

My thoughts about the Great Depression and my folks carried me all the way to Boscobel. I rode down Wisconsin Avenue and asked the first person I saw to recommend a good place to eat. He asked me if I liked history. I told him that indeed I did—I'd been thinking about the Great Depression all morning. "Then you're going to like the Unique Café; its walls are covered with history. It'll take you right back to the thirties."

He was right—the walls were covered with photos and signs from the early twentieth century. A well-preserved J.I. Case sign from Racine, Wisconsin, was the first thing to catch my eye. A classic eagle-perched-on-the-globe sign, all six feet of it, hung on the far wall in the restaurant. It looked just like the sign that graced my dad's farm implement business throughout the fifties and sixties. Oh, how I wished I'd had the foresight to keep it, but all I have left from those days is a pair of coveralls with that same logo sewn on the back and my name stitched on the front. I treasure those coveralls; they were the work clothes I wore fifty years ago when I helped my dad in his shop.

Why hadn't I asked my dad as many questions about starting his business as I'd asked Steve? The signs throughout the café brought to mind memory after pleasant memory of my father. I was surrounded by the logos of the products my dad sold to the farmers of the county. Maybe that's what eternity is for—to ask the questions we wish we'd asked when we had the chance.

I also wished I had chosen the special at the Unique Café. Only after ordering a cheeseburger did I see a heaping plate of goulash that would easily have fueled me all the way to the Mississippi River. While waiting for lunch, I noted in my journal that I'd arrived at the café at noon, having ridden just short of thirty miles during the morning, which wasn't too bad considering how long I'd visited with Steve and his family. I also wrote a note to myself: *Always order the special!*

I tried to capture in words the unique flavor of this, my third day on the road. I noted how different each of the days had been. This day had gotten off to a bizarre start with the old man and the turkey and stayed true to form with the cleaver-wielding, Halloween-celebrating, half-Polish-half-Ojibwa businessman. As I hopped on my bike and crossed the Wisconsin River to continue my journey on the north shore, I wondered just what this rather strange day was going to send my way in the afternoon.

It didn't take long to find out that the day had definitely developed a unique personality. A few miles down the road, about halfway to Prairie du Chien from Boscobel, is a beautiful, well-maintained cemetery with a single white cross and a small unassuming sign: Stuckville Cemetery. The place had a stark, haunting beauty—the earthly resting place of a single soul.

I settled beneath an oak to absorb the beauty for a few moments. My thoughts went again to my parents—how different their lives had been from mine. My mother, except when she had to live near one or another of her children as her health failed, lived her whole life in Hayes County, Nebraska. My dad moved around a bit more. He was born in Kearney, Nebraska, in the middle of the state, but he too spent, except for periods of sickness, most of his adult life in either the Sandhills of Nebraska near Arthur or in Hayes County, on the southern edge of those rolling, sandy hills that stretch over a hundred miles to the north. He started life as a cowboy—an honest-to-goodness bronco-riding cowboy—and he had a crooked left arm that wouldn't fully straighten to prove it.

I, on the other hand, quit counting a few years ago when I discovered that I'd lived in more than two dozen homes in my life and had even lived in a foreign country with my young family as well as spending time in a half-dozen foreign countries for periods between a few weeks and a few months while I was in the army. I have traveled in every state of the union and many foreign countries as well since getting out of the service. Mine has been a peripatetic life indeed, to throw out a two-bit word I learned while studying vocabulary books on lonely assignments in Vietnam and Korea.

John Steinbeck noted in 1962 just how mobile we had become as a society, but *he hadn't seen nothing yet.* He worried about the effect of such alienation—the loss of a sense of place—and I worry about it too. Sitting under that lone tree, looking at that single white cross, I wondered where I'd want to be buried if I were to die soon. Steinbeck grew up in Salinas, California, but died while living in New York. His funeral was held at Saint James Episcopal Church in New York City, but he asked for his ashes to be spread where he had developed his strongest sense of place—near his boyhood home in Salinas.

Until I sold the farm, I had imagined that I would be buried in Wisconsin. But like Steinbeck I feel a deep connection to the hills that I roamed across as a child. My parents purchased extra space next to their cemetery plots, and I wouldn't mind if my kids and grandkids came once in a while to that gravesite, just as I do occasionally, and plan to again when and if this journey passes by that windblown hilltop cemetery on the way to Hayes Center a few weeks down this road.

The thirty-four-mile ride to the Mississippi that afternoon carried me along the Wisconsin River on a smooth highway with a wide shoulder, affording plenty of space and time to enjoy the view and reflect on my first three days of riding. I was on a journey hoping to take the pulse of America. So far, most of the people I had met had voiced some level of frustration with the way things were going in the country. I had met a caregiver upset with the provisions of Obamacare and a businessman who wasn't hiring because of regulations associated with the so-called Affordable Care Act. I had met an entrepreneur who didn't like "white man's laws and regulations."

Despite these concerns, my overall impression was that people still feel that America is a great place to live and raise a family. But an undercurrent of concern for our country bubbled along just under the surface, even among those who had not been outspoken in their worries. They fear America is changing, and no one so far had voiced the opinion that those changes were good for our country.

Even though my journey had just begun, the days had developed a rhythm, and so had my riding. I was eating an energy bar each morning, a moderate-sized meal at noon, and a fuller meal in the evening. I carried apples and Snickers candy bars to bump up my blood sugar level if my energy dropped. Pulling a fifty-some-pound trailer, pushing against a wind, and propelling myself along at just under fifteen miles an hour burns around a thousand calories an hour. I have been adding fewer calories to my body than I've been expending. My weight has dropped— and my waist is smaller.

The other good news was that I had developed no sore spots, nor were my legs hurting—I was feeling good and I was feeling strong. Pushing too hard in the early part of a bike ride can lead to problems— hot spots and blisters can develop, especially saddle sores if you spend too many hours riding in the early part of a trip. For most people the weak link in the bicyclist's arsenal is the *derriere,* as the French call it.

On day one I rode only forty-four miles. On day two the total was fifty-some. And today the GPS indicates that I'll hit Iowa at sixty-some miles for the day's ride—a slow increase that should be a good foundation for the thousand-plus miles I hope to cover.

By the time I got to Prairie du Chien I was running low on "fuel." The cheeseburger had not delivered enough calories to get me all the way to the river, so I stopped at my favorite Wisconsin franchise, Culver's, to eat a bowl of vegetable beef soup—resisting the urge to have a scoop of frozen custard. I figured the soup was all I needed to get me across the Mississippi to Marquette, Iowa. One state down and three to go—the mileage when I stopped to take a picture of Wisconsin from the apex of the bridge was 162.4 miles—I was more than one-tenth of the way to the mountains of Colorado.

I had heard years before that just across the river was a small town with a very interesting used-book store. I couldn't remember the name, but it seemed like a reasonably good bet that the bookstore was in Marquette. A helpful lady at the only stoplight in town told me she knew of no bookstore in Marquette but that I'd find one in McGregor. I must have looked pretty disappointed, because she reached out as if to console me and said, "It's only two miles down the road. And well worth the ride."

And with that I was on my way to a pleasant surprise. Even the two-mile ride to McGregor was memorable—a slender slice of a highway squeezed between a railroad track hugging the shore of the Mississippi on one side and on the other, a sheer cliff cut through the riverbank. As promised, two miles down the road, the riverbank opened up into a small valley, and a unique town came into view, one that preserved the character of the area and the era in which it came to life. Were it not for the cars and motorcycles parked on the main street it would have been easy to imagine that in those two miles I had traveled back almost two hundred years. There was even a well-preserved hand-hewn cabin welcoming me to McGregor.

The bookstore was indeed a treasure. I should hasten to add that I think just about every bookstore is a treasure, but this one could have kept me thoroughly engrossed for hours if it were not for the fact that closing time was fast approaching. And were it not for the fact that I had no room in my trailer, I would have bought several books.

The whole town was a treat, especially if you like architectural character and are especially fond of the style of houses and public buildings that were constructed in the 1800s and early 1900s. The grain elevator with the classic silhouette rusting next to the single train track reminded me of the early history of McGregor. The historical plaques in the area revealed that the town's original name was MacGreggor's Landing—a reference to the ferry that Mr. MacGreggor operated between

Prairie du Chien and the Iowa shoreline. Sadly, most folks traveling though the area won't see the town of McGregor unless they've been specifically told of it—the highway bypasses the town. My wife and I have been crossing the Mississippi at Prairie du Chien for decades but had not once set foot in McGregor. That is the legacy of our efficient highway system—it's so easy to pass right by some of our most interesting towns and historical locations.

Beyond McGregor's welcoming cabin was a beautiful park surrounded by tastefully painted Victorian-era shops and homes, many of them having been converted to B&B's offering tourists and travelers an early-1900s hometown ambiance. I would have taken advantage of that offer, but the price tags weren't in keeping with my "mom-and-pop motel" budget.

After much searching, I discovered a motel on the edge of town that reflected the mid-twentieth century. It was dedicated to engineering efficiency, not architectural grace. I made the manager an offer he could easily have refused, but he didn't. He had a spartanly furnished room that he was willing to rent at my mom-and-pop price. It had other problems in addition to austerity. It wasn't on the ground floor. I had to climb an open steel-girded stairway to the second level and then walk the length of the motel to get to my room, but it saved me about seventy-five dollars, so I accepted the inconvenience and climbed the twisting stairs twice with heavy loads—first with the trailer on my shoulder and then with Friday high above my head.

After washing off sixty-some miles of road grime, I walked around town looking for a place to watch the Obama/Biden speeches at the Democratic National Convention and eat a good meal. But I found only one place with a television—a bar/café recommended to me by the manager of the motel for its food. Unfortunately, when I returned later that evening a rather vulgar "reality" show was on, so I went to the Mexican restaurant at the Alexander Hotel and enjoyed a quiet meal, but no conversations with other guests about politics or anything else.

I returned to my motel room and watched the convention alone. I was disappointed not to see the reactions of other people to the speeches of President Obama and Vice President Biden, but in the quiet of my room I was able to concentrate on what the men were saying, and I tried to figure out what Steinbeck might have thought about their message. On his travels he had timed his stops at motels to coincide with the Nixon-Kennedy debates.

All of Steinbeck's books, in one way or another, were about the American condition. I've always felt that he was honored for his writing because he was good at taking another view of life, even when it was unpopular. He was deeply concerned about America. *Travels with Charley* was the clearest representation of that theme, but *The Winter of Our Discontent,* published the year before *Charley,* was an essay in novel form about morality, which he defined as *taking out more than you are willing to put in.* Steinbeck's final book, *America and Americans,* published in October 1966, just two years before his death, approached the theme of America's possible decline directly. In it he wrote, "Paradoxes are everywhere: We proudly insist that we base our political positions on the issues—and we will vote against a man because of his religion, his name, or the shape of his nose."

If, like Rip Van Winkle, Steinbeck had awakened one morning after almost fifty years of not following the course of American political thought, what would his reaction have been to the vision Obama laid out in his speech? Would it seem all that different to him, or would it just be more of the same? Would he have thought Obama's rhetoric matched Obama's record? That was what struck me about the speech. It sounded good, but as I listened, I remembered what Jim and Rose had told me a couple of days earlier.

"If I wanted to destroy a nation, I would give it too much, and I would have it on its knees, miserable, greedy, and sick," Steinbeck wrote to a friend on November 5, 1959.

Steinbeck was fond of trying to take the long view, wondering how the sober judges of history would consider our presidents. "Strangely it is our mediocre Presidents we honor during their lives," Steinbeck wrote in *America and Americans.*

Despite writings that some perceive as evidence of hostility toward faith, Steinbeck often framed situations in Biblical-sounding language. In *East of Eden* he wrote, "An unbelieved truth can hurt a man much more than a lie." I don't know what "unbelieved truth" Steinbeck had in mind, but in the world of faith, such a sentiment is hard to argue with. He wrote in a private letter late in his life, "Our moral system came in about two hundred years ago and will be gone in twenty-five more." And in a rather prescient observation, he wrote the following chilling words in *Travels with Charley:* "You can't forbid people to be born—at least not yet."

The seventies confirmed Steinbeck's status as a prophet. Abortion was declared legal in America less than five years after he died. No-fault divorces, instituted by the Bolsheviks in Russia in 1918 to weaken families and prepare the way for socialism, made their way to America in 1970 when Ronald Reagan signed the Family Law Act that brought no-fault divorce to California only a little more than a year after Steinbeck was gone. When Steinbeck declared that our moral system would be gone in twenty-five years, the number of children born to unmarried mothers was statistically insignificant. Today almost half of America's children— three-quarters in the black population—are born to unmarried women, and in New York City more than half of all pregnancies end in abortion.

As I pondered these things I came to a fuller realization of why I so admired Steinbeck—why he had inspired me as a teenager and why now, as a senior citizen, I was still being influenced by him, still trying to do what he had done. I realized that my journey across America, and the book I planned to write about it, could be summed up in one revealing sentence Steinbeck had penned in a letter to his wife: "I'm trying to write history while it's happening and I don't want to be wrong."

As I fell asleep that night, I sensed that I was trying to do the same thing. I was celebrating the fiftieth anniversary of my first long-distance bike trip, but this trip wasn't just about adventure and proving that I was still in good shape. I, like Steinbeck, wanted to know what America was thinking, and as much as possible I wanted to hear directly from the people, and from as many of them as possible.

To write history as it is happening is a daunting task, but one that Steinbeck did not shy away from. He accomplished it in *The Grapes of Wrath,* and I don't think he ever quit trying to bring clarity to the issues of the day by distilling the disparate elements of daily life to their essence. He was imbued with a deeply held conviction of right and wrong, and he never wavered in his belief that America's future depends upon a population that will never lose sight of the certainty that right and wrong do in fact exist. His stories were a way to impart that conviction to others.

Chapter Four

Start by doing what is necessary,
then what is possible,
and suddenly you are doing the impossible.
SAINT FRANCIS OF ASSISI

Getting on the Road Early

The next morning, I got up before the sun. As I was packing Friday, my thoughts carried me up and down the back streets and main street of McGregor. I unplugged my phone from its charger and took a look at the photos I had taken. A movie producer looking to recreate a late 1800s or early 1900s period film would save a lot of money and time in this river town. The stores, the homes, the businesses— even the fire station— could be filmed with little alteration. The Alexander Hotel, where I'd enjoyed dinner the night before, needed only horses and buggies tied up out front to complete the Victorian era picture.

But as I looked at all the perfectly preserved houses and buildings, it hit me that in all my wanderings about town, no conversations had sprung up—no *normal* conversations, that is. Certainly lots of "Hellos,"

"Good afternoons," and "Let me get that door for you," but nothing substantive. If I had to guess why, I'd say that we all just looked like tourists to each other. We were friendly, but we didn't engage each other.

I carried my bike and trailer down the darkened stairs, hooked them together, switched on Friday's lights, and pulled out of town just as the eastern horizon showed the first hint of a soft glow of orange. The day was coming alive, and I was about the only one witnessing it.

The first miles along the Great River Road were only a few feet above river level; the road curved gracefully around cliffs and crossed over small tributaries leading into the Mississippi. Feeling the pulse of the river took me back to my childhood and the Tom Sawyer/Huck Finn stories that carried me out of Nebraska and into the wide world. What grand adventures those boys got into. Maybe it wasn't John Steinbeck who first inspired my adventuresome streaks; maybe the blame should sit squarely on Mark Twain's shoulders.

Wherever it came from, the streak has endured. I love the feeling of getting on the road early when only delivery truck drivers and a few construction workers are moving about. The roads were quiet and so was Marquette when I passed through town on my way north to the route Jim had recommended. The river too was quiet. A lone fisherman in a flat-bottomed boat broke up the mirror-smooth surface, sending shimmering orange ripples all the way to the river's edge. The sun's low-angled rays created halos on fluttering grass along the shore and lit up the bluffs with a warm golden glow. The morning was also cool enough that I could ride hard without working up a sweat. Add a slight tailwind, and you have a picture of why I was calling the day "perfect."

"Cool enough didn't last long, though. A few miles north of Marquette, Highway 76 began climbing out of the Mississippi River Valley, up a long slope through thick stands of trees to Effigy Mounds National Monument. The park wasn't open, but I pulled in anyway so that I'd have a pleasant and safe place to take off a few layers. A park ranger noticed me reading some of the plaques by the front door of the visitor's center and stepped out to hand me a brochure. He advised me that the center wouldn't be open for a while, but that if I cared to look I'd find a mound only a short distance away and that I was welcome to head up the trail. He was also kind enough to assure me that my bike would be fine right where I had parked it.

A few hundred yards up the trail I found myself in a beautiful forest. As my eyes swept the woods I discovered a lone deer lying on the crest of a mound. She held her gaze and her spot while I snapped a few photos. Once I put my phone away, she quietly stood up and ambled off, apparently convinced that I meant her no harm.

The mounds were interesting and eerily beautiful; they reminded me that this land reveals the history of a culture that goes back many hundreds of years. But my main focus that morning was on the long, steep climb that lay ahead. I was hoping I'd have to make this climb only one time—that once on top I wouldn't have to cross a series of smaller valleys draining into the Mississippi.

I peeled off my leggings and stripped to a short-sleeved jersey even though the morning air was still quite crisp. I was going to be generating plenty of heat and creating little wind to cool me down. Even though the temperature was still in the fifties, I knew that within half a mile sweat would be pouring from my chin as I worked my way up the hill.

The road was narrow, but very few cars were traveling yet. A few lumber trucks were on the road, but with no traffic coming at them, they were able to give me a full lane. Because I have mirrors on both sides of my bike, I can both see, and hear, by the angle of the sound approaching me, whether a vehicle is giving me a wide berth. It was on this long, slow climb I began giving a wave of thanks to every car and truck that gave me the courtesy of moving over into the other lane when they passed me.

I can't say with certainty that every driver understood the reason for my wave, but I received enough short toots of the horn in return that I think that many did. I also got toots of appreciation from truck drivers when they saw that I had taken extra measures to give them a clear lane so that that they could maintain their momentum going up hills. Near the top of this climb out of the river valley, I could hear a heavily loaded truck approaching me. I couldn't yet see it, but I knew by the sound that I'd still be on a curve by the time it reached me. I knew the driver wouldn't be able to maintain his speed unless I got off the road, so while the truck was still singing along at full throttle but not yet in sight, I pulled onto the shoulder, got off my bike, and walked it into the ditch. By the time the truck flew by me, I had finished taking a drink and was ready to push the bike back to the road, hop on, and continue the climb.

To keep climbs from seeming interminably long, I developed a habit years ago of estimating the distance and time to the top. Even though I'm almost always wrong, I keep doing it because it helps me to realize that although I am working very hard, and the climbs seem long, in terms of actual clock time they invariably take only a few minutes.

The good news was that it took less time than I expected to climb out of the Mississippi River Valley. Once on top though, I discovered the bad news—the wind that had been a favorable early-morning breeze in the valley was now pushing right on my nose. However, the hilltop churches up there were a delight. I love how the Christian congregations of the nineteenth and early twentieth centuries chose high ground for their churches, often locating the structures far out in the country, visible for miles around, their steeples reaching many stories into the sky to serve as beacons for all within dozens of miles.

By mid-morning I was thinking of lunch and wondering if I would find a town with a place to eat. I was struggling against the wind when I noticed, some fifty yards from the highway, a farmer and his wife on a swinging lounge chair, absorbing what warmth was available on that chilly morning by sitting in the lee of their garage. I stopped mid-stroke and yelled across the distance, "Good morning! Can you tell me if there's anyplace to eat in Rossville?" The wind grabbed their answer and carried it across the fence line with the blowing corn stalks, so I dismounted and began pushing Friday down their rocky driveway. They gave me a hearty wave, leaving no doubt that they wanted me to join them.

When I got close enough that I too was in the lee of the farm buildings, the man yelled out again, "A few years ago you coulda got a bite to eat in Rossville, but not any more, not this time a day anyway." They struck me as friendly, hard-working folks like the salt-of-the-earth types I had grown up with, so I kept walking and he kept talking, telling me to just keep going until I got to Waukon, nine miles down the road. In that town, he and his wife assured me, I could get a great meal at Cynda's, "like Lynda but with a 'C.'" They took turns, talking over each other at times, telling me exactly how to get there—even what businesses I should look for before and after the small restaurant, although some disagreements arose regarding what was after and what was before. But I had no doubt they had given me enough information to find Cynda's.

I stored some key points of their directions in my memory bank and asked about rain. That opened up the floodgates. We talked farming for quite a while, about the drought, the farmers who are disappearing from the land, even about other bikers they had seen ride past their farm over the years. They weren't shy and seemed to be enjoying the chance to share their lives. They were proud to tell me they'd been married fifty-two years and were thinking about slowing down just a bit—not necessarily taking it easy, just taking time once in a while to enjoy the day, as they were doing at the moment. I was beginning to see that Iowa likes bike riders. Iowans take pride in providing bikers with a great experience crossing their state and are extremely proud of RAGBRAI (Register's Annual Great Bike Ride Across Iowa)—the ride Jim had mentioned—which is hosted by the *Des Moines Register* and attracts thousands of riders every summer. They enjoyed telling me about the never-ending lines of cyclists that have passed their farm over the years.

They didn't talk politics, at least not in the polarizing sense of setting Republicans against Democrats or vice versa, but they did talk politics in the sense of wondering how best to preserve America. They made it obvious they were worried about our country. They had enjoyed a good life, they said, but they weren't so optimistic about the future for their kids and grandkids. Debts, deficits, and morals were on their minds. They wondered if our leaders were up to the challenges—up to having the guts to call for sacrifice—just as they themselves had done so that instead of being saddled with debt in their old age they could sit in the sun on a chilly morning and just enjoy living. They knew what they were doing and what was good about their lives, and they were basking in it. As I pushed Friday down their driveway to get back to the highway I realized how fortunate it was that I hadn't been able to find a restaurant on my own that morning. It had been good to spend a few moments with members of a generation of people who are fast disappearing from America—who know just what a burden debt can be.

The subject of our nation's health came up again an hour later at Cynda's. A farmer sat down at the table next to me and opened the conversation by telling me he'd passed me on the way into town. He was curious about my destination, how far I traveled each day, and how far I planned to ride today. I told him that typically I rode anywhere from fifty to one hundred miles a day. I asked him how far I was from Decorah, which I knew from having driven through there a year ago had motels, campgrounds, even bike paths, and would be a great place to spend the night. He told me it was only nineteen miles. I made a quick calculation and realized that would put me into Decorah at well under fifty miles for the day. I told him I was following Highway 9 and wondered if he knew of any motels on the other side of Decorah along that route.

"I don't think you'll be able to find a motel until you get all the way to Osage," he said.

"And how far's that?" I asked, since I had never heard of the town.

"It must be, let's see, ah, it's sixty miles across there," he said, "and there's definitely no motels." He had added up the miles as he drove the route in his mind looking for a motel. I added that to the miles I'd already ridden and the miles to Decorah and realized that would bring the total to more than one hundred for the day.

Rather than think about such a long ride on just my fourth day of the journey, I changed the subject back to farming. He revealed, without saying so outright, that his was a rather large farming operation. He told me that on some of his land, the yields were quite good, while others were experiencing drought conditions. Normally that means the farm is either very large or quite spread out over the county or even adjoining counties—some of the land getting timely rain showers, other land getting few or none. I gathered from our conversation that he was an extremely thoughtful farmer, a good farmer, a prosperous farmer.

He was optimistic about farming, but he was scared to death of the nation's trillions of dollars of debt. He was doing well, a fact that was confirmed when I glanced out the window and saw the pickup that bore the name of his farm. Farmers in Iowa look like they're doing quite well. They certainly are land rich. But having said that, a big diesel pickup truck like the one he was driving costs over fifty thousand dollars. It may seem good that he can afford it. But the price of that truck is equivalent to the cost of four or five acres of good farmland. As he told me, land costing ten thousand dollars an acre may seem like a good thing, that farmers are getting rich, but what it really means is that our dollar is becoming worthless. Even the lunch I ate confirmed that fact--five dollars no longer buys a good meal in a small town restaurant as it did not too long ago. It now takes ten dollars—and if you have a piece of pie and something to drink, as I did that day, by the time you leave a tip you're going to have to leave fourteen or fifteen dollars on the table. What I enjoyed that day in Waukon would have cost me only a buck twenty-five when I was a fifteen.

When I was a kid, the coconut cream pie I enjoyed at the café my best friend's parents owned cost me just fifteen cents. I paid almost twenty times as much for a piece of Cynda's pie. Both were absolutely delicious—the difference was price and size—today everything is supersized. I see the need for large portions if you happen to bike fifty miles to lunch, but not many people expend that kind of energy every day. Even farmers, most of whom had good reason to eat hefty portions fifty years ago, no longer work as hard physically in 2012, so like the rest of us they too are getting "supersized."

My disgruntled farmer friend, who, incidentally, was quite trim, sent me on my way with two recommendations—one for Obama and Federal Reserve chairman Ben Bernanke and one for me—*Quit monetizing the debt by printing increasingly worthless money* and *Head straight out of town on the road you're on instead of returning to Highway 9.* He assured me it would be a beautiful ride, well worth the extra hills I'd have to climb. Before I took off, I thanked him, tipped the friendly waitress who had peppered me with questions about Italy each time she filled my Pepsi glass, and grabbed my doggie bags—as hungry as I'd been that morning, and as long as I'd lingered over lunch, I still couldn't eat it all.

It didn't take long to discover that the farmer knew what he was talking about. The views of the hilltops and valleys from that county road were stunningly beautiful in a rolling-land kind of way. I love the variety of such landscapes—the shapes of fields and pastures dictated not by straight lines and grids but by rolling hills, meandering rivers, and woodlots. If you want to a take journey, and not just get from place to place, there's no better advice to follow than to eat where the locals do. Following my original plan would have put me on a course of straight-line but boring efficiency. The farmer had suggested a road that was built when the lay of the land dictated where it would go, and because of that, the road had integrity and the beauty of a thing done right.

As I rode into Decorah, I spotted a bike shop. Rich, the owner, yielded a gold mine of information. He too was a long-distance biker. He confirmed that I should be prepared to either camp or ride all the way to Osage, another sixty-some miles. I had the word of a farmer and a bike shop owner—two very reliable sources on local road conditions.

I should have taken their warnings more as commands, but earlier that morning I'd done what I said I wouldn't do. I had accepted Jim's invitation to spend the night at his house and had told him I'd arrive on Saturday afternoon. Jim had been kind enough to extend a hand of hospitality, and I was looking forward to getting to know him better, meet his family, and get a feel for the community he so obviously loved—and there's no better time than the weekend to do that.

But that decision required me to cut short the time I spent at the bike shop. Rich had questions for me—he wanted to know why I had chosen the Bike Friday over other bikes on the market that are geared toward bikers who want to travel by train or plane for portions of their journeys. From the way he studied the bike and the trailer it was obvious he had more than a salesman's interest, and I asked him about it. He led me to the back of his shop and showed me his creations. Over the years he had designed and built a number of bike trailers, small and large. One was big enough that college kids could rent it to move furniture; others were the right size for pulling kids, dogs, and groceries.

Rich was near my age, and he'd spent his adult life serving the bicycling needs of his community. I loved getting to know a bit of his history and the town's relationship to bicycles. Decorah has an extensive network of bike trails throughout the city and along the Iowa River. The resurgence of the bicycle industry is thrilling, especially when I think back to my college days.

I am old enough and have been committed to bicycling long enough that I remember when biking by anyone old enough to have a driver's license was not cool—when people hurled insults at me as I biked around Lincoln, Nebraska, as a freshman at the University of Nebraska in the mid-sixties. Mine was the only bike on campus. Bike riding was so nerdy, so frowned upon, that my fraternity pledge father told me that if I insisted on riding a bike, I was not to embarrass my brothers by pulling up to the front of the fraternity house—I had to come through the alley and park my bike at the back door.

But since then, bicycle riding has had a resurgence, and its popularity grows every year, especially in towns and cities with college campuses, like Decorah, the home of Luther College.

Rich directed me to a path along the Upper Iowa River that carried me safely and quietly though the city to a county road affording me a quiet ride in the country past beautiful farms, elegant churches, and quaint country cemeteries.

As I continued west, the land continued to roll, the wind continued to blow out of the north, and I continued to ask the folks I met if they knew where I could find a motel. But not one person I talked to knew of one unless I was willing to travel a significant number of miles either north or south. My destination, unfortunately, was due west—and I needed to continue riding in that direction or I'd never make it to Jim's house in Forest City by Saturday. So I decided to keep pedaling straight west as fast as the wind would allow me.

This was day four of my journey—a Friday. I'd already ridden farther than I had on any of the previous three days and was still almost fifty miles from Osage. As I struggled along I considered my options. The option I didn't want to exercise was to call Jim and tell him I wouldn't be able to make it to his place the following afternoon. If I could make it to Osage I'd have less than fifty miles to ride on Saturday. I hoped to able to arrive by mid-afternoon to give me time to enjoy the day with Jim and his wife, Cheryl.

But my average speed was dropping from thirteen to twelve, and by late afternoon it was at eleven. The crosswinds were brutal, and on the rolling hills my speed dropped to four miles an hour. I continued to explore my options but found few. Neither did I find many people to talk to. I don't know whether it was the wind or the remoteness of the area, but few people were out and about. I think that having a specific destination cuts a bike rider off from opportunities to interact with people. I also know that people are more open to conversation on nice, sunny, pleasant days than when a cold, north wind is blowing.

But if day four was brutal, it was because I made it that way. Had I not been committed to being in Forest City on Saturday, I could have changed my destination to give myself a bit of a tailwind. I could have ridden south, or at least southeasterly, when roads heading that direction were available. Lincoln, Nebraska, one of my interim destinations, was, when I left Decorah, almost three hundred miles west and two hundred miles south. Turning south out of Decorah would have given me a quick ride. I could have flown along at twenty-plus miles an hour and probably put on almost one hundred miles that afternoon with the wind at my back and still had time for lots of breaks along the way.

But I had committed to riding west—and without realizing it until too late, I had committed to a route with no motels—a bad combination. I turned my attention to finding a campground, but that didn't go well either. I learned that there might be one in Riceville, but that was seven or eight miles north, right into the teeth of the wind. The only other choice, in the waning moments of the day, was to keep riding west. Osage was almost twenty miles away, and the sun was low in the sky. No one I had talked to was sure that Riceville even had a campground, but everyone was certain that Osage had a motel—probably two or three.

I checked my phone to get the time of sunset in Osage. I factored in my current average speed and the fact that the wind usually falls off a bit as the sun is setting. Factoring all the variables, it was clear that I couldn't make Osage before sundown but that I could reach the edge of town before dark. My smartphone also told me that my total distance for the day would be right around one hundred miles, depending upon which motel I chose.

Considering how hard the wind was blowing, the fact that I was pulling a fifty pound trailer, and that on the three previous days I'd ridden only half that many miles, committing to a "century ride" carried some risk. However, I'd eaten a big lunch, I had apples and energy bars, and I had plenty of water, so I hoped I wouldn't "bonk"—deplete my energy supply so completely that my body would shut down. But the winds that continued to gust in the thirty-mile-an-hour range made all my reasoned calculations inconsequential—my speed at times dropped well below ten miles an hour, especially on the hills that kept rising up. I couldn't make up on the downhill runs what I was losing on the uphill climbs. The wind was so strong that even going downhill, pedaling as hard as I could, my speed was less than twenty miles an hour.

One writer has quipped that there is only one human constant—a universal hatred of headwinds. On that day I offered no argument. As I headed straight west toward Osage I watched that big orange sun sink lower and lower until it had sunk so low that it was obscured first by trees and then by silos. I was still miles from town; the race had not yet been decided, but thankfully my energy level was still high. I forced myself to take sips of water before I was thirsty to lessen the chance of bonking. I discovered years ago while bicycle racing the devastating effect of running out of fluids. If your body hits the "wall," as mine was threatening to do, the muscles in your legs refuse to cooperate and your speed, despite all-out effort, can be cut in half instantly—the bike riders I was comfortably keeping pace with moments earlier in that race pulled easily away from me as my body shut down.

As I made my way toward town, I turned on the strobe on the back of my bike even though the sun hadn't quite set. It flashes a beam of bright light to make certain that drivers whose windshields might not be clean can see me. But I didn't just rely on that strobe. I watched the approaching cars in my rearview mirror to make doubly sure that drivers doing battle with the setting sun saw me. And thankfully they all did. They either slowed as they went around me or, if there was no traffic in the approaching lane, gave me the whole lane.

Rather quickly, it seemed, the sun sank so low that houses were now obscuring it. Then it sat on the horizon for a while before settling out of sight. At that dreaded moment I had only three miles to go—a distance I'd normally cover in about twelve minutes, but with the winds only slightly diminished from the thirty-mile-an-hour gusts of the afternoon, it looked like it was going to take me more like twenty minutes to reach Osage. Normally a few minutes wouldn't make a big difference, but approaching darkness makes every minute precious when you're biking.

When finally I reached the edge of Osage, the bike computer clicked over the ninety-ninth mile for the day, and it looked like I'd definitely hit the one-hundred-mile mark before I reached the Super 8 Motel's sign, which I could see glowing in the dusty distance. What I hadn't yet noticed, even though it was closer, was a much smaller sign for the Osage Motel and Lounge. It stood in front of a mid-twentieth-century pull-up-to-the-door-and-walk-right-into-the-room motel. The Super 8 would have pushed my mileage to the century mark and slightly beyond, but I'd ridden enough centuries in my life—doing it one more time wasn't a motivating factor. I just wanted to put an end to a brutal day on the road.

I parked Friday between two huge pickups loaded with fuel barrels and tools. On unsteady legs, which had forgotten how to walk, I made my way to a door marked "Office." I saw neither a "Vacancy" sign nor a "No Vacancy" sign, but the parking lot was so crowded I was worried that the place was booked solid with construction workers. Inside I discovered a huge lounge/bar full of men drinking beer and eating pizza—except for one young man working on a big plate of pasta.

"What can I do for ya?" I turned and saw a middle-aged rather severe woman with long straight hair who seemed impatient for my answer.

I motioned toward the plate of spaghetti and asked, "Is that the special tonight?"

"For him it is, but for you it's pizza. That's my son. We only serve pizza here."

"I see. Actually I was looking for a room."

"You have ID?"

"Yes. Yes … I do."

"Well, then we have one room left. Can I see that ID?"

While I was pulling my billfold out of my fanny pouch I asked, "How much?"

"Just you?"

"Yep."

"Then it's forty including tax."

"OK."

I showed her my driver's license, counted out forty dollars, and let out a sigh of relief. My brutal day in the saddle battling the wind would end with a hot shower and a good night's sleep. No matter what happened in that lounge, or how loud they played the music, I was certain that nothing would keep me from getting a good night's rest.

I pulled my bike up to number 4, unhitched the trailer, pulled it inside, then wheeled the bike into the room on its back tire and parked it on the other side of the bed. I stripped off my dirty clothes, carried them into the shower with me, and began scrubbing my socks, biking shorts, and jersey. The day wasn't over—I still needed to eat—but once the clothes were hung up and drying, I considered my work done for the day. It had been a punishing day in the saddle, but it now seemed certain that I could get to Forest City easily the next day even if the wind kept blowing. It was still blowing hard as I made my way to a Mexican restaurant half a mile down the road, walking through acres of farm machinery—some pieces of equipment as large as small buildings.

I'm not sure why I didn't just eat at the lounge and call it a day, but for some reason I didn't want pizza that night. Maybe I just thought that after spending so much time in the saddle it would be good for my body to take a long walk. Or maybe I just felt like rewarding myself with a margarita. Or maybe I thought I'd meet some people. Or maybe I just wasn't thinking so straight after such an exhausting day. The only thing I got was a walk, a fairly good enchilada, and a so-so margarita—and the conviction that in almost every town in America today with a population of at least one thousand people, it is possible to find a restaurant operated by recent immigrants.

I walked the half-mile back to my room and fell into bed. As I was connecting my phone to the charger I noticed that I had a voicemail. I heard Jim's voice say, "Sorry, James, but I forgot to check with my wife. We're not going to be in town this weekend—my brother-in-law is in a stock car race Saturday night. I just completely forgot. Hey, maybe some other time. Give me a call."

I couldn't believe it! Why couldn't he have called when I was in McGregor, or even Decorah—I felt like I'd been kicked in the gut. I grabbed my journal and wrote, *A brutal day—I tried to dictate instead of letting the day come to me. I missed out on staying at Carol's cabin.* [A friend of my sister-in-law was following my journey on Facebook, saw that I was in McGregor, and had offered me her place on a high bluff overlooking the Mississippi River—but I'd been in such a rush most of the day that I hadn't taken the time to read my emails and learned of it fifty miles too late.] *Or I could have spent a pleasant afternoon in Decorah. Instead I pushed myself to exhaustion and rode against a miserable crosswind for fifty miles—and for no reason. Jim is going out of town this weekend.* I concluded my journal notes underlining the following admonition: *What a great lesson. Don't dictate! Go with the flow.*

I felt like an idiot. Most of the last fifty miles had been miserable. I could have stayed in Decorah, or I could have turned south and flown down the highway at twenty to thirty miles an hour. My regrets reminded me of an incident in *Travels with Charley*. Steinbeck wrote of charging across what was left of Montana and across the whole state of Washington so that he could meet his wife in Seattle. She was flying out to meet him, but she had to change her plans at the last minute, and he spent three days hanging out in a motel near the airport thinking about what might have been had he not been in such a hurry.

I didn't kick myself very long, though. I turned the light off and fell asleep before the room turned dark.

Chapter Five

*Maybe the hardest thing in writing is simply
to tell the truth about things.*
JOHN STEINBECK

One of My Own

I woke up to a very different day than I was expecting. If I hadn't fallen asleep so fast I would have gotten the message from Jim telling me to disregard his earlier message—he'd just heard that his brother-in-law had blown up his engine in the qualifying heat and wouldn't be racing, so he and Cheryl were going to be home after all. I put down my phone and laughed at myself. I was sure glad I hadn't lost any sleep or altered any plans. I was, however, resolved more than ever to let the events of the day, to the extent possible, dictate my actions.

Day five, Saturday, September 8, started off very cool—forty-six degrees, according to the bank across from the Kwik Star. I had stopped in to buy a banana and an apple. I had thought that all convenience stores carried fruit, but on this journey I discovered, as I came out empty-handed from store after store, that only Kwik Trip in Wisconsin and Kwik Star in Iowa could be counted on for good fruit. My wife had cautioned me not to neglect my potassium intake. She insisted that I eat at least one banana every day. Apples I find to be an excellent source of both water and energy—and most of them taste pretty good these days, especially Fuji and Pink Lady. And if you can afford them, Honey Crisp apples are exceptionally sweet and at the same time slightly tart. Fruit and energy bars are my emergency rations. Each morning begins with a check of my inventory.

I also take a look at my maps as I start each day to find out if anything in the area might be of special interest. Many states have dedicated bike maps, and the Iowa Department of Transportation's map is one of the best. I checked the Osage area and discovered a "green multi-use trail"—although a serpentine trail a mile or two west of Osage was clearly marked, not one person at the Kwik Star had heard of it. I wasn't entirely sure why I wanted so badly to find that trail, especially since it would take me a few miles north of Highway 9, but it had caught my eye, and I was determined to be open to whatever the day might have in store for me.

My interest in the trail may have been for no other reason than it appeared to follow the Cedar River, and I thought that might be a welcome respite from the many miles of straight roads I had followed over hill and dale the previous day. So when I saw the Cedar River Valley and a road snaking off to the right, I followed it. It was every bit as beautiful, peaceful, and restful as I'd hoped it would be. I also discovered why no one knew about it—the green wavy line didn't mark a dedicated bike trail—it just drew attention to a beautiful river road to bike along.

I hadn't planned to spend as much time on that river as I did, but before I'd ridden a quarter of a mile I discovered on a gentle turn that my front tire was soft—a much better way to discover your tire is about to go flat than on a high-speed descent clocking almost thirty miles an hour—exactly what I'd been doing only a few moments earlier as I descended into the valley.

Flat number one of the journey. I pulled to the side of the road, chose a downed tree trunk for a workbench, and went to work repairing the tube—and enjoying the gently flowing river. A jogger happened by who didn't stop to talk but did say hello. A man out walking his dog was next—he stopped and we chatted a bit. He was a part-time farmer who also worked in town to support his habit of being on the land. Like many part-time farmers, he was looking forward to the day when he could "retire" to the farm and quit commuting to town. He stayed long enough to see that my repair held air before resuming his walk.

Just as I was putting the wheel back on the bike, a kind-faced man driving an older minivan stopped and asked if I needed anything. I had spent the past ten minutes working with my undersized pump to bring the pressure up to about forty pounds and cussing myself for not packing my full-sized floor pump—it would have had the tire up to sixty-five pounds of pressure in less than thirty seconds. I asked if he happened to have a tire pump.

"Indeed I do, sir!"

And with that he pulled his van up next to my bike and hopped out. As he opened the back of the van he said, "My name is Harold," and then he went on to tell me that he had just moved to Iowa from Washington, DC.

"And how have things been going for you since moving west?" I asked.

Harold paused to look at me; his face lost its gentle smile. "I don't want to play the race card, but it hasn't been going well. I haven't been able to find work."

"What kind of work are you looking for?" I asked.

"Oh, I can do most anything," he said. And I didn't doubt it as I watched him pull out a small compressor from the well-organized supply of tools arranged on the floor of his van. But I wondered if prefacing his observations with a mention of the "race card" might tend to contradict what he was saying. I could think of a number of reasons that finding work here might be hard for anyone. Topping the list was our nation's high unemployment rate. I also knew from firsthand experience that being new to an area makes getting a job much more difficult, especially when you're looking for work in construction or as a handyman. A person whose family history is known is much more likely to be hired than a stranger or newcomer. The fact that he was of African ancestry might have had little or nothing to do with his lack of work. Lots of factors go into decisions about who gets hired. But I said none of that. Instead I offered encouragement and prompted him to tell me more. And he did. Harold, I had little doubt, was from a story-telling family. His sentences flowed with a gentle rhythm that drew me in.

He had moved to the Osage area for a number of reasons; family and his failing health topped the list. He told me he had "lots of children and grandchildren, but they are still in the DC area." He went on to tell me of his efforts to find work and that he'd even had to begin picking up cans along the road we were on—both to make some money and to keep the river beautiful. "I love it here. I come down here to fish just about every morning—I know the good spots and the bad spots, where the fish are biting and where they're not. I feel like this is my river and I want to keep it nice for everyone."

Harold's air pump worked away while we talked, and within a few minutes the pressure was up to sixty-five pounds. We continued talking while he put the pump away. I noted how much he valued self-reliance—taking care of himself and teaching his kids to be disciplined and at the same time decrying the trend he was noticing for others to raise children who were dependent, spoiled, and unwilling to work hard.

His delivery was slow, delightful, and nuanced with a Southern ease—and he had a tendency to inexplicably put a high-pitched emphasis on what to my ear seemed random words. "I've been going through many adversities and I needed SOMEONE to talk to. I reach out and the man up at the church on the HILL has been very helpful to me—helping me with my bills and everything. I come through here a lot of times and pick up the cans and BOTTLES 'cause I can get CHANGE for 'em. I come through here and pick 'em up so it won't look so BAD out here 'cause I know the kids COME through here and throw 'em out, so I just get 'em OUTTA HERE. Say, it's been good meeting you. You TAKE care of YOURSELF."

And with that rather long parting soliloquy, Harold was gone. I hadn't expected our conversation to end so abruptly. We'd been talking for an hour, and I wouldn't have minded hearing even more of Harold's story, but I think the fisherman in him was ready to get on with the day.

As I packed up my tools, I thought about the man I'd just met—how strongly he'd voiced principles of self-reliance and at the same time a dependence on God. Early in our conversation he had told me how disgusted he was that the DNC had voted three times to take God out of their platform—he was flat out mad about it. But Harold made it clear that despite his grievances with the Democratic Party, he was still going to have to vote for "one of my own. I don't like a lot of what Obama's doing. But I don't know Romney."

Harold's sentiments were backing up what the polls among African Americans indicate—President Obama has overwhelming support, in the area of ninety percent. I asked Harold if he thought he might change his mind about Romney after the debates. He said he might, but the way he said it made me think that the ten-second sound bites and the thirty-second commercials had told Harold all he thought he needed to know about Romney to decide he didn't like him.

Harold was a great reminder of why we should not get stressed out when "bad things" come our way. I would not have chosen "flat tire" had I been given my choice of experiences for the day, but that flat made it possible for me to look at the election and our nation from a viewpoint I hadn't expected to find in Iowa. Harold gave me a big-city perspective on America and the election—an African American perspective and a perspective from a person who was, at that moment, unemployed.

The day had gotten off to a good start even though I'd traveled only two miles in two hours. The flat tire and the conversation with Harold had given the sun time to climb high enough to warm up the day, so I peeled off a layer of clothes and continued riding along the river. Harold wasn't the only fisherman out that morning. Just as I started out again, a boat floated into view with two fishermen making slow, deliberate casts into the shallows. I'd traveled less than two hundred yards since the flat, but remembering my promise to let the day come to me, I stopped.

The scene was just too pretty to pass up. The boat presented a nice focal point for a photo of the Cedar River—a memory of the morning that I could post on Facebook—and it would also tell my wife I wasn't getting very far very fast.

For all the concerns about the loss of privacy that Facebook has brought to the world, I must say that on balance, I feel, at least at the present time, that it's a good thing. People knock living in small towns because everyone knows your business, what you're doing, and who you're doing it with. That's not necessarily a bad thing. I like that aspect of small towns. And my Facebook friends are like a small community. Maybe if I were doing things I didn't want others to know about I wouldn't feel so kindly toward either small towns or Facebook. But knowing what people are doing is precisely why I like Facebook. I like knowing what my kids and grandkids are doing, what they like, and what they did at school or with their friends. On this day Facebook allowed me not only to let my wife and family know what I was doing, but also to let them know where I was, and when you're traveling solo across America, that's a very good thing. But if the world gets turned upside down and the good thing I'm doing becomes a bad thing in somebody's mind—somebody with power and control over me—what then?

I began the day thinking I'd be riding west all day. And that's the direction I resumed traveling after the pleasant interlude following the Cedar River northwest for four or five miles. Even though it was still early in the morning, the wind was starting to blow, but unlike the day before it wasn't coming out of the north—it had shifted ninety degrees and was blowing straight down the road at me. What had started out promising to be a half-day ride was now looking like anything but. The wind was almost as strong as yesterday's gale, and it was right on my nose by the time I had climbed out of the Cedar River valley. Once again I was committed to heading west. I had ridden less than ten miles and already I was tired of the wind.

I saw an SUV about half a mile away coming toward me. I was only a hundred yards from a major highway intersection that we were both approaching. I pushed hard against the wind. I wanted to beat the SUV to the intersection, roll through the stop sign, and wait across the road for it to pull to a stop so that I might talk to the driver. But it reached the intersection first. The driver turned left in front of me just as I got there, winded from the effort to beat her. She waved and smiled, but she seemed to be in a hurry, so I didn't bother to flag her down to ask if she knew of any restaurants in the area.

I continued struggling west against the wind and soon noticed a well-dressed, well-groomed man in his late thirties or early forties and what I presumed to be his daughter transferring pumpkins and gourds from a 1950s-era restored Chevy truck to a late-model pickup parked close to the road. The wind had convinced me that it was not too early to begin thinking about brunch. Roads with no traffic make for pleasant days of riding, but often the small towns that country roads pass through no longer have enough people to support restaurants and cafés. I had opted to leave Osage without sitting down for breakfast, so if Grafton, a small town about ten miles up the road, didn't have anyplace to eat, my next option would be Manly or Kensett, another dozen or so miles to the west, and now that I was battling a fierce wind, these little towns were separated from each other by at least an hour of riding.

I pulled off the road and stopped right in front of the old Chevy. The man had not heard or seen me yet. "Good morning. Nice-looking truck you got there."

"Thanks," the man said, somewhat surprised but still he continued transferring pumpkins.

"I was wondering if you'd be able to tell me whether I could get something to eat in Grafton?"

He quit taking pumpkins from his daughter and turned to face me. "No, not any more. You're heading west, I take it."

I nodded. "Yeah, right into the wind."

"Stiff isn't it? There are few ... actually, I can't think of anyplace to eat west of here. What about going north?"

"I'm trying to get to Forest City. How far north?" I asked.

"St. Ansgar's not far. They're having a big festival—food booths up and down the street. It's a neat little town. You'll like it. It's a big biking town—the spinning classes are packed. Just ride back to 218—that's the highway you just crossed."

I glanced at his daughter, who was still loading pumpkins into the pickup.

"Did I by chance just pass your wife?"

"You probably did. She just left. She's on her way to St. Ansgar with a load of pumpkins. You can't go wrong going to the festival—the food is great."

"How far did you say it was?"

"Not far, six miles. How'd you know it was my wife? Did you see the pumpkins?"

"No. Just took a guess." I smiled and looked at his daughter. "She was a spittin' image of your helper." And I tipped my head toward her. She stopped picking up pumpkins and said a quiet hello. I said, "Hi," and looked back at her dad.

He was looking at her with an admiring smile. "Yeah, they do look a bit alike, don't they." It was obvious he was proud of them. They were both beautiful, bordering on movie-star gorgeous. But I didn't praise her beauty—I commented on how fortunate her father was to have such a good worker. She had continued working while her dad and I talked. I've picked a few pumpkins in my life, and she was lifting some pretty big ones with relative ease.

"Yeah, it's great to have the help. Where you riding to?" he asked as though he was considering joining me.

And the conversation turned to my travels and his life. He too was a part-time farmer. His other job was state senator. He described himself as a bit of a traditionalist and proudly handed me a campaign button that looked like a throwback to the mid-twentieth century.

He was concerned enough about the direction the country was going that he decided to get politically active. I sensed that he would have liked to spend a lot of time talking. He was very interested in my trip and the fact that I was a writer. He was hoping that someday he'd have time to write a book. I would have loved to learn more about what changes to Iowa and to America he wanted to bring about. But he had a lot of pumpkins to deliver, and my miles were going to be hard to come by once more.

When Josh mentioned again that Saint Ansgar was the only place nearby where I'd find food, I felt that was a good exit to the conversation. I thanked him, said good-bye to him and his daughter, coasted with the wind back to the intersection, and turned north. Getting to Forest City by early afternoon was now completely out of the question, but I was determined not to repeat the mistakes of yesterday. By turning north I was committing to a detour of at least a dozen miles—and who knows how much time I'd spend at the festival. But what better way to experience America than to mingle about in a town that celebrates not only its history but two of my other favorite things as well: biking and food.

Even though it was only six miles, the crosswind convinced me to stop a couple of times for short breaks. I even stopped on the edge of town to take a picture of the banner advertising the Fall Fest and learned that St. Ansgar was the "Garden Spot of Iowa." The town was just as Josh promised—overflowing with people and a good place to be on a Saturday morning. I cruised up and down the street a couple of times scouting out the various offerings. By the time I finished my second pass, I still hadn't seen any booths selling sandwiches or meals, only lots of stands selling sweets, so I asked for a recommendation at the honey booth. Two customers instantly sang out, "Paradise Pizza." They did it with such conviction that I had no doubt I was going to get a good meal. I thanked them and went off in search of it.

I found Paradise Pizza at the end of Main Street. I parked Friday on the far side of the building and made my way through the sidewalk booths and into the café. The conversation was lively. The folks were having fun celebrating their fall festival. The woman serving me seemed so competent and attentive that I assumed she was the owner. It turned out she was a relative of the owner. I asked how things were going, and she told me that despite the downturn in the economy, their business was doing quite well. "Commodity prices are up, and a lot of farms and the communities around here are doing just fine," she said, "but that doesn't keep us from being a bit worried about the way things are going in the rest of the country."

One of the women who had recommended Paradise Pizza came in just as I was switching from the all-you-can-eat salad bar to an Italian sandwich. She wanted to know more about my story. I must have talked to a dozen people in that place, and just about every one of them commented that they were amazed that someone my age was up to the challenge of biking solo across the country. Josh had been right—the town did seem oriented toward biking. And just about everyone also echoed the sentiments of my waitress: guarded optimism about the country's economy. I would have liked to spend more time celebrating fall with the good folks of St. Ansgar, a town very proud of its Norwegian heritage, but I could see by the banners fluttering outside the window that the wind wasn't letting up, so I said good-bye to what had become a room full of friends and took off.

On the way out of town I got a sense of why they call their little village the "Garden Spot of Iowa"—the Cedar River, which had provided such a beautiful backdrop to my early morning tire change, seems to play no small part in the lush vegetation of the town. It would be hard to fault the local folks or accuse them of hyperbole—the town really was pretty. And I got a good look at it—I ended up crossing the bridge on the west edge of town three times.

As I was climbing out of the valley my thoughts went back to the conversation with my waitress about the pride of the townspeople as I paid her at the cash register. I then remembered that on the way back to my table with the change, another table of friendly people asked about my adventure. That conversation played through my mind and took me all the way back to my table, gathering my fanny pack and water bottles, and leaving the restaurant—*without leaving a tip!*

By then I was two or three miles out of town—miles ridden against the wind and up the hill out of the valley—a slow go. Giving up progress against the wind is a hard thing to do when you know you're going to have to fight the battle again on the way back, but there was no way

I was going to let that keep me from returning to Paradise Pizza and tipping the waitress who had helped make my lunch so pleasant.

The ride back to town was thrilling—with the wind at my back my speed shot up from seven miles an hour to twenty-three. Riding across Iowa from east to west is difficult enough to be called masochistic. RAGBRAI has it right: start at the Missouri and head for the Mississippi— the ride will be shorter by many days. Within a few minutes I was once again riding past booths and sidewalk vendors and families with strollers. I parked my bike and trailer where I had before, but this time I noticed that my bike was almost blocking a takeout window—another indication that my mind wasn't very sharp that morning. I walked into the restaurant hoping that my inattention wasn't setting a pattern for the day. The first person who caught my eye was my waitress. She looked at me with a questioning smile as I entered. I held her gaze, walked over and, handed her a tip, and gave her a sheepish smile.

"I forgot to tip you," I said. "I'm sorry."

"No problem, I hadn't even noticed," she said. Whether that was true, I couldn't tell, but her smile told me she was touched that I had come back. And I was glad too. Even if she hadn't noticed, I had, and it would have been on my mind much of the day and maybe longer.

As I biked down the main street of St. Ansgar for what I hoped would be the last time, an incident in *Travels with Charley* came to mind. Steinbeck wrote of a waitress who had ruined his morning in Maine, I believe it was. To describe her, he first placed in the reader's mind a different kind of waitress—one just like the one who had made my day at Paradise Pizza with her energy and good humor: "Strange how one person can saturate a room with vitality, with excitement. Then there are others, and this dame was one of them, who can drain off energy and joy, can suck pleasure dry and get no sustenance from it. Such people spread a grayness in the air about them." My waitress had spread joy, and I was glad my addled brain had prompted me to realize I hadn't tipped her—and that it had done so before I'd ridden twenty or so miles down the road.

I started to look for Josh and then remembered he'd said he was heading for a different town—a different festival—so at least for now my thanks to him would have to wait. I recalled that he was a state legislator—finding him on the Internet would be easy—and I had that campaign button to remind me and voters that he was a bit of a traditionalist. It was obvious that folks in this area valued tradition. Josh had chosen well going for an old-timey campaign button. As I think back over my childhood, I am coming to the conclusion that the reason small towns and rural states tend to be conservative is because the people who remain in small towns value tradition and want to preserve what they grew up with.

Those who want change head to the city—I am beginning to see this, especially as I look at the voting blocs on the electoral maps. If you want to see where Obama's votes are most likely to come from, look for the areas heaviest in population. In Iowa that means the city of Des Moines and the Quad Cities area. Counties where towns like St. Ansgar are located tend to vote for people like Romney and Ryan. Some folks value tradition. Some folks don't. Signs along the road proclaiming allegiance to Romney outnumbered those promoting another four years for Obama. Even though the disparity was great, I realized I shouldn't be surprised, nor should I read too much into it. I was avoiding large cities, which are typically Democratic strongholds.

My rural route was taking me right through the heart of an Iowa corn harvest. As a farm boy I've seen a harvest or two, but the size of the equipment, now that I was riding past the larger fields of Iowa, was staggering. The combines were massive. And no one uses farm trucks anymore—the combines auger the corn into monstrous wagons with huge balloon tires or straight into semis. I saw no Chevy, Ford, or International trucks with sixteen-foot beds capable of hauling three hundred bushels from the field to the grain elevator. In 1962, when I took my first bike ride to Colorado, semi trucks were used to haul grain *away* from elevators, not to take it *to* them. Back then combines had a capacity of sixty to seventy bushels. A farm truck could unload a combine five times before heading to the farm granaries or elevators.

Today's combines have a capacity of two hundred bushels—a farm truck would be almost full after unloading only one combine. A few miles outside of St. Ansgar I came across a scene that seemed to perfectly capture the change in the landscape of America's farms. A John Deere 9530 was sweeping through twelve rows on each pass through the field. Lined up along the edge of the field were two huge semis painted a matching glowing green, quite a few shades lighter than the John Deere green of his equipment. The trucks left no doubt that the farm was prospering. Those three pieces of equipment represented an investment of over half a million dollars—possibly as much as a million.

The farmer in me couldn't resist stopping to take a picture. The farmer in me also couldn't help noticing that in the background, in an adjoining field, was an old combine, possibly thirty or forty years old, with a corn head capable of handling only four rows at a time— not unlike what I would have seen on my 1962 ride. It was a strange picture of past, present, and future. To make the scene even more surreal, the slowly turning blades of dozens of wind turbines were beating out a lazy rhythm on the horizon.

I hopped back on my bike and resumed my wind-battling, westward ride. But I didn't get far. A pickup slowed as I approached and came to a stop, partly in my lane. I wasn't sure what the driver wanted, but there was no doubt he wanted me to stop.

"My son, Joe, he's in the combine out there ..." the driver looked out toward the field where the monster combine was pulling back into the field after having dumped its load in the lead semi. "He said you stopped to take a picture. I'm curious. Why?"

"I was struck by how good your trucks looked parked by the side of the field. I thought it would make a good picture as he was pulling up to unload."

"You like those trucks?"

"You bet. Love the color," I said.

"Where you heading?"

I gave him a quick and somewhat nervous summation—I could see a car approaching in my mirrors and we were blocking the highway. He noticed it too. As he pulled away, he yelled back at me, "If you want to take a break, or want a soda, stop in for a moment."

I pulled to the side of the road to give the car plenty of room to go around and thought, *Why not?* I didn't want a repeat of yesterday's afternoon grind that had me pumping long and hard all day long with hardly any contact with people. I saw that the farmer had already turned into a driveway less than a hundred yards back. Even though I wasn't making very good time and I'd already added around eighteen miles to the day's total with my swing through St. Ansgar, I rationalized that I should still be able to ride sixty-some miles by late afternoon. So I checked my mirrors yet again, swung around in the road, and turned in to the farmyard. At first I didn't see the farmer's truck among all the vehicles, so I kept riding, past the house and past another monster combine, and then I saw his pickup parked in front of a big machine shed. I parked my bike and went looking for him. I found him within seconds in front of the combine.

He smiled. "What kind you want—Coke okay?"

"Sure, that'd be great."

He pulled a dollar out of his pocket and fed it into a machine by the side of the building. Out popped a cold can that he handed to me. He didn't get one for himself.

"Say, you ever ridden in a combine?"

"Matter of a fact I have. In a former life I was a Nebraska wheat farmer."

"You're kidding. So maybe it's not such a big deal to you but I thought maybe you might like to ride a few rounds. How long's it been since you were in a combine?"

"Never been in one this big." We were once again standing in the shadow of his big green monster next to his pickup truck. "Love to. You got time?" I asked.

"Sure, if you don't mind riding in a messy truck. Imagine you can drive this rig, right?"

"Yeah, no problem."

"I'll take you out to the field, then. One of the semis is full; I need to get it. You ride with my son as long as you want, and when you're done, just drive this back to the yard. That work for you?"

"You bet."

I was amazed at how quickly he had extended an invitation to me—for both the Coke and the ride in the combine. I wondered why he was taking time out of his busy schedule. Every minute during harvest time is like gold—farmers have to get the crop out of the field or risk losing it. As we were driving to the field he began answering my questions—it was almost as though he had read my mind.

"I have lots of different landlords. Some of them know next to nothing about farming; they just inherited the land. I make it a point to invite them onto the farm. I want the people who trust me to farm their land to get to understand farming as much as possible. I've found that they love it—love that I take the time to do that for them."

He went on to tell me that he takes pride in building bridges between farmers and non-farmers. "You'd be surprised at how many people have never set foot on a farm—they don't know the first thing about a farm, yet they own one. I want to do my part to change that."

And from what I could see, he was an ambassador of good will extending hospitality to anyone who expressed an interest in farming. "The more we know about each other, the better the chance that we'll be able to get along," he added.

I certainly couldn't argue with that. His timing was good, too. Just as we drove into the field, his son was pulling up to the first semi to top off the load. While the corn was streaming out of the auger, I climbed the ladder up to the cab. Joe was just as welcoming as his father, Jim, was—and so was the cab of the combine. It had everything, including a jump seat. It was like an airplane cockpit in other ways as well—computer screens and high-tech wizardry throughout.

Joe pointed out all the monitoring he could do right from the cockpit. Yields are available to him. He can get even yields in a troublesome part of a field such as a low spot where water collects or a particularly sandy ridge. The moisture content of the corn is also recorded.

But the most mind-boggling feature to me was the "autopilot." Joe pointed out the "feelers" on the corn head that literally steer the combine down the rows by making minute microsecond-by-microsecond corrections from information supplied by sensors that feel the stalks passing by. The similarities to an airplane were stunning. GPS technology has moved into farming in a big way, especially in recordkeeping—it helps farmers to determine the effects of the fertilizers and the poisons they put on their fields.

I rode a couple of rounds, marveling at the changes that have taken place in farming in the past fifty years. I was so overwhelmed that my over stimulated brain ran out of questions to ask Joe. During the lull I found out that he was pretty observant and sharp-eyed—he'd noticed the little Italian flag flying from Friday's six-foot poly pole and asked me about it. Turned out that he and his wife had recently spent a delightful few weeks in Italy, in the Lake Como region. Also turned out that Joe is a bit of a chef. And a businessman—he makes and sells a barbecue sauce that is doing quite well. As I hopped off the combine, I thought how very different the day was turning out from what I expected as I set out from Osage. It began as the coldest morning of the trip. I'd hoped to get a lot of miles down the road before the forecasted high winds picked up. But ten minutes later I was fixing a flat while both the temperature and the wind speed climbed steadily. And now at two in the afternoon the wind was howling out of the west, and I was only eight miles closer to my goal for the day after eight hours on the road. That's not great progress, but the day had been fun, interesting, and full of stimulating conversations. However, sundown was only five hours away, and the wind was bearing down on me at speeds approaching forty miles an hour. I hopped in the old pickup and headed back to the farmstead. Jim met me as I stepped from the truck and handed me a bottle of his son's special barbecue sauce.

"Tell your friend in Forest City that if he'll supply the burgers you'll bring the sauce. You've got room in that trailer for a bottle, don't you?"

I took a look at it and said, "You bet, I'll make room." The label proclaimed "Farm Boy BBQ" It even bore the iconic image of a John

Deere combine. I declined Jim's offer of another Coke, explaining that because of the wind I had to get going but I was extremely glad he'd stopped me on the road. And with that I pushed my bike back out to the county road and leaned into the wind.

An hour later I had managed to get only another ten miles closer to Forest City. I was making such slow progress that I was again thinking of where I'd find another restaurant. I was carrying leftovers from Paradise Pizza, but I was making so little progress that I didn't want to eat my reserves until I knew I'd be able to find something to replace them. Long-distance bicyclists look at food just like automobile drivers look at gasoline. You need gas to keep that engine running, and a bicyclist can travel only so far on empty before the engine just shuts down.

I found nothing in Bolan. In Kensett, the bar was closed. The only food/energy available was a can of Pepsi from the pop machine on Main Street. I took it to the park to drink it and consider my options. I had two routes to Forest City—one on county roads, one on Highway 9. Via the county road, Joice and Leland were my options for food. On Highway 9, Manly and Hanlontown presented the only possibilities. Checking the map, I discovered that both Joice and Leland had populations of less than three hundred people—almost exactly the size of my hometown.

The population of Manly topped one thousand, but I didn't want to ride on the busier state highway. I decided to gamble that Joice and Leland, like my hometown, supported cafés. I hoped I wasn't being too optimistic. The wind was not letting up—in fact, the speed was increasing—Weather Bug, my favorite weather app, now listed gusts of up to forty-five miles an hour. I did some quick calculations and discovered that unless the winds dropped off dramatically or shifted to blowing out of the north, getting to Forest City was going to be a race with the setting sun yet again. Adding to the difficulty of reaching Forest City was the high probability that I had some climbing to do—my route would lead me across the Winnebago River twice.

My route also took me across the Shell Rock River. A couple of good ol' boys were leaning over the railing of the Shell Rock River Bridge peering into the water. I stopped to find out what they were looking at.

Lonnie and his friend were passing a lazy afternoon wondering whether to go carp fishing. I leaned over and looked too. The surface of the water was rippling with the movement of hundreds of monster carp just below the surface. I saw individual carp pass through pools of clear standing water—they were gigantic—more than two feet and maybe as much as three. I didn't ask what they were fishing with, but I didn't see any poles. I didn't stay long—I don't think they were looking for company that afternoon, and I wasn't in a real talkative mood either. I had a lot of miles to go and a lot of wind to push.

By the time I reached Joice and discovered that there was no restaurant, my calculations showed that even if there had been, I didn't have time to sit down and eat—I had to keep pedaling against the wind and hope its direction would shift. Four miles west of Joice, the county road gave me a bit of breather by turning south for a mile. My speed almost doubled, and I realized I'd been so focused on watching the sun sink in the sky that I hadn't noticed that imperceptible shifts in wind direction had given me a touch of tailwind as I headed south.

I was still a dozen miles from Jim's place with only an hour of daylight, and I was averaging less than ten miles an hour against the raging gale. My only hope of getting there before dark was a dramatic increase in speed—and that could happen only if the wind shifted even more. A crosswind would be helpful, but without more of a tailwind, I'd be riding through Forest City in the dark looking for Jim's house.

As I struggled along working hard to get my speed above ten miles an hour, I looked for flags in the farmsteads that would show me that the wind was shifting. I watched the paths of leaves blowing across the road—anything that might give me hope that the angle was increasing. I still had four more miles west to ride—and each one was taking about five minutes, sometimes as many as six. Roger Bannister, when he set the record for the mile run when I was a kid, beat my pace. Heck, citizen marathoners click off miles faster than I was going that afternoon.

But when I made that ninety-degree turn south half a dozen miles north of Forest City, my speed jumped up to that of world-record holder Usain Bolt in the one hundred meter dash. I was clipping off each mile in just over two minutes—at speeds above Bolt's 27.45 miles-per-hour record pace. I got to the restaurant in Leland so quickly that I had time to go into the roadside bar/café to see if I could get a takeout serving of pie. I'd been carrying thoughts of that pie all day. I think it was Josh early that morning who first mentioned the pie I'd find in Leland, and he wasn't the only one to bring it up as I made my way slowly westward. Unfortunately, those recommendations were a little dated—the waitress informed me that they'd quit baking pies four years earlier. But before she let me go, she insisted that I let her fill up my water bottles. Nice touch—good way to keep recommendations coming their way even if they were no longer serving the best pie in upper Iowa. I hopped back on Friday and flew into town sporting an average on the plus side of twenty miles an hour for the six-mile run since I had turned south toward Forest City. I was on the bike long enough to take only one swig of that water the waitress had given me.

Despite my worries, I reached Jim's early enough that I had plenty of time to unpack, settle in, and shower before he threw the burgers on the barbie. Running true to form for the day, I totally forgot to tell Jim and Cheryl that I was carrying Farm Boy BBQ sauce to share with them. But I did share with them stories of all the people I had met that day. Jim told me stories of his RAGBRAI rides and chided me for riding the wrong way across his state. I had to agree as I told them about the two days of riding against an unforgiving wind to get to their house. Jim had his own stories to tell. I suspect that every bike rider who has ridden Iowa has at least one horror story about struggling against gale-force winds. The state tilts at windmills for a very good reason.

And that reminded me of Don Quixote's battles with windmills. I wanted to know more about why John Steinbeck had chosen to name his "horse" Rocinante. While we watched NASCAR on TV, I Googled Rocinante and was struck by the way Wikipedia put it: "In many ways, Rocinante is not only Don Quixote's horse, but also his double: like Don Quixote, he is awkward, past his prime, and engaged in a task beyond his capacities… *Rocín* in Spanish means a workhorse or low quality horse, but can also mean an illiterate or rough man."

I wondered if Steinbeck had really felt that way about his journey and about himself. If he had, it had been lost on me the first time I read *Travels with Charley*. I suppose when I was younger I focused on the adventure of it all and passed right over lines that revealed the author's doubts—lines that jump out at me now. This is one of the reasons that every time I read a book I date it. I also date the notes I make in the margins as well as the passages I highlight. Those dates help me better understand my journey in life—what has caught my eye and what I didn't even see on previous readings. Reading the book as a sixty-five-year-old, I noticed, highlighted, and commented on this line: "Am I learning anything? If I am, I don't know what it is."

I was especially intrigued when Steinbeck repeated this thought a page later. He liked lean prose, so I doubt that the repetition was an oversight. Most likely, it was a point of emphasis. People weren't talking to him as much as he had hoped they would, and he couldn't hide his disappointment. I hadn't been on the road a week yet, so it was probably too early to generalize, but I was pleased with how willing people had been to talk about themselves and their country—and their feelings about our future.

Has America changed? Are we now more open to strangers? Or is my little Bike Friday the difference? Like Steinbeck, I too had embarked on a quixotic adventure, but my interactions with Americans were giving me hope for our country. What I had been hearing was not the channeled, episodic, lockstep thought of the evening news of NBC, ABC, and CBS. The Americans I'd been meeting may seem invisible, or inconsequential, to the people in power in Washington and New York City, but in truth, these unseen people were and still are the backbone of America, people who give more than they take, people who love God and country and are willing to take a stand for the idea that is America. They are the basis for believing that our best days may yet be ahead of us. But it would be a mistake to not recognize that there is a battle for the soul of America—two philosophically different visions—and they aren't compatible.

Chapter Six

America will never be destroyed from the outside.
If we falter and lose our freedoms,
it will be because we destroyed ourselves.
ABRAHAM LINCOLN

For Such As These

The next morning, which happened to be National Grandparents Day, I woke up early and decided to go for a walk on the grounds of Jim and Cheryl's beautiful home, a place that seemed perfect for family get-togethers. First I walked down to a pond that serves as a focal point for all the acreages in their subdivision. The water was vibrantly alive with geese. I got lost in thought watching them glide gracefully across the sparkling surface—I was trying to imagine how long ago this land had been farmed. It still had vestiges of the farm it used to be—windmills and hayfields—but now instead of corn and cows, the land was raising kids and grandkids. The morning light was too gorgeous to let go of just yet, so I continued walking. At the crest of a hill I heard a vehicle coming up behind me. I moved over to let it pass, but it slowed and stopped. I turned to look and was surprised to see Jim smiling at me. He and Cheryl had driven out to find me and tell me they were going to church. It seemed like a good morning to do exactly that, so I asked if I could tag along. They were a bit surprised, but they recovered quickly, and Jim said, "Sure can!"

Cheryl scooted over next to Jim, and I hopped in the front seat of the pickup truck. We headed south past farms and cornfields on a quiet country road to Jim's hometown, to the Lutheran church he had been attending almost his whole life. It was built when he was in grade school. He had hoped to sit next to his grandchildren, but we were a little late and had to sit at the very back of the church. It was so crowded we even had to sit in separate pews. But we were close enough that Jim was able to point out a few of his grandkids up near the front.

The sermon was about children—*for the kingdom of God belongs to such as these.* Indeed, the whole service was devoted to children. The name of each child in Sunday School was called out and he walked alone to the front of the church to receive the book he would be studying for the year. Some were shy, some were outgoing, but all seemed proud to be recognized. It reminded me of the services I attended as a child when each of us had to make that self-conscious walk to the front of the church to receive recognition or to sing in the Christmas or Easter program.

I was reminded again of my childhood when the church gathered in the basement after the service. The kids were playing games, the parents were talking, and everyone was eating. It was a scene right out of my childhood in the basement of the Congregational Church. Jim knew everyone and everyone knew him. I was amazed at how comfortable I felt and how much I identified with the kids in the room. The smells and sounds and big thermos jugs of Kool-Aid also took me back fifty-some years. I probably shouldn't have been surprised, but I was. Except for a couple of folks checking phone messages, it could easily have been the late fifties or early sixties. No wonder the America I've been seeing on this journey seems so familiar if, despite all the technological changes, church congregations are still gathering like this all across this country.

Jim introduced me to his children who were there and told me about those who weren't. He also pointed out his grandchildren. They were doing just what I did as a kid—racing around the room getting rid of pent-up energy from having sat still for the past hour. We watched them and talked of earlier days while we ate corn dogs on a stick, then we grabbed a bag of popcorn and headed out for a tour of the town.

Jim wanted to show me the homes of his kids and the schools of his grandkids. He and Cheryl have nine grandchildren in the same school system and another eagerly anticipating kindergarten. I told them they were fortunate, but I think they already knew that—they knew that a lot of grandparents don't see their grandkids as much in a year as they do in a week.

Jim also wanted to show me Pilot Knob State Park just east of Forest City. It's famous for a tower built by the CCC—the Civilian Conservation Corps, a program in the early thirties that provided work for young men whose families were on relief. While Jim was speaking proudly of the work the CCC had done, I remembered that my parents had done the same thing when visitors came—they drove guests out to "the lake" to show off the handiwork of the CCC. The Corps was no longer operating by the time I was born, but I heard the stories of the shelters the men had built and how Franklin Delano Roosevelt had instituted the program. Jim knew these stories as well, but we went ahead and told them to each other just because we liked them so much and because it's so hard to imagine such a program today.

To be eligible for the CCC, men had to be between the ages of seventeen and twenty-eight. The pay was thirty dollars a month, but the young man could keep only five dollars of it—the rest of the money had to be sent home to his family. It's hard to imagine that such "discrimination" would be allowed in today's politically correct world. In addition to their pay, the men received shelter, food, and clothing. Just about everybody loved the CCC. Communities benefited from well-built structures that promoted the use of nearby parks, and the men received valuable job skills and a boost in morale—and since most of the work involved manual labor, they came out of the CCC extremely fit. The program also contributed to a heightened appreciation of our nation's natural resources.

I think the CCC was responsible for some of the best stonework in America's public parks. As I've traveled around the country, I'm surprised by how often I see a CCC project that today, seventy-some years later, still makes a community proud. Jim and Cheryl were certainly proud to show the tower to me—it was a special place because it was the second highest point in Iowa—it reached thirty feet above the hilltop and two or three hundred feet above the surrounding countryside. From the top, it felt as if you were looking at Iowa from a small airplane but without the noise of the plane's engine. The CCC program was successful because the government received something in return for the money it used to help families, and besides money, the young men learned a strong work ethic and earned the pride that comes from building something with a touch of immortality. The CCC lasted about ten years and helped a lot of young men, one of whom, I was proud to tell Jim, was an uncle of mine.

In contrast, and in what sounded like a dig at Barack Obama for his "You didn't build that!" statement to business owners a couple of months earlier, Jim said he wanted to show me something the government *hadn't* built. We dropped Cheryl off at the house and drove to Jim's factory. On the way we drove by the plant where Jim used to work—a company that has given back to the community as well as the whole area. Jim told me that the founder of the company started a foundation that, among other things, had built a church for just about every congregation in the town of Forest City. Score one for capitalism, Jim said—and for keeping wealth from being confiscated by big government.

Jim's factory was in Britt, a small town a few miles from Forest City. From the street it was nondescript, the kind of building people drive by without wondering what might be inside those walls. But once inside, I began asking how a young guy with only a high school education and a few years' experience working in a motor home factory could have built such a successful business. Jim's company supplies pickup toppers that are sold and shipped throughout the United States, and he competes with some of the largest companies in America for market share.

"How did you learn how to use all these machines?" I asked.

"I didn't," Jim said. "I just hired people who knew how to run them—smart people, good people, hard-working people. I knew enough to know what I was looking for."

"Yeah, but at the beginning, I'm sure you didn't have many employees. You had to do most of it yourself."

"You're right. I had learned how the company I was working for was making toppers and I thought I could make a better one," Jim said as he switched on a bank of lights that illuminated a huge painting bay.

"When I started this company I could hardly read," Jim said, "but I had discovered that I was an outside-the-box thinker." Jim also had a Norwegian father who had told him, "You can do whatever you put your mind to, Jim. You'll be successful. We don't fail." And that gave him the confidence to think he could create a business. After he'd created the business, he found that he had to go back and pick up some of the skills that had escaped him in school. "Now I'm a terrific reader—an avid reader—and I use math all day long. Funny the way things turn out." He smiled. "I have to process a lot of information every day—profit and loss statements, reports, and what have you."

Jim has gone through good times and really tough times. One of the worst was the day his whole factory burned to the ground. He lost everything—buildings, inventory, materials, and all of his records. He had five hundred orders at the time—and even that information was lost—phone numbers, names, everything. "You just can't believe how many things you take for granted until you lose it all," Jim told me. "It's the little things that get you." He told me he was ready to throw in the towel until his employees came to him and told him that they'd build the business back if he'd supply the capital—they loved their life, they loved working for him, and they didn't want to go to work anywhere else. "I had no idea it meant so much to them," he said. That gave him energy he had never felt before. What had been a devastating setback in the hours after the fire became, in the days and weeks that followed, a do-over—"A chance to do it right this time."

I didn't get to meet any of Jim's employees, but I did walk around the offices and glance at the clippings, the memorabilia, and the awards—and it sure looked like the company was doing things right and the employees were still glad they were working for Jim.

I was glad Jim had gone out to get ice that evening we met at the Sugar Maple Inn back in Kendall, Wisconsin. Because of a late afternoon storm and a two-hour wait I got to meet a man who is living the American dream. Jim has not only created a job and a good life for himself, but he's also doing the same for his employees. And he's doing it in his hometown. He also has what just about everyone aspires to—kids and grandkids surrounding him.

It seemed odd to me that someone like Jim would be demonized for "not paying his fair share." Here's a guy who is able to create more jobs, *wants* to create more jobs, has the money and the customers to create more jobs, but our government is taking away his will to create those jobs. "I'd be risking the jobs of my current employees—my whole company—if I grow my business and take on more employees. My accountants, my lawyers, have all looked into the new regulations, and they tell me it is just too risky."

As I listened to Jim, it struck me that his story must not be unique. There must be "Jims" all over America who are afraid to grow their businesses—who are ridiculed instead of praised. Has America changed so much that success stories like his are no longer celebrated? I sure hope not, but that's certainly what Jim feels.

I'm sure that those who feel the rich aren't paying their fair share consider themselves fair in demanding that Jim pay more taxes. I'm sure the people who support the Affordable Health Care Act feel they are being fair. But Jim and his advisers have looked at the thousands of pages of regulations and taxes, and Jim sums up their conclusions by saying, "The Affordable Health Care Act is everything but affordable; it would bankrupt my business."

I asked Jim what he planned to do. "I don't know. None of the options look good. The only thing I can do is to wait to see how the election turns out." He could sell his business and retire, but it doesn't seem like he is ready for that just yet.

When we got back to Jim's house, I challenged him to a game of shuffleboard; his game room sported a full-size wooden shuffleboard complete with electronic scoring, just like the one I learned to play on at Casey's on R Street in Lincoln when I should have been studying.

We were well matched—at least I don't think he threw the first game just to be a good host. We battled back and forth, knocking each other's pucks off the board and sticking our own for points until at last the match was tied one to one. Cheryl had by that time joined us. She noted how fiercely we were competing and steered us toward leaving it at a draw. She quietly reminded Jim that it was "movie night," and they still had a few things to do first.

Over the years, Jim and Cheryl have established a tradition of going to a movie once a week. And they kept their date that Sunday. I stayed home to catch up on my notes and get ready for an early morning departure. I fought off sleep until they got home so that I could say good-bye and thank them for their warm hospitality, and for what turned out to be, in many ways, an unexpected journey to my own childhood.

I slept well that night. I even dreamed of my hometown—of a day, which I hoped would not be too far in the future, when people could make small communities more attractive to innovators because of advances in technology. I woke up long before sunrise and quietly tiptoed out of the house without waking Jim and Cheryl. A waning crescent of a moon greeted me in the still-black sky. I switched on my lights and biked away from what I had begun thinking of as a family compound— similar to the Kennedy compound, famous for its hard-fought family touch football games in the early sixties. I also couldn't help thinking of Kennedy's famous words: "My fellow Americans, ask not what your country can do for you, but what you can do for your country." What a contrast from Obama's words fifty years later—"You didn't build that." One quotation carried a grand vision; the other seemed petty. That's certainly how Jim saw it, anyway.

First light would not grace the eastern horizon for half an hour, and I had about four miles to ride south on Highway 69 before I could turn off on what Jim had promised would be a lightly traveled county road—B14. He was right—just about the only thing moving on the road that morning was the wind and my eyes as I watched the reflection of a halo on the horizon turn into a sunrise in my rearview mirrors. The eastern horizon tried on every color in the rainbow as the sun slowly made its grand appearance. I hopped off the bike every mile or so to take a photo, hoping to capture the brilliant colors I was seeing. But the camera's sensitivity was no match for nature's beauty. That gorgeous morning is etched only in my memory.

Thanks to Jim, my morning was carefully planned. Britt was my first goal. I had been to the outskirts to see Jim's factory, but today I was looking forward seeing the heart of the town, eating breakfast, and finding out how Britt came to be known as Hobo Capital of the World. I also had more questions about Jim's business. I wanted to see if a small business like his, which didn't call attention to itself, would be mentioned if I asked folks about the local economy.

At the edge of town I noticed a city worker with a transit—I stopped and asked him where I would find a good breakfast. I also asked him how the economy was doing and who were the biggest employers in town. The economy was doing okay, he said. The biggest employers, he thought, would have to be the hospital and the local government. Jim's business didn't come to mind and I didn't ask him specifically about it. He mentioned again the directions to the Heartland Café, and I thanked him for his time. I would probably have chosen the Heartland without his recommendation—it was the first place I came to and there were enough cars parked out front and enough people inside to convince me the food was good. I ordered biscuits and gravy.

While waiting, I looked up the employment numbers for the local hospital and discovered that it did indeed employ more people than Jim did, but only by a couple of dozen. I was surprised that Jim's factory didn't get a mention from the city worker, but my guess is that unless you work for Jim or you know someone who does, it would be possible to overlook the contribution of his factory to the local economy. And if someone from Britt doesn't think about Jim's business when asked to name the biggest employers in the area, it's not surprising that businesses like Jim's are not recognized by politicians in Washington either.

John Steinbeck would have loved the Heartland Café. He went in search of America's political pulse, and he would have found it here even if he hadn't been looking for it. An older man at a nearby table, who had been reading the *Des Moines Register* while I browsed the Internet, folded his newspaper when I laid my phone down and asked if he could join me. "You bet!" I said and moved my handlebar pack so he could sit down.

He introduced himself as Everett. It bothered me to do it, but I couldn't help using his nose as a mnemonic to help me remember his name. He had one of those noses that, unlike the rest of the body, just keeps growing as you get older, and it brought to mind Mount Everest. Everett wanted to know how many miles I typically rode in a day. When I told him, he said, "You must be in pretty good shape."

"I've just never quit riding." I said.

He then told me about the hobos who have made Britt famous and the Britt Draft Horse Show held every Labor Day, which features hitches with as many as sixteen horses. After we talked horses and hobos for a while, I asked him about local employers. He mentioned an egg factory and the local grain elevator, but he didn't mention Jim' factory. I asked if he'd gone to school in Britt.

"Yeah. I was born here. How old do you think I am?"

To be safe I said, "Fifty-five."

"Not quite. I was born in '35."

"You're a little older than I am," I said.

"Seventy-seven. So how old you then?"

"I'm sixty-five."

"You do *all* that ridin' yet—ain't that *hard* on your knees?"

"I'm doing okay so far," I said.

"Boy, I couldn't do that—got a bad hip."

"What happened?" I asked.

"I was down in Texas, used to go every winter for eight or nine years. A guy was going too fast—an illegal Mexican—he lost control—tried to miss one car—then jumped the curb and came way over in the other lane and got me. They had to cut the top off to get me out—I was in the car for an hour—and in the hospital twenty-three days—the bill was over a hundred thousand dollars."

"Wow. I bet that set you back."

"Ain't set me back at all yet—I had good insurance. But they're still trying to collect from that guy."

"So you're retired now? How long ago were you hurt? I asked.

"Eight years I been waitin'. And yeah, I had to retire, but you can't live on Social Security, I know that. I get about nine hundred thirty and my wife gets thirteen hundred and we can't live on that."

"So you get a little over two thousand a month."

"Yeah. We had about everything paid for, about, but with insurance, taxes, licenses—we just can't live on that. I used to get odd jobs, but I can't anymore."

"So what do you do?" I asked.

"We have to take it out of savings. And we're running our Visa card way up, too."

"Oh, that's not good," I said.

"I know it, but what are ya gonna do?"

"What did you used to do?"

"I farmed," said Everett and then he went on to describe his farming operation before turning to the state of the economy. "Neither one of them runnin' is gonna do nothin'. Obama ain't done nothin' in four years. Zero."

And then he went on to complain about all the expensive trips Obama and his wife take. While Everett continued to list his grievances with Obama, I did a little *double-tasking* and tuned in to the conversation of four women at a nearby table. One was maybe in her late forties or early fifties; the other three were in their sixties, maybe early seventies. They were also talking economy, making a strong case against "Obama's socialism—he's going to bankrupt this country." I was able to catch only snippets of their conversation; Everett's delivery was pretty strong—you might even say worked up. But I was hearing enough of what the women were saying to know that none of them seemed to be defending Obama or finding anything good to say about what he was doing to the country. Everett was not defending him either, but nothing he said, despite his passion, was belligerent or profane.

I tuned back in to Everett's voice. "Obamacare is gonna get more people dependent on government. There's jobs all around here, but nobody will take 'em when you're gonna make more money on welfare.

There's lot a Mexicans coming up here and collecting welfare—no license, no insurance, no nothin', but they're collecting welfare. And now we're sixteen trillion in debt. To get himself elected Obama told us he was going to cut our debt in half, but instead he doubled it. And now he wants us to elect him again. I dunno."

Everett turned for a moment to talk to the owner of the restaurant, who was walking by with a pot of coffee, and I tuned in again to the four women at the nearby table: "... there's nothing wrong with her, she could be working. But instead she sits around all day watching TV and collecting welfare. She's living off our taxes instead of getting off her butt and taking care of herself."

One of women seemed to know the young woman they were talking about quite well. "They offered her a job, but she refused to take it ..."

The youngest of the four interrupted: "It's just another Obama giveaway. It's unbelievable what we're paying in taxes. Before long half the country will be on welfare. I can't believe what is ..."

"James, this is Merv. He made the biscuits you just ate," Everett said, forcing my ears to turn back to my own table.

"Hi, Merv. Those were really good. Did I hear Everett say you used to be a Wisconsin farmer?" I asked, standing up to shake his hand. His handshake was solid, and his hand was huge—the kind of hand you find only when you shake hands with a farmer. Even most construction workers don't have such a solid tool of a hand as an old dairy farmer.

"Yeah, I was until the government bought me out," said Merv with a hint of apology—or maybe it was regret. He looked like a farmer—a man who had spent long days squinting into the sun. He had an open face with a ready smile and piercing blue eyes. He looked good standing there, but I'll bet he looked better and felt more at home with acres of land at his feet.

"This is quite a change from dairy farming. You miss it?" I asked.

"Yah, I do, but the government made me an offer I couldn't refuse."

"You mean the money was too good—or they were going to break your legs?"

"No, it was the money. It was too good of a deal to pass up."

"How did you happen to end up in Britt?" I asked.

"My wife's from here. We had seen this old A & W standing empty, so we made them an offer," Merv said. "It wasn't an offer they couldn't refuse, but eventually we did come to an agreement."

"And now we have a great place to eat," chimed in Everett.

"And it looks like the town has a place they like coming to for morning coffee," I added. For the past hour, I had been watching Merv interact with his customers. I'd heard little of their conversations, but by their body language I could tell that Merv had created an atmosphere that people enjoyed.

"Yeah, it seems to have worked out," admitted Merv. "Although it's not quite what I had in mind for my retirement years."

"Sounds like you still miss farming," I said again, because it was obvious to me that playing the part of farmer was the perfect role for him.

"I guess I do, but this is good too. We like it here. Thanks for stopping in—ride safe." Merv tipped his head toward Everett and walked back behind the counter.

"I got to get going too. Sorry to have kept you so long," said Everett.

"No, not at all. Glad you introduced yourself," I said as I folded up my map.

"Be sure to stop by the Hobo Museum," Everett added as he headed toward the door.

"I will. Thanks."

But the museum wasn't open and the waitress at the Hobo Café didn't offer to open it, as Everett suggested she might if she saw me looking at the paintings on the wall—an extensive collection celebrating the lives of famous and not-so-famous hobos. I left the café, crossed the street, and peeked into the museum but decided against asking to have it opened. I'd already spent almost two hours in Britt and could probably have spent another hour in the museum. It was time to hit the road.

I hopped on Friday and took a few strong strokes of the pedals but quit when I noticed a tall, thin, athletic-looking man my age or a bit older looking straight at me. I let the momentum of the bike carry me

down the street and right into the parking lot where he was standing
next to the front door of the bank. When I was about twenty feet away
he asked, "How far you going?" in a deep timber of a voice that sounded
as though he might have been, or maybe still was, a radio announcer.

"Heading for Colorado."

"I keep thinking that I'll get in shape and ride across the country
too."

"What bike you have?

"A Long Haul Trucker by Surly. I bought it from a guy who rode it
across the southern part of the U.S."

"Well, then, you're all set. Why don't you join me?"

"No—I'm not in shape. You look fit," he said.

"You look like you could handle it," I said and meant it.

"Uh, I don't think so. But it's definitely on my list. I'd love to find
the time one of these years."

"You from Britt?"

"I am. Definitely. The room I'm sleeping in is the same room I was
born in. I'm seventy-four years old."

"Not many people can say that," I said. "That's amazing." I was
referring to both the room he was sleeping in and his age.

"There weren't any hospitals then."

"No, I mean about sleeping in the same room you were born in.
You married?"

"Yes. Just celebrated our fiftieth wedding anniversary."

"Well then, you were kind of old when you got married," I joked.

"Yeah, I was, let's see, twenty-four. But you're right, back then a lot
of people got married at eighteen, nineteen, twenty years old."

"You have kids?"

"Yeah—one lives in Denver. And the other, actually, lives with us
right now. He paints. He was painting in Phoenix but that dried up with
the economy. And then he went to Des Moines and that dried up. Now
he's painting a one-hundred-year-old Victorian called the Armstrong
House that's going to be turned into a museum right here in Britt."

"I'm impressed by this town. Seems like there are a lot of stories here, a lot of characters. And it sounds like you may be one of them. Did I get that right, you're still sleeping in the room you were born in?"

He nodded his head slowly and emphatically. It seemed he was used to people not quite being able to believe his story.

"How long ago did you lose your parents?"

"I haven't. My dad's still alive."

"My golly!" I said with more than a little gusto. This man neither looked like he was seventy-four, nor moved like he was seventy-four, and now he was telling me his dad was still alive. I was almost ten years younger than he was, and my dad had died a long time ago. Wow—I couldn't imagine still being able to share my life with my dad.

"He's going to be one hundred next year. His mind is still sharp. He's probably healthier than I am." I just smiled and shook my head. He was smiling too—obviously pleased to be able to be telling me his story.

"You retired?" I asked.

"No, not really. I'm farming three hundred twenty acres."

"That's a nice-sized farm," I said.

"Yeah, you're right. A lot of people think it's too small, but it's enough to make a living on." The more we talked, the more I liked the guy. I like farmers who farm small enough that they can take good care of their land.

"You sure you don't want to come along?" I asked again.

"No, I'd love to go, I sure wish I could."

And I wished he could too. We finally got around to introducing ourselves—putting names with the stories. I could have talked to him the rest of the morning—easily. I wondered if his dad was living so well and so long because he hadn't killed himself trying to farm more acres than a man rightly can, as I believe my favorite author, Wendell Berry, puts it. At least that's what I would have asked Wayne if he'd decided to hop on his Surly and bike across America with me. I think I'll definitely ride RAGBRAI next year and stop in, if the tour goes through Britt, and ask if Wayne would introduce me to his dad. He's the kind of farmer I would definitely love to meet.

Leaving Britt was hard. I wouldn't have had to meet but one or two more of the town's characters and I would be going back to the Heartland Café for lunch.

A brutal wind blowing right down Highway 18 greeted me when I turned west. A surprising number of the people I met during my first days on the road echoed Wayne's sentiments—wishing they were either in good enough shape or that they had enough time to take off on an adventure like mine. Standing in the lee of buildings on the main street of a town, they can say they'd like to ride with me, but most would probably lose interest a couple of miles out of town, especially on a morning when a steady wind of twenty miles an hour is blowing— and gusting to thirty-five. I didn't make it very far before I was ready to take another break. Five miles from Britt, I stopped next to one of those massive concrete grain elevators that tower over just about every Midwestern town. This one was in Hutchins.

I had to take off my wind pants—even though the morning was still a little cool, my legs were developing plenty of heat to keep me warm. An employee of the elevator, dressed in a blue denim company shirt, was the first to notice me. He introduced himself. Mark was wistful—wishing he could take off on an adventure. We talked a bit. He reminded me of Dwight, a high school classmate who had gone to work at the elevator in Hayes Center. He not only looked like him, and wore John Lennon-like small, dark glasses, he was built just like Dwight too—about five foot eight and wiry. And like Dwight, he too had served in the Army— twenty years, much of it in Korea. He even got up to the DMZ—the demilitarized zone. And also like John Lennon, Dwight had died much too young. I hoped that was where the similarities ended.

A semi truck pulled in. Mark went to unload it. The driver hopped out and immediately began asking me questions. He wanted to know where I was headed and why I was flying an Italian flag. He had been to Italy—Rome and Venice. We talked about the friendliness of the Italian people. We talked for a long time about Italian food. He was the only guy I'd ever met who didn't think Italians ate enough—he thought the portions were too small.

"But they've got to be small if you're going to get through five or six courses every time you sit down for a meal," I protested.

"I don't know. I was hungry the whole time I was there. But I loved it. I'd go back in a heartbeat," he said.

John was driving a semi, but I didn't think he was a truck driver. The Pioneer Seed Corn cap and the pliers on his belt made him look more like a farmer. He was also wearing a Hawaiian shirt, that didn't quite cover his belly—didn't quite meet up with his well-worn jeans. Heck— he was dressed, even down to the pliers, just like I dressed all those years I was a wheat farmer in southwestern Nebraska.

Turned out that John had also been to Hawaii. I told him that I too had been there; in fact, I'd lived there when I was in the Army. But our conversation about Hawaii was cut short. His truck was empty and he had to get going to make way for the next semi in line. He said good-bye and drove his truck across the road to get his empty weight. I stuffed my wind pants into my suitcase, took a drink of water, jotted a few notes, and prepared to do battle again. But just as I was getting ready to pull out I saw John jump down from the cab of his truck and run toward me.

"What's your phone number?" he yelled as he was crossing the road.

I grabbed a business card, a miniature of the cover of *An Italian Journey*, and handed it to him.

"I want to stay in touch," he said. He didn't say whether it was because of Italy or Hawaii or just because he liked to travel, but something about my story must have resonated with him.

As he ran back across the road I yelled, "You can follow me on Facebook. The address is on the back. I post photos just about every day—you can see if I make it to Colorado."

"Thanks. I'll do that," and with that he hopped back in his truck. I turned and waved at Mark and started pushing against the wind again. Wesley was only five or six miles west, but I had no doubt that I'd be ready to take another break by the time I got there. Some days are a struggle. Some mornings you make a lot of miles, and some mornings you don't. This was shaping up to be one of those "don't" mornings. And it was also shaping up to be one of those mornings that year after year make me want to take off on yet another long-distance "life-is-like-a-box-of-chocolates" bike ride. I'm used to bike rides bringing surprises to my life, but I could hardly believe how many unique personalities I had met in just one morning.

The wind was not letting up—if anything, it was blowing even harder. I pulled into Wesley at a speed just above a fast walk. I had my eyes on a beautiful steeple that had been pulling me toward it since the moment I had first noticed it not long after I pulled out of Hutchins, six miles back. I turned south on East Street to go park in its shadow and take a photograph of its uplifting architecture. While I was still cooling down in the shade of Saint Joseph's Catholic Church a huge man with wavy hair, a sleeveless shirt that revealed a big tattoo on his massive arm, and a ready smile pulled over to ask where I was heading. Darryl turned out to be one of the friendliest people I'd ever met. He had just picked up his son from school and was heading to Minneapolis to see a Twins game. His boss had given him two tickets and the rest of the day off. We talked about Colorado and baseball for awhile, and how much fun it was when we were kids to get called to the office, knowing that our dad was pulling us out of school for the afternoon just so the two of us could be together. I glanced at his son in the back seat—he was smiling too. As Darryl was pulling away for the three-hour drive to the Twin Cities, I asked him where I might find a good place to eat. He directed me back to Old 18 and Johnny's.

The place was quiet. The room was dark and cavernous. I worked my way slowly to the bar, fearing that my shins would meet up with a chair. When my eyes had adjusted, I saw that except for the waitress, there was not another soul in the place. Normally that would have concerned me, but both Mark and John, back at the elevator in Hutchins, and now Darryl, had recommended the place, so I just figured I was a bit early for lunch.

"What can I get you?" I looked toward the sound of the voice. My eyes had not adjusted enough that I could not make out her features, except she was tall, had long hair and sounded like she was in her thirties.

"Am I too early for lunch?"

"No, not at all. The special should be ready in just a few minutes. Here's a menu."

I took a look and noticed that I could order a baked potato à la carte. That sounded real good to me. A potato and a Pepsi. Even though I'd been riding hard, I had traveled only thirty miles that morning. The biscuits and gravy from the Heartland Café, topped off with a cinnamon roll, were taking good care of fueling my engine. While I was waiting for the potato, an older customer walked in. From the conversation that started the moment he came through the door, I gathered that he was moving to his favorite spot at the bar, and that he and the waitress were picking up where they'd left off the day before. In fact, the waitress was diagnosing his medical condition, telling him how best to take care of himself—that instead of swallowing an aspirin he should apply it directly to the infected area. At least that's what I think she told him. It was obvious that she knew him well and that they had discussed his condition many times, and it was getting better.

After he had left, I asked if she was a nurse—I'd been very impressed with her comprehension of the situation, her diagnosis—and her *barside* manner.

"No, but I've raised three kids, and besides, my mother's in the kitchen. She's raised even more kids. She has a remedy for everything."

"Even for what to do with aspirin?" I asked.

"Yeah. Even for the many ways to use aspirin," she assured me. I had hoped she would tell me what aspirin applied externally would cure, but she didn't, and I didn't want to violate *doctor/patient* confidentiality, so I pried no further. I did learn many months later, much to my surprise and delight, that aspirin moistened, and rubbed on insect bites relieved a terrible case of itching on my feet and legs from no-see-um bites that was just about to drive me nuts. If the man who came into the bar that morning was suffering anything like I was before I rubbed aspirin on those welts, it's no wonder he was happy to report to the waitress that she had cured his problem.

In my first seven days on the road, I ate in more family-owned restaurants than I probably had in the past seventeen years. I felt like

I was back in my hometown of Hayes Center. I grew up overhearing conversations like that. I realized as I was sitting there that I really miss the interactions of people whose lives are intimately entwined. The waitress was taking great care of me as well—she topped off my Pepsi several times and gave me extra butter. She loaded me up with sugar and carbohydrates and fat—enough to drive food police like New York City Mayor Michael Bloomberg and First Lady Michelle Obama nuts. But then I look at food and freedom a little differently. I look at food as fuel. Calories are a good thing. And so is the freedom to eat or drink them if you choose. Eat less food if you don't need the energy. But if you do need energy, eat food with the good stuff still in it.

In addition to her barside manner, the waitress had *roadside* manner as well. She told me that McGregor road ran parallel to Old 18 and that I'd find it just a mile south of town.

"That would be your best road into Algona, not much traffic. But be prepared to hit the ditch—there are a few people around here who drive it like it was the Autobahn—like it's their own private drag strip," she told me as she was bringing my change back to the bar. I left it all there and added a little to it—a hundred percent tip, but it was still one of the most inexpensive lunches I had eaten on the journey.

As I was walking out of Johnny's I saw a man walking up to the door as though he were coming in, but then he veered off toward my bike. I could feel a question coming on. And sure enough, when I got outside, he was just standing there, staring at my bike.

"Weird-looking, isn't it?" I said, startling him. He hadn't noticed me approaching. "It's my airplane bike," I added.

"My son rides bikes. He has all kinds, but I've never seen one like this."

"Yeah, it's a little different. It folds up—and it all fits into that suitcase I'm pulling—including the trailer's wheels. I bought it to travel around Italy a few years ago. My name's James; my bike's name is Friday."

"My name is Gene. My relatives have been to Italy. My cousins just loved it. We've all got to get over there—it sounds like they had a great time," Gene said and flashed me a shy, quizzical smile. He was in his seventies; a humble man—the kind of guy people immediately take a liking to.

"Your son's around here—and he rides a lot?"

"No, he's in Kansas City. He races bikes—he was number two in Missouri a few years ago."

"Really!" I said. "I wasn't second in the state, but a couple of years ago, I was second in Aspen, in the old guy's group."

"Well, you should ride RAGBRAI. You ever heard of it?"

"Yeah, I have. But I've got to ask you. Do they really get fifteen thousand riders crossing the state at one time? That's got to be a bit of an exaggeration, isn't it?"

"No, I don't think so. They've been though Algona a couple of times, and they just shut down the town."

"Who feeds them?"

"Volunteers. Spaghetti suppers, what have you."

"That sounds pretty good."

"Where you heading today?" he asked.

"Hoping to get to the Grotto in West Bend. Is that a good thing to see?"

"You bet. You've got to see that."

And Gene went on to tell me all about it. How it's listed as one of the wonders of the world. He confirmed that there was indeed a motel in the town and it was pretty nice. We talked about how long it would take to ride to Colorado, and how hard the wind had been blowing the past week, and what a good road McGregor would be to get me to Algona.

"Where should I eat in Algona?"

"You might try Premier Pizza. It's right downtown."

"I just ate, but I imagine I'll be hungry by then. How far is it, about fifteen miles?"

"A bit less than that."

"And to West Bend?"

"I'd say another twenty."

By then Gene and I had been talking half an hour or so, mostly about his son, our mutual Irish heritages, and Colorado, where his son used to live. I looked over his shoulder and noticed a late model John Deere tractor pulling a silage wagon zipping through the intersection.

"Wish I could find one of those heading down McGregor Road going about nineteen miles an hour," I said.

Gene turned back to me with that quizzical smile of his again, then tilted his head slightly. "Those things travel faster than that—about twenty-four or twenty-five."

I think Gene was still thinking he was talking to a city boy.

"Yeah I know. That's why I'm wishin' I could find one truckin' down the road at less than full throttle so I could tuck in behind him. I just can't stay up with one going top speed. With nothing to break the wind today I'll be lucky to make much over nine or ten miles an hour."

"Yeah, I know. That's a stiff wind." I didn't know for sure, but the look on his face as he said it made me think that Gene was a retired farmer and had spent his share of days out in just such a wind. Although he hadn't shown any sign of wanting to end our conversation, I thought at that moment I saw him step back a bit, so I said, "Hey, it's been good talking to you."

"It's been real nice visiting with you. If you don't find a room in West Bend, you can ride back to Algona and we'll put you up for the night."

"You—you live in Algona?" I was watching him intently—looking for clues that I had heard him correctly.

"Yeah," he said and nodded his head quietly.

"Do you really …," I was stalling trying to think through all the ramifications of what seemed to be a sincere invitation.

"Yeah, we do," and he nodded a little more emphatically.

"Well, I don't think I'd bike twenty miles back, but if I got to Algona, and saw that I was tired of battling the wind, I just might take you up on your offer. Do you want to give me your …?"

And before I had said the word "address" Gene had given it to me, and his cell phone number.

"Are you serious?" I asked.

"Yeah," he said, and thrust his head down and forward to show emphasis, but in his own quiet way.

"Well, I just might take you up on it—I love meetin' people along the way—that's the fun part of it."

"Like I said, you get to Algona, and you're tired ... I'll be back home by three or four o'clock."

"I'm not sure I'll be there by then, but I should be—guess I don't even know what time it is. "

"Well I'll for sure be home by four. Just give me a call."

"Well, I will. One way or the other, whether I decide to stay or go on—but with the wind whipping up like it is I suspect I just may take you up on it."

"That would be great. You can get up and ride to the Grotto tomorrow morning before the wind picks up too much."

As Gene turned to go, a farmer in coveralls got out of his truck to head into Johnny's "Which way you going?" he asked.

"Colorado."

"You'll be battling it then. It's going to be even windier tomorrow," he said as he disappeared into the restaurant.

And with that bit of timely advice, I was becoming more convinced that I should resign myself to two short days in a row, and spend the night at Gene's place. But I didn't tell Gene that, just in case something changed my mind on the way to Algona. However, I had no idea what that would be short of the wind doing an about-face in the next couple of hours.

"Thanks Gene."

"Give me a call," he said as he got into his car.

"I'll do that. Thanks for stopping to look at my crazy bike."

Something had prevented me from committing to accepting Gene's generous offer, but before I'd logged five miles, I was certain I was going to seriously consider yet another day of less than fifty miles. The wind was not letting up. The wires were singing a high-pitched whine as I made my way slowly down McGregor Road. My average was again flirting with ten miles an hour.

The land had flattened out. There weren't as many rolling hills, and the intersections reminded me of scenes in Alfred Hitchcock's *North by Northwest*—a stop sign standing like a lonely sentinel at the point of intersection of two long straight lines—I could see Cary Grant standing there looking off into the distance and slowly realizing that a crop duster that had been flying low over the fields was now coming right at him. That's how desolate it was out there that afternoon. Although few cars were on the road, during one brief stop I made to take a drink of water, two semis pulled up to the stop signs at the same time, one on either side of the intersection. Nothing else was moving, except far off on the horizon I could just make out, through the dust-filled air, wind turbines spinning in slow motion. Despite the warning from the waitress at Johnny's, not once on this road had I been forced to dive into the ditch to avoid a speeding Autobahn driver or a drag racer. The only things moving on that road were trucks, and they were giving me a wide berth.

I don't know how long it took to ride the thirteen miles between Wesley and Algona, but it felt like two hours. On the outskirts of Algona I got a bit of a break. The trees and the houses cut the wind speed down from hurricane level to gale force. I rode up and down the main street looking for Premier Pizza. On the second pass I found it, but not before noticing that most of Algona's restaurants were closed for the afternoon— observing a Mediterranean siesta, apparently. I felt as though I was back in San Gimignano, Tuscany, wandering empty streets, wondering when the shops and restaurants would reopen following the afternoon nap.

The only place I found open in Algona was the Sum Hing Chinese Restaurant. I grabbed my handlebar bag so that I could write notes on what had been a rather remarkable day that was only a little over half over. Once inside the restaurant, I discovered that again I was the only customer. Pinky, my waitress, was from Hong Kong and had plenty of time for me. I chose a huge bowl of corn/egg drop soup. Pinky was surprised that I was able to finish it, and she was also surprised at how much water I drank. I think she decided that rather than come back to fill up my water glass, she'd just stay and talk while I polished off yet another twenty-ounce tumbler. She wanted to know where I was headed, and I wanted to know more about her. She had come to America as a foreign exchange student in high school, loved America, and wanted to go to college here. Her host family helped her.

Fast-forward eleven years. Pinky is married and co-owner of a Chinese restaurant that is struggling to make a profit in a small Iowa town. It wasn't always that way, she told me. She blames a lot of it on a changing workforce. "My employees tell me, 'I have too much hours, they're going to cut it off if I work too much hours for you.' That makes me so mad. I work my butt off twelve hours a day, and have to pay my own insurance, and everything for my kids, and they tell me that they can't work a few hours extra for me because it will cost them."

"You mean they will lose their welfare check if they work too many hours in a week for you? Is that what you mean?" I asked.

"Yes! It's horrible. Nobody wants to work. They get a check for doing nothing. Why they work for me?" she asked, the pitch of her voice rising in indignation.

In the short time she has been in America she has seen the work ethic erode, she told me. The entitlement culture, as she called it, has left her with a workforce unwilling to contribute. "I can't compete with the government," she said. I asked her about the work ethic in China.

"They have all these people wanting work. China is productive. You have to work to eat, to live. You cannot really compare China to America. They are so different. That is why so many Chinese students come to America. China does not have enough colleges for everyone."

Although she talked for some time about the problems of China, and how happy she is to be able to raise her children in America, I could feel a "but" coming on.

"I love this country, our freedoms, our human rights. But I'm worried. A lot of people don't get married so they can get bigger checks from the government. And a lot of people don't work so they can collect more money. So I am worried. How long can America do this?"

I didn't have an answer, but it seemed like a good question for a recent immigrant to ask. Indeed, if the people I had met today were a typical cross-section of America, an awful lot of people are concerned about America's future. They're asking how long can we afford to pay people, who could be working, to not work—putting the burden on others. Pinky had made me see that the burden put on others was not just in taxes, but also in the long days that she was forced to work even though she wanted to be home taking care of her children. She pointed out to me—in colorful, distinctive language—all the unintended consequences of do-gooder bureaucrats. Her story was not anything like Jim's, but her feelings about the government were certainly similar.

The people I'd met on this day were extremely friendly, but in our conversations was an undercurrent of fear that at times turned into anger. Pinky was the youngest person I had met who had expressed fear, but she had the advantage of understanding at the gut level what is unique about America—she had lived without the freedoms that America offers and she feared the loss of them. I guess that's one of the things I've always enjoyed about travel. It takes you out of your own world, away from the things you're so close to, that you can no longer see them clearly.

The long talk with Pinky and the wind that was continuing to howl were conspiring to convince me to take Gene up on his offer. But I was still curious. Had I judged him correctly? What kind of man can so quickly decide to invite a stranger into his home? I've always felt that I was a pretty good judge of character, but there are plenty of stories floating around to make you realize that sometimes people are fooled by kind strangers.

But even as I was contemplating my options I didn't think that giving the matter any more thought would make me change my mind about Gene. I was certain that he was as he appeared—a friendly man who enjoyed people—who had enjoyed our conversation and wanted to share his life and his home. Within two minutes we had established what we needed to know about each other. I immediately knew I greatly liked this man asking me questions about my bike and my journey— he seemed to have no other agenda than to learn something new from a fellow traveler in life. He was not condescending, critical, or judgmental—by the way he spoke of his son I learned a lot about the man with the shy, quizzical, but knowing smile.

I called Gene while I was waiting for Pinky to bring me my bill and told him that I'd made it to Algona, had grabbed a bite to eat, and that the wind had convinced me to quit riding for the day. He told me how to get to his place from the restaurant. I was glad to find out that I wouldn't be backtracking; his place was tucked away in the woods on the edge of town—the edge closest to West Bend and the Grotto.

I found Gene's home at the top of a high hill overlooking a beautiful wooded valley. I found Gene sitting in his garage whittling a walking stick. Bicycles had brought us together, and now walking sticks were cementing our bond. His sticks were true works of art, and he was appreciative of my admiration for his craft. I told him of a walking stick I'd discovered ten years ago on a hike in the mountains of New Mexico that I had crafted over the years into one of my most prized possessions. Its handle, by virtue of being gripped so many times over the years, has taken on a sheen and smoothness that is sensual beyond what I ever imagined wood could be. The stick feels so comfortable in my hand and is so perfectly balanced that it became an extension of my body during all the years I traipsed around the steep hills of my farm.

Gene put away his tools and led me into his spacious home to introduce me to his wife, Sharon. She showed me around their comfortable, made-for-extended-family home, which was a museum of their family history. Like many families, they had photos of the kids and grandkids. But unlike most families, Sharon's collection included photos of all the generations of her family and Gene's family since photography had been invented. The display didn't stop with photographs; she also had artifacts from each generation—the toys, the tools, the weapons, even the marriage certificates were on display. It was a fascinating journey through the past one hundred fifty years. I couldn't quit looking at what were museum-quality displays, even though Sharon had long ago headed upstairs to make the final preparations for dinner. I needed a shower, but I couldn't tear myself away. I got interested in the giveaway items from my childhood—the screwdrivers, pens, bottle openers, and even political buttons and posters. Sharon had it all on display, her home was large enough to absorb it, and it was irresistible.

In addition to celebrating family, panoramic photography was celebrated as well. Sharon was especially proud of a photo that showed her family's home place with everyone standing out in the yard. She also had on display a beautiful photograph of her father's whole school—1st through the 12th grade. It was fascinating to study all the faces—and the clothing the kids were wearing. I remember how important the choice of what to wear on picture day was when I was a kid. That photograph made me think that it's always been a big thing.

Gene and Sharon's house was designed to absorb people, and to make them comfortable—it's beautiful, warm, and inviting—a home for kids, grandkids, and friends. In addition to me they had invited neighbors over for dinner—Paul and Pat. Pat talked little. She seemed to be suffering, possibly from the loss of her first husband, even though it happened many years ago. She and her first husband had been married thirty-three years. It wasn't surprising to me that she found comfort in having Gene and Sharon for friends.

I couldn't say for sure, but I suspected that Gene might have a strong faith—that he most likely was Christian, possibly Roman Catholic. He hadn't used any foul language or used the Lord's name in vain, and I knew that family was important to him. That's not a sure sign that a person is Christian, but it certainly points to that possibility. When you add a deep sense of hospitality to the mix, the odds are even better.

Three years earlier, I had set out on a journey through Italy to try to find out what makes Italians the way they are—so darned friendly and hospitable. When I was a kid, my best friend was Italian. I had read lots of books about Italians, the friendliness of the people, and, of course, their love of food. I spent seven weeks touring Italy, picking olives for Italian farmers, sharing meals with them at their kitchen tables, and loving every minute of it. But I came home without discovering a reason for their friendly ways. It wasn't until a couple of years later, when I was watching a World War II Italian movie made by an atheist, that a possible reason for the hospitality of the Italian people finally dawned on me—in fact, the filmmaker stated it unequivocally.

The director, Roberto Rossellini, began his film with a short prologue about the bravery of the Italian peasants, who, in the face of certain death at the hands of the Nazis if they were discovered, nevertheless took into their homes and hid escaped Allied prisoners. Mr. Rossellini, despite his lack of belief, nevertheless attributed their bravery to their Christian beliefs. I had witnessed Italian hospitality, and had benefited from it, but I had not attributed it to their religious beliefs. Roman Catholicism is so engrained in the Italian culture that it is tradition. I didn't recognize it because not once when I sat down to eat with my host families did anyone offer a prayer. But despite the lack of outward signs, the inward influence of the centuries-old Catholic traditions and beliefs still infuses the daily lives of Italian families.

My suspicions about Gene's faith were confirmed when we sat down to dinner. Gene offered a short prayer, a Roman Catholic prayer, and then we began talking about family. It would be hard not to in that house—I had so many questions about all the interesting photographs on display. We also talked of farming. I was right; Gene had been a farmer. He was just enough older than I am that he had stories to tell of farming with horses—of Bess and Baldy, a pair of big Belgian draft horses that scared the heck out of him when he was a little boy.

We talked of the changes in farming—of the six thousand dollars he paid for his first tractor and of the quarter of a million dollars that a tractor can cost today. He confirmed my estimate that it's possible to blow a million-dollar bill on a combine and a couple of semis. He told me that some of the farms in the area had just hit the ten-thousand-dollar-an-acre mark and have operating loans of four million dollars. None of Gene and Sharon's kids went into farming, but Gene made it possible for a young man just getting started in farming to take over his operation when it came time for Gene to retire.

As might be guessed in a home so devoted to family, the plight of the American family came up. "We know a teacher who has eighteen students in her classroom, and eleven of them are living with only one parent," Sharon said.

I quickly thought back to my graduating class and could think of no one who wasn't going home each evening to a home with two parents. We talked of all the changes—of the old Pontiac Catalinas we'd driven—the ones with the pointy V-shaped fins—of prom nights, and of going to town at night to shop before TV came and changed everything. And we wondered if it was a good thing that we hadn't asked our kids to work as hard or as long as we had worked as kids.

"I spent a lot of hours with a pitchfork and a scoop shovel in my hand," Gene said. "But I didn't want that for my kids. I wanted them to play basketball, compete in track, be in the band, whatever they wanted."

I guess it's inevitable to wonder if the country isn't getting a little soft—and to worry about it just a bit. On this night the worry about America turned to money—and to the debt that America is facing. I'm sure there must have been a lot of people who didn't know during the presidential election of 2012 that America was over sixteen trillion dollars in debt, but I don't think I met any of them that day.

After a while we forgot about the problems facing America and talked about virgin olive oil, and Italy, and travel—about where we'd love to go and what we'd love to do. Soon after we had shared our dreams, Pat and Paul said it was time for them to go. But Gene and Sharon and I still felt like talking. The conversation turned back to family and I asked about the design of their house, which was perfectly suited to hospitality.

"That's what attracted us to it, the layout—that it was big enough to entertain people, to make them comfortable. We've always liked the biblical verse: 'Do not neglect to show hospitality to strangers, for by this some have entertained angels without knowing it,'" Sharon said. I wasn't surprised that she was comfortable about mentioning her faith and that she should mention that verse.

I didn't mention it to Gene and Sharon, but I've wondered whether the converse may be true as well: *Do not neglect to accept the hospitality of strangers, for by this some have been entertained by angels without knowing it.*

I think I could make a strong case that something like that happened outside of Johnny's Restaurant in windy Wesley, Iowa, on the tenth day of September 2012. And that meant that on September 11, when I awoke to eat breakfast, I was among friends. Sharon and Gene sent me out into the world on the anniversary of that terrible day in 2001 to take on the wind and the world, fueled with hopeful discussions about America's future and a farm breakfast like those we had grown up eating.

I also felt as if I had found something that Steinbeck had gone in search of but failed to find. Was Steinbeck's view of America in the sixties accurate? He had gone in search of men with convictions—in fact, a friend of his had advised him, "If anywhere in your travels you come on a man with guts, mark the place. I want to go see him. I haven't seen anything but cowardice and expediency. This used to be a nation of giants. Where have they gone?"

Steinbeck responded to his friend's concern: "His obvious worry in this matter impressed me, so I did listen and look along the way. And it is true I didn't hear many convictions."

Is the view of America that I was getting accurate? The kinds of people that I have been meeting are for the most part unseen by those in the halls of power, both in government and in the media. Their opinions are given little notice and even less airtime. But, and this is the big difference, people of conviction are gaining a voice—the powers of expediency and power itself are being opposed by the people who believe in something—in the ideas that made America great.

Steinbeck asked, when he found no one of conviction, "What am I doing wrong?" Having traveled among Americans then, and having traveled among Americans now, I'm not sure that Steinbeck was doing anything wrong. I believe that only in the last few years have Americans begun to realize that they have a voice, that the Internet has given power to the once powerless, and that no longer do people have to turn to the once almighty broadcast media to find out what's going on in the world. No longer can any of the big three nightly newscasters say, "And that's the way it is," and expect to be believed by any but the barely informed. If interested citizens want to find out exactly what is going on, they have discovered that it is absolutely essential to look elsewhere. The powers of NYC and Washington, DC, may soon be powerless to stop the voices of the rest of the country from being heard.

Chapter Seven

I'm fighting so I can die a martyr and go to heaven to meet God.
Our fight now is against the Americans.
OSAMA BIN LADEN

And just as the terrorist seeks to divide humanity in hate,
So we have to unify it around an idea.
And that idea is liberty.
TONY BLAIR

These terrorists aren't trying to kill us because we offended them.
They attack us because they want to impose their view of the world
on as many people as they can, and America is standing in their way.
MARCO RUBIO

A Day Unlike Any Other

September 11, 2012 was very different from September 10, 2012—so different that I am completely unable to account for it. All I can do is to attempt to describe it.

On Monday the tenth, at least a dozen people engaged me, stopped me on the street, invited themselves to join me at my table, pulled up alongside me in their cars, and stopped to ask where I was heading;

waitresses took time to question me and share their lives with me, a farmer delayed his race back to his fields to ask how he could stay in touch with me, and of course Gene and Sharon opened their home and lives to me.

But on Tuesday the eleventh, as I was checking in to my motel, I realized that not one person had engaged me during the day. Had there been a seismic shift in the mood of this part of Iowa in just one day? Both days were windy. I struggled to make headway. Both days were sunny. Yet on Monday everyone wanted to talk. A day later no one took the time to talk—not one person opened up to share his life. I was dressed the same. I stopped to rest often. Looking back, I could think of nothing that was different, except the date.

I was reflective, and maybe everyone else was too. Maybe we were all looking inward on that day, thinking of the dangers that confront us in the world and the challenges that face us in America. I saw lots of people. I ate lunch among tourists touring the Grotto, and I toured it as well. I shopped at the local grocery store, and checked in to a motel, yet unlike the day before, not one conversation of substance developed. Did I somehow seem closed off to others, or were we all too just introspective because of the horrible attack that America had suffered on that day eleven years earlier.

My journal for September 11, 2012, notes that an "ambassador has been killed and Obama refused to meet with Netanyahu." It is interesting to travel back in time to read my journal notes in the light of what we now know of the attack in Benghazi, Libya. My journal also noted that the White House issued an apology to the Muslims of the world in the wake of the attack on our embassy in which Ambassador Stevens was killed. Following a chorus of criticism, the White House apologized for the apology. In reading my notes for September 11, I see that the Obama administration's explanation of the Benghazi attack and its reaction in the aftermath wasn't passing the smell test. And the media didn't smell so good either. The mainstream media was accepting the disinformation the Obama administration was putting out rather than demanding to know what had happened. And since Romney questioned the wisdom of apologizing to the Muslim world in the wake of an attack killing Americans, the media attacked Romney. From the start, this whole incident smelled fishy, and it also said a lot about America and Americans as well as a lot about those in power in America—especially the media.

I had not been aware of the attacks on our consulate in Benghazi when I set out from Gene and Sharon's home the morning of September 11. A reporter for the local newspaper had stopped by to interview me about my adventure. Sharon and Gene joined me for the reporter's photograph. The reporter took a picture on my camera as well. I treasure that photo for what it says about hospitality and friendship—about people sharing their lives with each other. The photo represents a summation of the many great qualities that I've come to appreciate about America. I've traveled in all fifty states, but I learn the most about Americans when I travel and live abroad. We Americans are a unique people. The difference most often mentioned by the people I meet in other countries is our friendliness and openness—the very qualities that brought Gene and Sharon and me together for that photograph.

As we were saying good-bye, Gene warned me that I would have a steep climb soon after leaving his house. Despite the steepness, the climb did not last long, and I was soon out of the Des Moines River Valley and heading west through miles and miles of corn. I took two photographs that summed up that morning of riding. One was of a monster containment facility. I couldn't tell what kinds of animals were spending their lives in that building. I only knew that the exhaust fans were gigantic—almost twice my height—and fourteen of them stretched across the end of the building. Whatever animal was contained in that building, it never felt the wind or saw the sky.

The second photo showed my bike pulled up to a stop sign at the intersection of two lonely highways—the flag on my bike standing straight out. At the other stop sign—a big semi loaded with corn was pulling through the intersection—cornfields as far as you could see in all directions. Completing the scene was a warning below the stop sign next to my bike: CROSS TRAFFIC DOES NOT STOP.

Scenes like those carried me all the way to West Bend. I arrived there just before noon. But the wind didn't carry me at all—I had to battle it all the way. WeatherBug informed me that it was "27 mph SW gusting to 36 mph" at the intersection where I photographed the semi. When finally I got to West Bend and turned north, I checked it again—"32 mph SSW gusting to 43 mph." The southerly component was now even stronger, and I rode the wind into town flying almost thirty miles an hour. But for the morning my average was just 9.9 miles per hour, and I had traveled just twenty miles.

Gene had told me that I'd find a nice motel—a convention center near the Grotto—and that I should consider spending the night so I'd have plenty of time to tour the Grotto. After yet another morning battling the Iowa winds, I was quite certain I was going to take Gene's advice.

I didn't stop at the restaurants on the main street. It seemed better to immerse myself in the experience of the Grotto by eating lunch there. The lunchroom was not overly busy, just a few tourists scattered about the dining room. I ordered a cheeseburger special and sat down to read the brochures and learn about the priest who, in a moment of desperation, had made a vow to God and then had spent his lifetime keeping that vow. What would take me only a few hours to tour took forty years of Father Dobberstein's life to build—in fact, he died while working on it. Others took up the challenge and completed his homage to the New Testament in stone.

I was the last to join the tour. We were a shy group. Few of us had questions. Maybe on these tours no one ever does, but on this day we all seemed to be within ourselves. Maybe, on a day when our thoughts were with the three thousand Americans killed on one horrendous morning, it was good to be touring a site dedicated to the next life—to eternity. On that morning eleven years ago, Americans were attacked by people who had a very different view of eternity and the journey to that eternity. Maybe all fifteen or twenty of us touring the Grotto that morning were wrestling with conflicted thoughts, but for whatever reason, we all seemed to prefer to remain within ourselves—in our own thoughts.

On September 11, 2001, we lost our bearings, and as a nation, we turned toward God. Alan Jackson summed up the mood of Americans in his moving song, *Where Were You When The World Stopped Turning?*

He was pitch perfect in asking us:

> *Did you stand there in shock at the sight of that*
> *black smoke rising against that blue sky?*
> *Did you look up to Heaven for some kind of answer*
> *And look at yourself and what really matters?...*
> *Did you call up your mother and tell her you loved her*
> *Did you dust off that Bible at home?*
> *Did you notice the sunset the first time in ages*
> *Or speak to some stranger on the street?...*
> *Did you go to a church and hold hands with some stranger*
> *Stand in line and give your own blood?*
> *Did you just stay home and cling tight to your family*
> *Thank God you had somebody to love?*

And we felt better when he told us:

> *But I know Jesus and I talk to God.*
> *And I remember this from when I was young.*
> *Faith, hope, and love are some good things He gave us,*
> *And the greatest is love.*
> *Where were you when the world stopped turning that*
> *September day?*

It felt like we were right back there again wanting to ask the big questions—and that's why we were so quiet.

As soon as the tour was over, I retraced my steps, looking for a quiet corner with a bench that I'd noticed during the tour, but by the time I found it, someone else was already absorbing the peace of that spot. I moved on to let that person revel silently in the moment and went in search of another reverent place to contemplate.

I found my quiet place below the hill that the priest constructed as Golgotha, reminding us of the cross of Christ and His sacrifice. In the late afternoon the cross and the hill were backlit, providing a dramatic visualization of the day. It was a stark reminder of all the people whose lives had been lost eleven years before. But the story the priest told didn't end there on Golgotha—he went on to tell the rest of the story—the story of the risen Christ.

In the increasingly secular culture that has been overtaking America these past fifty years, the mention of Jesus Christ grates on the ears of a portion of our population. The PC police have not removed Jesus completely from the public square, but it was refreshing to hear the name of Jesus mentioned so nonchalantly as our tour guide helped us to see the story of the New Testament that Father Dobberstein had spent his lifetime creating.

I sat praying and contemplating—getting lost in thought about past and future until a gust of wind brought me back to the present. I looked up to see violently fluttering flags and decided that on this day of reflection, twenty miles were indeed enough to have traveled. I didn't want to break my mood. The miles were not as important as the fact that I seemed to be where I should be. So I broke the spell for a moment to go check in to the motel, lest the place get filled up and force me to hit the road again.

I walked back to where I had parked my bike, and felt a blow as though the wind had been knocked out of me. My bike was gone. I ran quickly to the road, grabbing for my camera, hoping I could get a picture of whoever who had stolen it. I got to the street and looked toward town—not a soul was moving. I turned and looked the opposite direction, toward the motel, and discovered my bike right where I had left it. I had gotten so involved in thinking about September 11, that I'd forgotten that I had moved the bike between lunch and the beginning of the Grotto tour.

I let my heart rate settle a bit, then hopped on my bike to ride the few blocks to the motel. It seemed strange to quit riding with the sun high in the sky—very different from the two days when I had raced the sun to the horizon. Fifty years ago I would have pressed on. Heck, only two days earlier I *had* pressed on when I probably should have stopped. But on this day I was listening to that voice within, and it was telling me that I was where I needed to be, that I had gone as far as I needed to go.

But when I walked into my motel room and saw that the maid was still cleaning it, I began rethinking my decision. Maybe I should say *Forget it, I think I'll just keep riding a little longer. I've seen the Grotto, time to move on.* But that was before the couple at the front desk had apologized for the mistake that had been made. For my trouble they insisted I should take a look at another room. If after looking at that room I still wanted to get on the road, they'd understand and refund my money.

As I opened the door to the new room, I discovered the reason for the money-back guarantee. My eyes fell on a huge whirlpool tub facing a wall-sized TV. Any thought of heading out the door to do battle against the wind again immediately disappeared. I wanted to yell, "I'll take it!" but I waited until I had walked back down the stairs. I probably wouldn't have had to say anything to the bemused couple—I'm sure my smile gave me away. They were smiling too—they had already recognized my enthusiasm for hopping in that tub and soaking my tired legs.

I grabbed my suitcase and carried it to the room—my bike I parked below my window where I could keep an eye on it. After half an hour of soaking my muscles, I planned to return to the Grotto to absorb more of Father Dobberstein's creativity and inspiration—what many in this part of America had taken to calling the Eighth Wonder of the World.

But my thoughts, as I sat in that tub, were about what had just happened. Even though I had opted not to pay the premium for the suite with the hot tub, I ended up with it anyway and at no extra cost. I would not have gotten the suite if I had checked in half an hour later. The maid would have had my room cleaned and I would have walked in and thought nothing more about it.

But it hadn't happened that way, and I was the beneficiary. Probably no one in that motel would have appreciated being given that suite more than I. How did it happen? I don't know, but I've spent the last half of my life noticing improbable sequences of events that line up to bring about strange outcomes.

The first half of my life, if I noticed such strange outcomes, I just chalked them up to coincidence. But that word doesn't really explain much. Coincidence is just a word to label what we can't figure out—an event that should not have happened, yet nevertheless did. If you have no belief in God, or believe in a god who has no influence over the events on this earth, then a coincidence is what these improbable occurrences remain. But if you believe that God has power over this world, then you scratch your head and say, *How in the heck did that happen?*

And that's how it came about that I wasn't out on the road riding my bike until sunset on September 11, 2012, and instead was soaking in a hot tub watching a special broadcast of a look back at 9/11—a day I remember better than just about any day in my life that happened over a week ago.

On September 11, 2001, I was waiting at my airplane on the ramp in Rock Hill, South Carolina, for a courier to arrive with leather pouches filled with hundreds of pounds of checks that I would load into my twin-engine Piper Seneca and fly to Knoxville, Tennessee. It was a blue-sky perfect morning; gorgeous for flying and anything else a person might want to do. We just didn't know yet what some people might want to do on such a day.

The courier arrived, and as we were throwing the leather pouches into the plane, he asked me if I'd heard the news. I told him I hadn't heard anything. He told me that an airliner had flown into the World Trade Center in New York City. He said it as though he thought it was an accident, which I thought was odd. An accidental collision with a building didn't make sense unless the pilot and copilot were both incapacitated. By the time we had finished loading the plane, we'd heard that a second plane had crashed into the World Trade Center.

Without really thinking about it I knew I needed to get into the air as soon as I could. After I was airborne I began to understand the implications of what I "knew." On a severe clear day such as September 11, 2001, I had the choice of flying under visual flight rules (VFR) or instrument flight rules (IFR). Since Rock Hill was an uncontrolled airport (no air-traffic controller), all I had to do was announce my departure and taxi to the end of the runway. I completed my preflight checklist and run-up as I taxied to save time. Since wind was not a factor, I could establish the active runway. I chose Two-Zero—it was closest to where the plane was parked on the ramp. By the time I got to the end of the runway, the plane and I were ready to go. I advanced the throttles, maneuvered the nose gear onto the centerline as the plane began slowly moving, waited for the speed to build up to seventy-two miles an hour, and then rotated by pulling the yoke back enough to coax the heavily laden Seneca into the air. I called my turnout and headed straight toward McGhee Tyson Airport in Knoxville, one hundred eighty air miles away, just across the Great Smoky Mountains.

I didn't want anyone to notice me. I was going to stay off the radios as much as possible. I planned to monitor as many frequencies as possible to determine what was going on, but I wanted to draw absolutely no attention to myself. I had begun flying this route exactly one week before, but my company and this plane had been on this route for years. Since the plane flew this route five days a week every week, an observant controller would know just where it was going once it was identified, but until then I'd be just a target on his radar screen, albeit one he saw every day going the same way at the same time. But until I was identified, he had no reason to know that for sure.

I was thinking all these thoughts because I knew that with things going so terribly wrong in New York City, things could also be going terribly wrong in other parts of the country, and if and when they did, I wanted to be in Knoxville with my work done for the morning—my checks delivered to the courier on that end. If forced to land short of Knoxville, I'd have to rent a van and drive untold hours over mountainous roads to deliver my payload to the clearinghouse in Knoxville.

There was one other complication: in the plane I also had my road bike. I had no idea what I'd do with my bike if I had to stop short of Knoxville. I had planned to ride my bike to pass the hours until my return flight at three thirty that afternoon.

As the minutes passed slowly by, I began to realize that the airspace of the United States just might be shut down—that every aircraft in the country might soon be grounded. If that happened, I knew that controllers were going to be extremely busy, even overloaded. So I called in and obtained an IFR clearance to Knoxville. As that realization occurred to more and more pilots, the airwaves began buzzing, but I stayed quiet. And I planned to stay silent until at least Asheville, North Carolina, near the halfway point of my journey. But halfway was not where I wanted to be. I wanted to stay in the air long enough to get high enough that Knoxville would be the closest practical airport where I could land if the call went out for all aircraft to get on the ground.

At 0949, just as I was being handed over from Greer to Asheville, the FAA grounded all aircraft within the continental United States—every airplane was to land as soon as it was practical to do so. At that moment it could have been argued that Asheville was my closest destination, but it wasn't the most practical destination. I knew I'd have to circle to lose altitude in order to get into Asheville. Within another few minutes I'd be over the "hump" of the mountains and could lose altitude instead on my descent into Knoxville. I kept quiet.

I was certain that fighter aircraft were being scrambled all over America, and I imagined what it would be like to be escorted to a landing in Knoxville, if only I could get that far. I watched Asheville slide under my right wing and then reappear behind the trailing edge of the wing before disappearing again behind the fuselage. If I could get just a few more minutes in the air before I declared myself, I hoped the controller would have no choice but to grant my request to land in Knoxville. He began talking to another aircraft in my area. Staying quiet for a few more minutes would be no problem—the frequency was busy.

I didn't know the details of what had happened in the world since I'd taken off, but I did know that it was very serious because of the tone that had been established on the radio. The airwaves became quieter and quieter as fewer and fewer planes were left in the air, and I was getting closer and closer to Knoxville—close enough that I figured my request to land there would not be denied.

I called Asheville, identified myself, and told the controller that Greer had cleared me to Knoxville. The frequency went quiet for fifteen seconds and then Asheville called out, "Seven Six November—can't allow that. You got two options—land at Asheville or continue VFR."

I made a quick calculation and keyed my mike: "Seven Six November—cancelling IFR."

"Roger Seven Six November—cancelling IFR—have a good day." I climbed to ten thousand five hundred feet and got the plane ready to descend once I'd cleared the peaks. The moment I cleared the peaks I called Knoxville and told them I was forty miles out, landing.

"Roger Seven Six November—you're number five—fly heading of two eight zero and descend at pilot's discretion to five thousand feet." They were vectoring me to an eight-mile final to Five Left. On a typical morning I would have been cleared straight to the airport.

When I finally landed, my courier was waiting for me, and that's when I heard the rest of the story, at least as much as was known at ten thirty that morning. I knew there was a very good chance that I wouldn't be flying the return route to South Carolina that evening, so I changed into my biking clothes and set out to explore the Great Smoky Mountains, which I had just flown over in my fifteen-minute descent. I'd probably never have a better chance to ride deep into those mountains—normally I'd have to be back at the airport by mid-afternoon

I certainly wanted to know more about what had happened, but at the moment I just wanted to be alone in nature. Within an hour and a half I was in Pigeon Forge, and after two hours I passed through Gatlinburg on the way to the entrance to the Great Smoky Mountains National Park and a rendezvous with a family of bears.

And that's how I spent September 11, 2001, at least the daylight hours. So much of that day is indelibly imprinted on my mind as I climbed switchback after switchback on that rocky road working my way slowly up the mountain that I'd flown over so quickly a few hours before. A favorite memory of the day is the family of bears that brought the whole park to a standstill—causing a massive traffic jam that I was able to maneuver through on my bike. The sight of those animals frolicking in the woods without a care in the world represented something completely incongruous about that day—the idea that "this too shall pass." Those bears knew nothing of the attack on America and I wondered as I worked my way out of the park and back to Knoxville, if any of the people I was riding by on the road that day were also unaware of what had just happened—were they too just delaying dealing with the tragedy, or were they like the bears, blissfully ignorant.

It was a strange thought, but that whole day was strange. I had seen none of the images that are now so firmly embedded in my mind. I talked to no one except the courier. I just rode and absorbed and put off thinking about the attack that had been launched on America. It was as though I needed a huge dose of nature to prepare myself for exactly what I didn't know—I just knew it was big. *The tree had fallen in the forest*—and even though I wasn't there, I knew it had made a sound.

And for seven hours straight that night I listened to that sound and I watched those images as the horror of the morning revealed itself before my eyes. Unimaginable. Unbelievable. Unforgettable. Yet it had happened. And in America. We discovered that day that we have enemies intent upon unleashing incomprehensible terror upon us. America still suffers from that day. Every time we board an airplane, the inconvenience of the security check is a reminder of the day when we learned just how vulnerable we are to people who wage war with no regard for their own lives or for the lives of those they have deemed to be their enemy.

Americans fought kamikaze pilots in World War II, but these people who attacked us with our own airliners were willing to kill themselves not to win a war but to inflict terror upon our citizens. That day we entered a new era of unspeakable horror. We wondered if we would ever feel safe or complacent again and we pulled together as a nation.

But we are no longer together. We are as divided as we were one hundred fifty years ago, when we fought each other to propagate the principle that no man should be a slave of another—that we should all be free. Today we are once again engaged in a battle for our freedoms. And we are engaged in a battle for the truth—a truth that is no longer honored and is with increasing frequency trampled upon.

And that is exactly where I felt we were as a country when I went to bed after soaking all evening in a motel hot tub watching a TV special that had taken me back to that awful day. At the conclusion of the show, I was brought back to our uncertain present when I learned that our consulate in Benghazi had been attacked and our ambassador had been killed. But it was not being called an act of war. And as far as I could tell nothing was being done about it. Even though the Libyan government blamed the attack on Islamic militants and Ansar al-Sharia took credit for the attack, the Obama administration chose to blame the ambassador's death on a riot sparked by an Internet video about Muslims.

I wrote this in my journal just before I turned off the light to put September 11, 2012, to bed. *Interesting to have access to TV on a day when Hillary Clinton said, 'There are no red lines in the sand regarding Israel,' Obama refused to meet with Netanyahu, and an ambassador has been killed. Oh yes, I forgot about the apology that the White House sent out to the Muslim world in the wake of embassy riots. After the fallout the White House sent out another apology, this time to the American people saying that the first apology wasn't cleared before it went out.* Fishy indeed.

What a strange day September 11, 2012, turned out to be—for me and for America. I don't think Americans have heard the last about what happened on that day. Both September 11, 2001, and September 11, 2012, will long be on the minds of Americans—the first because it was the date of an attack from without, the second because it will be seen by history as an attack from within.

I had ridden into the heart of America to take its pulse. I hadn't realized when I departed that I'd be on the road on the anniversary of 9/11, but now it seems entirely appropriate that this day of reflection occurred during my journey. And considering that America was attacked again on 9/11, I'm also glad I was journeying and journaling—I have a record of what I was feeling that day. I have words not colored by subsequent revelations and revamping of the story to keep the truth from the American people. I know what I felt at the time. I knew we were being misled by President Obama and his secretary of state. I knew I could trust the words of the Libyan president more than I could trust the words of the commander in chief of the United States military.

Our government has not come clean about what happened on September 11, 2012, nor has it come clean about what happened on September 11, 2001. Immediately after the original 9/11 attack, approximately three hundred Saudis, including twenty-four members of Osama bin Laden's family, were allowed to leave America bound for Saudi Arabia on sixty-one chartered jets with either no interviews or only cursory examination of their background by the FBI. Some reports indicate that these charter flights began picking up Saudi citizens in various parts of America while our airspace was still officially closed. Whether they flew before or after flight restrictions were lifted, these aircraft were among the first to become airborne following the grounding of all aircraft on September 11, 2001. Discovering who authorized these evacuations is extremely difficult. Was it the White House, the Department of State, or the FBI? The answer might be contained within the twenty-eight pages redacted from The 9/11 Commission Report.

I don't understood the impulse of leaders to cover up the truth or to lie to the people, especially in America. The truth is much easier to absorb, much easier than lies to forgive and learn from, yet still our leaders, and those who work for us in government, lie to us. To demand the truth is not to posit a conspiracy theory. Conspiracy simply means that two or more people got together to bring about some end—whether it was to conceal mistakes, commit intentional wrongdoing, or take part in illegal activity. Two or more people agreeing to withhold the truth or cover up lies is a conspiracy, especially if they are in positions of power.

The First Amendment was written to prevent abuses of power by government and to prevent lies by people in power. I went to bed on September 11, 2012, firmly convinced that the American people were being lied to in a most egregious way about Islamic terrorists. But I also went to the bed that night with the conviction that in America still live a people who provide the best hope to the world of righting such wrongs. I would not have known about the lies of the Obama administration if it weren't for the reporting of people whose mission is to present the truth to the American people. On September 11, 2012, there were not a lot of people in the media providing the truth, but there were a few.

Chapter Eight

Go confidently in the direction of your dreams.
HENRY DAVID THOREAU

Probably Never Heard of our Country

Even though rain was forecast for later in the day, I was not eager to hit the road early. I wanted to sit in the Jacuzzi one more time. I doubted I would again find a hot tub waiting for me if I kept to my mom-and-pop motel budget. I wanted to eat a leisurely breakfast and chat with the managers who had surprised me with the deluxe suite. I got my chance when I stopped by the continental breakfast bar to pick up an apple and a banana. I thanked them for giving me the hot tub suite.

Almost in unison they asked quietly, "Did you like it?"

"Yes, yes I did. It was wonderful."

"We thought you might like it."

"Loved it! By the way, my name is James," I said.

"My name is Divi. My husband's name is Krishna," said the woman, smiling warmly. I was expecting names like Carlos, or Juan, or Maria—names from this hemisphere. "Krishna" sent me to the other side of the world—to memories of being in India filming a documentary about religion. Krishna, I learned then, was a Hindu god.

"Where are you from? You don't sound like you're from India."

"No, no. You've probably never heard of our country," Divi said.

"An island, maybe?" I guessed.

"Yes! We're from Mauritius," Krishna said.

"I've heard of it … but exactly where it is I can't say."

"It's off the coast of Africa," Divi said.

"Oh yes—dodo bird. Right?"

"That's it," said Krishna. "How did you know?"

"Just one of those curious bits of trivia I remember from high school. It was uninhabited when European sailors first landed there, right?" I asked, remembering that with no fear of man, the dodo was easy to catch, good to eat, and before too long, it was a goner.

They were pleased that I had heard of Mauritius and began speaking glowingly of their tiny island nation—so glowingly in fact that I wondered why they had come to America. They were proud that Mauritius had been classified as the most democratic nation in the African region. Their pride aroused my curiosity, and I learned a lot about the island from them. Its government is strongly influenced by British law. The official language is English, but a form of French Creole is spoken. France lost control of the island during the Napoleonic Wars. It has a very interesting history, they told me, but the most important thing for the world to know about Mauritius was that it is a great place to visit—beautiful beaches and moderate temperatures year-round.

"Why in the world are you here, then?" I asked.

"We love America," Divi said with a wistfulness that came from the heart. But they were also speaking of Mauritius with such fondness that I was certain there was more to the story.

"But what about your family?" I asked.

"It is true. We will go back," Divi said. "We will stay here only a few more years, then go home to retire."

"I am fifty-five. I will go back to Mauritius at sixty to collect my pension," Krishna said.

They told me that Mauritians are well taken care of by their tourist economy and that they won't have any worries in retirement. They also told me that homelessness is virtually unheard of in Mauritius; so rare, in fact, that if a newspaper reporter learns that someone is homeless, his or her plight will be published in the local paper.

"We just heard a few weeks ago from relatives that a newspaper published the name of an old woman who was having a tough time, and so much money flowed in she was able to buy a very nice home," said Divi.

They also spoke glowingly of the health care system in Mauritius. It reminded me of my experience in New Zealand some twenty-five years ago. I told them that I had been biking in Auckland when my front wheel dropped into a hole in the road and flipped me onto my back. My head was split open and I could barely breathe because of the pain. A kind soul was happening by and saw the crash. He helped me into his car and took me to the hospital. At the emergency room, I paid five dollars to register—as a nonresident of New Zealand on a temporary work visa, but it would have been the same if I had been a tourist. That was the extent of my payments—for the examination, the stitches, the painkillers, the wrappings for my fractured ribs—and that included the follow-up examination a week later to remove the stitches.

"Would they have done the same for me in Mauritius?" I asked.

"Yes. No matter who you are, where you came from, you would be taken care of," said Divi.

They were speaking so highly of Mauritius and so disparagingly of the poverty that they were seeing in America that I asked again why they had come to America.

"We thought all Americans were rich," said Krishna. "We had never met a poor American. I don't think there *are* any poor Americans in Mauritius. We were not thinking clearly. It takes a lot of money to get there. And a lot of money to stay there—the hotels are expensive. How could a poor person get to Mauritius? How could a poor person stay in Mauritius? So it is no wonder we never saw a poor American in Mauritius."

Divi added, "The poverty we saw when we got here was a shock. We were not expecting that. But we love how friendly Americans are—and their ingenuity. Americans make things—and they make things happen. We love that."

I loved hearing them speak well of America—loved hearing them speak realistically of America. They seemed to love America, in spite of our problems. I could easily have spent the day talking to them. They invited me to visit them in Mauritius. Who knows—that could be a great journey. They'll be back on their beautiful island in 2017. I've got it on my calendar.

But for the moment, I knew that a storm was bearing down on me and I needed to get on the road. Maybe I should have spent the day talking to them; maybe I should have asked them if I could stay another night in that Jacuzzi suite. If I had known how much I was going to suffer in the next ten hours I'd have done just that.

I even thought for a brief moment, as I was pulling away from the motel, that I could have been twenty miles down the road in the hour and a half I'd visited with Divi and Krishna. Then I remembered the invitation they had extended to try out the island life and I chastised myself for thinking such a thing.

Even though I knew talking with people was more important than getting from one place to another, I couldn't stop myself from pushing on. My eyes were on the rain clouds on the horizon and they pulled me right past a couple of farmers talking at the entrance to a field. I didn't stop, even though I wanted to ask them if there was a good place to eat in Plover, about five miles down the road. And the sight of those darkening clouds pulled me right on through Plover as well without so much as a stop to take a drink of water.

I also didn't stop in Pocahontas, another fifteen miles down the road, except to take a photo of a giant statue of the town's namesake greeting folks as they drive into town on Highway 3. I was surprised to discover that it had been created in 1948 by Frank William Shaw, erected at this site along the highway in 1954, and dedicated to his father, Albert Josiah Shaw, an early pioneer of Pocahontas county. I should have stopped to eat in Pocahontas and ask a few questions to try to figure out whether I was related. I knew there was a Frank Shaw in my family tree. Was this the Frank Shaw relatives had told me about who was an artist?

But that morning my thoughts were on the weather. I was benefitting from a bit of a tailwind. I'd ridden fifteen miles to Plover and another fifteen or so to Pocahontas. I was now at thirty miles for the day, and it was still mid-morning, so I kept riding.

The wind was out of the north and at times even had an easterly component. I pulled into Storm Lake, Iowa, at noon. Despite eating a leisurely breakfast, soaking in the hot tub, and talking to Divi and Krishna for over an hour and a half, I'd still managed to ride sixty-four miles that morning. A huge bike store caught my eye and I pulled in. A friendly young sales clerk offered to check my tire pressure. He wheeled Friday inside and topped off all four tires. I should have taken that as a clue that I'd found a good stopping place for the day. But something I seemed to have no control of was driving me, even though common sense, a huge dark cloud off to the west-northwest, and the radar map on my smartphone told me I was going to get rained on.

Instead of turning toward Storm Lake's downtown area, I pressed on, but not before stopping to check my map and eat my leftover chicken in a picnic shelter at the edge of the lake. I should never have eaten my reserves, but I was looking too far down the road that day. I rationalized that I was making good time with the wind at my back and that I could stay ahead of the storm. I'd been outpacing it all morning.

I continued around the edge of the lake clockwise, not fully committed to leaving town but not wanting to stay either. I was having a blast amassing so many miles in such a short period of time. By the time I got around to the south shore, the first of the raindrops hit me—not serious rain yet, but enough that I decided to stop at a public boat ramp and put on my rain gear. I still wasn't committed to leaving Storm Lake.

I almost rode right over a curb I hadn't noticed as I was pulling away from the dock. It was my first riding blunder of the trip, but still I didn't recognize it as a warning.

As I pulled away, I promised myself, *I'll stop if I see a motel.* But I saw no motel, not even any businesses on the south side of Storm Lake. Within a few miles I was in open country heading toward Ida Grove, over thirty miles away. At the pace I'd been riding I rationalized it wouldn't take me long to get there. And if it came to it, a couple of hours of riding in the rain wouldn't hurt me. But so far, it hadn't come to that. I was still only getting hit with intermittent drops.

So I let Storm Lake fade away in my rearview mirror. Five miles out of town the front caught me. The wind shifted and a cold rain began pelting me. My speed dropped from twenty miles an hour to just under ten—and as if that wasn't enough, the land began pitching up and down. The many rivers in the area all had tributaries draining into them from the high ground, and I had to climb out of one valley into another. There seemed to be no end to them. They were the kinds of climbs you hardly notice in a car, but on a bike, pulling a trailer, in the rain, against a headwind—you notice.

I kept expecting the rain to let up, but it never did. I had on plenty of clothes. I was expending energy. But I knew I had to keep moving—I couldn't stop—as cold as I now was, and as hard as the wind was blowing, hypothermia could set in if I quit generating heat from using my muscles. I ate Snickers bars to make sure I didn't bonk. But I never stopped for more than a minute at a time. Always I was looking for a small tavern—a roadside restaurant—a filling station—but nothing showed up. I even rode out of my way a couple of times, into small towns, to see if I could find a restaurant—but I found nothing.

One moment stands out clearly from that day. My eyes and those of an older woman locked briefly. She was driving an old Oldsmobile, gray, just like the day. She hesitated at a stop sign; too long it seemed, before pulling away. Maybe I should have stopped—maybe she wasn't worried about me—maybe she was the one who needed help. But I kept going and so eventually did she. I should have stopped though. I rationalized that she had hesitated because she was worried about me—and I knew that I was going to be okay—so no need to stop. But I'll never know for sure.

I rode more than thirty miles in the rain that afternoon. Not because I wanted to, but once I left Storm Lake, I had no choice. I was again in an area that didn't have towns large enough to support cafés or convenience stores—at least none showed up on my route. Only one person did I talk to that whole afternoon. I stopped a pickup truck to inquire of the driver where I might find a place to eat, and he told what I didn't want to hear—that I wouldn't find a restaurant until Ida Grove, which was still a long way from where I was in the little town of Galva. He did however mention a shortcut into Ida Grove that he thought would get me to a restaurant quicker.

The road from Galva to Ida Grove was like a long, spread-out roller coaster. At the top of each rise I'd look off to the next horizon about two or three miles away, and in between I'd see a mile-and-a-half-long run to the bottom of the watershed. Once I had made my way across the bridge at the bottom I'd be faced with an equally long climb to the next ridge. And when I'd eventually get to the top, I'd look off into the distance hoping that I was on a plateau—but no, I'd be facing another draw—another slow coast to the bottom and a long climb back to the top. The country was beautiful in a stark kind of way, but by the time I had seen the fourth tributary to the Maple River, I wished I'd chosen a road to Ida Grove that followed the river—even if it wasn't the shortest route. I was tired of climbing. I was tired of descending. I was tired of the rain. And I was tired of the wind. The miles weren't building up fast enough on my computer. I had eaten all the doggie bag food I had. I still had some water, and I still had Snickers bars and an apple, so my legs were still kicking the pedals over at a strong pace, but I was getting tired in the head, discouraged by the choices I'd made that day.

I wasn't racing the sun to the horizon and I wasn't looking for a motel before dark—I was just looking for a motel, any motel. Even if I walked I could get to Ida Grove before sunset. The race was against my body shutting down—against hypothermia. I was pushing my body to its limits. I was drinking water. I was putting energy into it. If given a choice, I would have rested it, too, but that was not an option. My clothes were soaked with rain on the outside and sweat on the inside. I needed to get to a place where I could get out of my wet clothes and into warm water. I'd lost interest in eating. But I was still, as best as I could figure, seven or eight miles from Ida Grove.

I had passed beyond the folds of my map—I couldn't see where I actually was. I was estimating the distance to Ida Grove based on calculations I'd made earlier in the day. I was just counting miles, knowing that Ida Grove was supposed to show up when my bike computer counted out the ninety-seventh or ninety-eighth mile for the day. If I had made a wrong turn, or if I had miscalculated, Ida Grove wouldn't show up when I was expecting it, and I'd be in trouble.

My mind was focused on seeing just one thing—the highway sign that would tell me to turn off M-25 and onto that shortcut to Ida Grove. I wanted to get to that turn badly, because then I'd know exactly where I was—I'd be only two miles from Ida Grove. That's what I was telling myself, but I hadn't been thinking clearly all day. What if it were three miles, or five miles?

No it can't be. It has to be two miles. I had noted that distance when I'd folded my map back in Storm Lake and put it in the plastic map carrier on my handlebar bag, but I couldn't confirm it—didn't want to confirm it. I didn't want to stop riding. I didn't want to stand still in the rain getting my map soaked. I wanted to just keep riding, hoping the sign would appear in the distance. I wouldn't even have to be close enough to read the sign. I'd know from its shape that it was a distance sign. That's all the hope I needed.

As ninety-four point three miles registered I came to the top of what I hoped was the last rise of the day. Far off, standing just before an intersection, was what had to be a distance sign—the shape was right, and the road beyond it turned to the right. I could see no town, but that was where Ida Grove was supposed to be. At mile ninety-five point six, I reached that sign and turned right. The sign had indeed said two miles. I should be no more than ten minutes from getting out of my wet clothes.

But as soon as I thought that thought I realized I still wasn't thinking clearly. If I were going to get out of my clothes that fast, I'd have to find a motel on this side of town. And I'd have to get checked in quickly, and if the motel didn't have a vacancy …

The thoughts reverberating through my mind were beginning to scare me. I was clipping off a mile every five minutes, but there were no telltale signs of being on the edge of a town. I could see a grain elevator far off in the valley, but where was Ida Grove? Finally, at mile two the road turned southeast and carried me over a ridge. Through the heavy haze I could see a town—at least the outskirts of one. My thoughts settled down, even though so far I could see nothing but houses and parks. It looked like a nice town, but I wanted to see a ticky-tacky entrance with fast food joints and motels and strip malls.

Not until I had ridden all the way though town to Highway 175— the east-west road through Ida Grove that I thought I'd been clever to avoid—did I find a place to get warmed up. At the intersection sat a most welcome sight—a Subway restaurant. I could see people inside ordering sandwiches. I parked Friday, slowly climbed off, and walked inside on stiff legs. Only two customers were ahead of me, but by the time I got to the front of the line I was shaking. I had lost interest in eating. Instead of ordering I asked the young girl waiting to take my order if there was a B&B or a motel downtown. She didn't know and turned toward the manager, who told me the nearest motel was two or three miles east.

"Nothing this way?" I asked and pointed to the west—the way I wanted to go—toward Nebraska and Colorado.

"I don't think so. No, your best bet is to head east on 175. There's a Super 8 out there, I know," he said.

That was exactly what I didn't want to hear—that I could already have been standing in a hot shower if I'd come into town on the main highway.

"Can I get you something?" he asked.

"Not now, I guess. I'm sorry, I'll be back," I said. "I need to get out of my wet clothes."

The odds of my coming back that night were not good—especially if I didn't find a motel close to downtown. I thought again of finding a bed and breakfast. The Subway manager knew of one and even gave me the phone number of the owner, but when I reached her I discovered she wasn't at the B&B and wouldn't be for another three hours. So it was back to the motel idea. I shuffled on cold legs out to my bike and headed east, looking not just for the Super 8 but for any motel. Block after block I saw not a sign of a motel. The traffic was heavy, and much of it was turning. I had to be very observant—very careful of cross traffic. I couldn't get up to speed—couldn't stay up with the flow. I was too cold—I was shaking too much.

When finally I got to the Super 8 I biked right on by it—I was no longer shaking, only shivering. The manager of the Subway had told me I'd also find an older motel half a mile or so past the Super 8. I wanted to get right into a room, and I thought an outdoor-entrance mom-and-pop motel would get me warmed up the quickest. I kept riding and riding until it looked as though I was heading back out into the country. I looked as far down the highway as I could see; I was on a big, sweeping curve. As I looked off into the distance, I realized that it had been a full hour since I'd turned onto the road leading into Ida Grove—the one I thought would lead me to a motel in ten minutes. My body started shaking again. I turned around and headed back into town—the truck traffic traveling that direction was even heavier. The shoulder was almost nonexistent, and traffic backed up behind me. The Super 8 seemed to have moved farther into town since I passed it. I thought I'd never get back to it. But finally it showed up—right where I had left it.

I pulled in, parked my bike, and with unsteady hands pulled out my check card. I was ready to call it a day. The computer had just clicked over the one hundred mile mark. But once inside, I discovered there was no room in the inn.

"Would you do me a big favor?" I asked the desk clerk. "Would you call the nearest motel and reserve me a room?"

"I definitely would. Miserable day, isn't it," she said as she began dialing.

"It definitely is," I said and closed my eyes, trying to think warm thoughts, hoping they would help me get control of my body.

"Got a room for you," she said interrupting my attempts to stop my shaking. I must have been really focused. I didn't think she had been on the phone long enough to have even gotten an answer, let alone a room.

"Where is it?" I asked. And she pointed down the highway toward where I had just come from.

"Oh no," I muttered. "How far is it?"

"It can't be much more than a mile, a mile and a half," she said.

I sighed and told her I'd just come from that direction and hadn't seen a thing. I described where I had turned around.

"You turned around too soon. It's the only thing out there. You just have to keep going," she assured me. "You won't miss it. Lots of people swear it's not out there, but it is."

I thanked her and climbed back on Friday to head through the rain once more. She was right. Had I ridden another fifty yards I would have caught sight of the edge of the rather sad-looking place. But there was no doubt it was in business—the parking lot was full.

I parked my bike under an oddly constructed overhang, walked in, and registered as quickly as possible. I couldn't believe the lady at the desk didn't ask why I was shaking. Maybe my shivering, my uncontrolled spasms, weren't evident to her—or maybe she chose the expedient of not opening up conversations—just get the people checked in—and go back to watching the afternoon soaps.

I pushed my bike all the way to the end unit. I was so tired and so cold that it was a struggle to get Friday through the small door. I walked into the shower fully clothed, turned on the water, and slowly began peeling the layers off my body. The clothes didn't come off easily; my hands were shaking and my body was trembling. Ten minutes passed before I quit shaking and fifteen minutes before I quit shivering.

I stayed in the shower for a full half hour—once the shivering stopped I began washing my clothes while I continued to let the warm water wash over my body and berated myself for my bad decisions. Leaving Storm Lake was stupid—I had arrived at noon and thought I needed to ride more hours. I should have been content with sixty-five miles. I thought I could stay in front of the front, but it swallowed me and almost chewed me up, before spitting me out.

Each day of this journey had developed a unique personality—today's ride reminded me of a hard-driving race across America. I took only the briefest of notes, recording wind speed and directions and noting the time of arrival in various towns. The last photograph I took that day was of the Pocahontas statue. I was shocked to discover that my average speed had been 14.6. That's pretty fast for 100 miles when over a third of it was battling wind, rain, and hills—no wonder my body was crying out for a hot tub again. I didn't have time to go out that night—cleaning my clothes and my bike and my gear plus studying the maps and trying to figure out the best route for the next day took about four hours. I ordered Pizza Hut delivered to the motel. Besides, it was still raining.

The conversation with Divi and Krishna had sustained me for much of the day. I thought of the stories they had told me—I even did some daydreaming about taking them up on their offer of hospitality and flying to Mauritius to get to know another island culture. I have had the privilege of spending time on two other islands, Waiheke Island in the Hauraki Gulf of New Zealand and Lefkada among the Ionian Islands in Greece. Both were fascinating. What I loved most about them was the sense of security the people felt—they seemed not to fear theft. Bikes, boats, and surfboards—pretty much everything—was left right where it was last used. The islanders knew it would be there when they needed it again. And if by chance someone did take it—it would have been because they needed it—and once the emergency was over, it would be returned.

When I asked an older man on Lefkada why people were so trusting, he just shrugged and said, "How you going to get it off the island? Besides, everyone will know it's not yours." Anonymity is not a good thing. An island society that holds its citizens accountable is a beautiful way to live. I liked the feeling so much that for a few years I fantasized about raising my family in such a culture—but I couldn't find one close enough to my extended family to take the plunge.

The story that Divi and Krishna told of homeless people being taken care of by the islanders fit right in with my impression of people I had known who had lived on small islands. I have to use the qualifier *small*, because my wife and I lived on Oahu when we were young newlyweds. That was where I first learned how violated you feel when something you treasure is stolen.

At the time we didn't own a car. We traveled about Honolulu on our twin Raleigh Superbe bikes. Hers was black and mine was green. A friend of ours surprised a thief in the act of running away pushing both bikes. He abandoned my bike and escaped on my wife's. It was never recovered. I didn't get the sense that the police much cared about our problem. That too felt like a violation—the people who I thought were there to protect us couldn't and didn't even seem to care that they couldn't. This was in fact true, I'm sure, but to a naïve twenty-four-year old from a small town in Nebraska it seemed wrong. I never heard of anyone stealing a bike in my hometown—just like on an island, everybody would know who the bike really belonged to—the sheriff wouldn't even have to get involved.

While I biked those one hundred miles I kept thinking about Divi and Krishna, wondering why they had given up their island life to come to America. I had so many questions I wanted to ask them. I had not focused enough on what must be the very good things about America that had drawn them to our country. Surely the friendliness of the people and the inventiveness of Americans wasn't enough to draw them so far from home.

Or was it? Our country has been a magnet since it was founded. America attracts people not just from impoverished lands, but from island paradises as well. And despite the things that many of us are beginning to see as being wrong with America, a lot of things are going well enough to keep attracting people to our shores—and our heartland. America is attractive enough that we draw people from the moderate temperatures of Mauritius to the bitter winters of a small town in upper Iowa. What is it about America that draws people like Divi and Krishna? I think I'm beginning to get an inkling by listening to the heart cries of those who have come here from other lands—Monday I spoke to Pinky from Hong Kong; Tuesday I met Divi and Krishna, and on Wednesday they shared their story with me. Whose story will I learn about tomorrow that will help me better understand America and Americans—that will help me understand why a country like ours has not only survived but continues to attract immigrants from all over the world?

I grew up thinking America's attraction had something to do with its size and natural resources. But the more I travel and the more I learn about other countries, other governments, and other people, I see that Americans are different—and uniquely so. Steinbeck, more than any other writer of the mid-twentieth century, focused on those qualities that made America unique—and he also fretted about those that would make America fail—its loss of morality. The theme that he wrestled with in *The Winter of Our Discontent* he took up again in his final book— *America and Americans*. In it he left no doubt that he was worried about the future of America. "When greatness recedes, so does belief in greatness," Steinbeck wrote. "It is hard criticizing the people one loves. I knew this would be a painful thing to write. But I am far from alone in my worry. My mail is full of it—letters of anxiety."

Steinbeck may have disliked criticizing his country, but his love for America was too great for him to remain silent. And if a note of discontent is detected in my words, please know that they are written in the conviction that America's best days need not be behind her—and they won't be if enough people keep their dreams alive.

Chapter Nine

I was born in a very small town in North Dakota,
a town of only about three hundred fifty people.
I lived there until I was thirteen. It was a marvelous advantage
to grow up in a small town where you knew everybody.
WARREN CHRISTOPHER

Main Street USA

Yesterday's struggle through the wind, rain, and rush hour traffic of Highway 175 convinced me that it would be a terrible road to take to Nebraska. But this morning, with the sun shining and light traffic, 175 is a joy. The heavy truck traffic is gone. Three miles west of Ida Grove, the trucks turned north on Highway 59 and left me a wide ribbon of highway with almost no traffic and four feet of paved shoulder. The few cars and trucks on the road gave me a wide berth, and I continued giving those drivers a thankful wave for their courtesy. For the first time in five days the wind was blowing lightly. And also for the first time the road was pointing right where I wanted to go—extend Highway 175 a couple of hundred miles and it would come within a few miles of my destination for the weekend—Lincoln, Nebraska, where I planned to spend time with friends from my college days. I was following the Maple River Valley flowing toward the Missouri—a light wind, a gentle downward run, and a road pointing southeast. Life was good—especially compared to yesterday's brutal ride in a cold, driving rain.

The road didn't climb up or down but stayed at the level of the river. The farms were prosperous. I stopped at one to photograph the tasteful displays of older pieces of equipment that were no longer in use on the farm—horse-drawn implements now serving as flower beds and paeans to a bygone era—at least in *this* part of Iowa it's bygone. Other parts of Iowa are home to Amish farmers still who still work the land with horse-drawn equipment, but I saw no Amish and no draft horses that morning. But I did see some beautiful churches that reminded me of the early twentieth century—the Catholic Church in Danbury caught my eye with its steeple soaring high into the sky. The church was set off by a huge field of green—a massive lawn that led my eye right to the front door of the sanctuary.

The early-American look of Danbury pulled me in. An old-fashioned grocery store—the kind that isn't surrounded by a parking lot—stood in the middle of the block between other stores on Main Street. I parked Friday at the curb, walked through the door, and was carried back fifty years to my hometown grocery store. The layout was exactly the same. The checkout counter was to the right of the door, the floors were made of the same planking, and the place smelled the same—as though they were using the same sweeping compound that Vernie used in Nelm's IGA, where I rushed each evening after basketball practice to pick up groceries for my family.

I pulled a couple of apples out of the cooler, noticed that Snickers were on sale, and grabbed a half dozen. My supply, after yesterday's long ride, was dangerously low. The cashier was very friendly. She had noticed the Italian flag on my bike and told me how much she hoped that someday she would be able to visit Italy. For many people, Italy represents a chance to recapture what they feel we've lost in America. They've heard that Italy still celebrates family and small towns, and they want to go there. I gave her a card and told her that if community was what she was looking for, she could still find it in Italy—food, family, and faith are alive and well there. I asked how those things were going in Danbury. She thought for a moment before answering, "Okay, I guess, but it sure used to be better." I had to agree with her. Many things are better in America, but on those three fronts, "used to be better" is as accurate a description as I've heard.

Not far out of Danbury I noticed another nicely manicured field. Unlike the large expanse of grass in front of Saint Mary's Church, this one was on a well-maintained farm. A handmade sign stood at the edge of the pasture: "Choose Life—Your Mother Did." On the other side the sign proclaimed, "It's a Baby—Not a Choice." The neatly manicured farm spoke of a farmer who took the Biblical mandate of stewardship seriously—and the signs proclaimed that he felt seriously about the stewardship of human life as well. As I was taking a photo of the farm, using the sign as foreground treatment, it hit me that I had seen a surprising number of signs proclaiming the rights of the unborn on my journey.

If you observe America only on network television, you'd think the preponderance of Americans are strongly in favor of being able to abort babies. Do all the signs opposing abortion along the roadways signal a change in American values? It's impossible to tell, but I think it would not be going too far to say that political correctness no longer holds as much power over people's thought in the heartland of America. My sense is that people are more willing to speak out—to say what they think. From what had been a low point in the seventies, when people seemed to be afraid to speak out about what the Supreme Court had done almost overnight in legalizing abortion, many today are showing courage. These people may be helping us avert the groupthink that

George Orwell's *1984* warned us about—the tyranny of the "thought police"—manipulators who attempt to change the meaning of words to keep us from thinking clearly. The sign that the farmer had chosen to put in his yard was fighting back by pointing out that abortion is not just about "choice"; that good-sounding word actually means *choosing death for what would, in a few months, be your baby—to love or to give to another family to love.* That too would be a choice—a choice that honors mother, father, and baby.

That farm—the beauty of it and the message it was proclaiming to all who drove by—spoke strongly to me about America. Steinbeck thought that people of courage had disappeared from America—and that America was becoming lazy. In one photo I captured a different America. A hard-working man of conviction and truth-telling lived on that beautiful piece of land. Within a couple of miles I stopped to take a picture of an equally good-looking town. Captivated by the inviting village, I turned onto the main street of Mapleton looking for a comfortable place to take a break. A bench on the sunny side of the street called out to me. I discovered after I sat down that it just happened to be in front of a barbershop. In making that turn off the highway I felt I had also turned back in time to a Norman Rockwell Main-Street-America scene. The street was full of cars—folks were walking on the sidewalk. Before even one minute had passed a thin woman with straight, short hair driving a motorized wheelchair stopped to ask where I was headed. She exuded warmth with her smile and her praise of the town for its friendliness—she had moved to Mapleton only a few years earlier and she was still, it was safe to say, feeling fortunate about her choice.

Two more women stopped to talk. One, who seemed very compassionate, asked the woman in the wheelchair how she was feeling, and after receiving assurance that she was doing fine, turned her attention to me.

"You're just passing through, aren't you?"

"I am." They wanted to know more, of course, and I shared the quick version of my story before I turned the attention back to them and their town. I asked if the vibrancy of their main street meant that the town had a vibrant economy. They thought for a while, but not one of the three seemed ready to say that things were going well. Their thoughts were not on what I was seeing that morning but on the way Mapleton had looked a year earlier—before it had been devastated by a tornado. I was shocked. I had noticed no evidence of destruction on the way into town, but I didn't have before-and-after pictures in my mind.

"It's recovering; we're doing better," said the woman in the wheelchair. When I commented again on how many cars and people were on the street, the compassionate woman came close to agreeing with me, but the other one wouldn't go there just yet. "I'm a tree lover," she said. "The tornado uprooted a lot of trees. I'm devastated. We have a long way to go to recover."

I wanted them to know how good it looked to me, though, so I persisted. "This town just has a good feeling about it."

"Oh! Well! That's wonderful," the compassionate woman said.

The tree lover finally admitted, "We *do* have a nice little town—and everybody gets along here."

"We have a lot of people who have been here a long time—there's a lot of history here," added the compassionate one as she and her friend turned to go.

"Thanks for stopping in our little town," said the tree lady.

"Ride carefully," the compassionate one sang out.

As they were walking away, the woman in the wheelchair was watching them and smiling, apparently in agreement with what they had said about the town. Then she turned to me and added, "We have a lot of churches here; it's a very Christian town. I think Christianity is the main reason the town is so vibrant."

"Christianity's that strong in this town, is it? Is that why you chose to move here?" I asked.

"I moved here because my husband was from here—his parents lived here—and we liked it," she said. She had moved to Mapleton only three years earlier, in 2009, and told me how impressed she was with the town's ability to recover from the tornado that had destroyed over half of it just a year earlier.

A man walking by caught my eye and asked, "Where you going?" He was dressed in a coat and tie and was walking briskly.

"Heading to Colorado. You want to come along?" I asked.

"Better not. Not sure my wife would let me," he said as he disappeared into the barbershop.

I turned back to the woman in the wheelchair, "How about you?"

"If we can stop every few hours and charge these batteries, I'm game," she said.

"I reckon we could do that," I joked.

"Then I'd better get going. I have a lot of errands to do before I can take off with you. Can I say a short prayer for you before I go?" she asked.

"Sure can," I said. And in a soft voice she prayed that God would bless me, grant me traveling mercies, and give me a rewarding journey. She offered a quiet amen and gave me another warm smile. I thanked her and she was off, wheeling quickly down the sidewalk toward the post office.

I followed her progress and saw a tall, lanky man walking toward me, a retired farmer I presumed, wearing a Triple F Feeds jacket. The jacket was open and he wore a wide smile. "Where ya headin'?"

Feeling his warmth and generosity, I moved into my Hayes Center voice and diction, "Just down the road a piece. Got my sights set on Colorado."

"That's more than a piece, my friend."

"Yeah, I suppose it is."

"Where'd ya start from?"

"Wisconsin."

"Well, heck, I see what ya mean. You're over halfway, ain't ya?"

"Just got that pesky Nebraska to get across."

He ignored my Nebraska comment. "Where you headin' to in Colorado?"

"Loveland for starters."

"Got a daughter lives there. Nice town," he said. "You have relatives in Colorado?" he asked.

"I do, but I'm going to Loveland to see a friend I haven't seen for years." At that point we introduced ourselves and I told him the story of my high school buddy Rossy, the other stops I had planned along the way, Lincoln, and my hometown, and that made him think of RAGBRAI.

"Iowa people are very friendly. A lot of people open up their homes to RAGBRAI riders," Clem assured me.

"Iowans open up their homes to just about anyone," I said and told Clem that I had spent the past three nights in the homes of Iowans I had not known when I set off on this adventure ten days ago.

"Anytime you come through a rural area, people are helpful and friendly," Clem told me. He then told me stories of neighbors coming to the aid of injured farmers. I told him that it's still that way in Wisconsin too. I told him about a farmer who had moved from Iowa to buy a farm in our valley and that within months of his arrival a tractor tipped over on him and paralyzed him from the neck down, and even though he had been there only a short time, his neighbors and the people of his church had been helping him ever since. Clem said it was just like that around here when he was a kid, and he was glad to hear that it was still that way in some places—but he wasn't sure it was still that way everywhere.

And with that, Clem and I got to know each other. We talked for more than two hours on that bench in front of the barbershop on the main street of Mapleton, Iowa. Clem shared with me things that I'll bet few people in town know about him, even his closest relatives.

I asked Clem if he raised crops or milked. He told me he raised soybeans and corn. "If I'd had to milk I would never have been a farmer. You're a slave if you're a dairy farmer. You can't get away, and I loved to travel. I had a camper van. We were nomads. Even drove all the way up to Alaska."

A couple stopped mid-stride in front of me, interrupting Clem's story. "Where you coming from?" the wife asked, smiling and stepping up real close. She seemed to have no fear of strangers.

Sensing that she, too, was very friendly I said, "Oh, that state Iowans don't much care for—Wisconsin."

"We like Wisconsin just fine, it's Nebraskans that we don't much get along with."

"Well that's where I'm heading," I said and started to admit that I had been raised a Cornhusker, but her husband cut me off.

"You just getting home from RAGBRAI?" he asked.

"Yeah, I'm a little slow," I said, playing along with him. Clem had just told me that I had only missed RAGBRAI by a few weeks.

The woman noticed my U.S. Air Force biking jersey. "I have a couple of sons in the Air Force."

I told her that a couple of my sons had been in the Air Force as well. "In fact, one of them gave this jersey to me," I told her with a touch of pride. She sensed it and told me how proud she was of her boys as well. We talked briefly of the benefits of military service in forging character, then they wished me well and moved on down the sidewalk to continue their shopping. It was that kind of morning. Clem and I would just get to talking again and more folks would drop by to either welcome me to town or ask where I was going.

Clem picked back up on his story of the things he liked to do other than farming, the reasons he wasn't a dairy farmer, and the reasons he didn't want to be tied down seven days a week, morning and night. "I love dancing. I'm eighty years old, but we still jitterbug—'Boot Scootin' Boogie.'"

And to prove it, Clem sat down on his haunches and smiled at me with the same look my four-year-old granddaughter Lilly flashed when she first rode her bike the length of the driveway without training wheels.

"Can I take a picture of you?" I asked. His smile was just as wide as his face—and his other cheeks were firmly planted on his heels.

"You bet! You heard of glucosamine?" (It rhymed with *mine* the way Clem said it.)

I nodded.

"I've been taking it for fifteen years," Clem beamed.

Clem then stood up with no trouble, with no help from his hands, like a man half his age. "Three fast dances and I was through when I was sixty-four. Sixteen years ago I wouldn't have wanted to sit down like that—I'd never been able to get back up. Hell, now I'm as loose as I could be."

"That's pretty good," I said as Clem sat right back down on his haunches to prove, I guess, that the first time had not been a fluke.

"For three years I took arthritis pills and they were eatin' up my stomach. Now I take glucosamine and I go right down on my haunches."

You couldn't help loving the guy. Here was a man with a spirit playful as a puppy—a man whose glow matched the blue-sky day I was enjoying on that liar's bench in Mapleton, Iowa.

"Up until about fifteen years ago, they had dancing in all the little country bars around here. But anymore the only dances are weddings. Timber Ridge had dances—but not any more." His face saddened, then just as fast lit up again. "We go to four dances a week when we're at our winter home in Arizona."

I had encountered in this town a man in love with life. He continued to tell me stories. And they reminded me of things from my own childhood I had not thought of for decades—seeing Clem sitting on his haunches had reminded me of a man I used to notice at the sale barn I went to with my father who chose that unconventional posture as he bid for cattle passing by him in the arena below.

Clem also told me that land in the area was selling for sky-high prices. We talked of corn prices—which were also sky high because of the demand caused by ethanol and the demand from China he said.

"Next year I'm going to get four hundred seventy-five dollars an acre just for renting my land. That's more than I paid to *buy* some of my land," Clem said, taking off his hat and scratching his head. Our conversation jumped from thought to thought. I learned that Clem had nine grandkids, and that he was kind of thrifty, but in some ways he was a big spender—he again mentioned the campervan, but this time he admitted that it was a big motor home that he drove all the way to Alaska.

He blamed his competing character traits on his Irish-German heritage. The Irish, he told me, built the big houses, and the Germans built the big barns. "And now the Germans own all the land. The Irish own the pubs and the grocery stores. You see, I know both cultures. My mom was Irish, Flood's the name, and my dad's German," Clem said.

I asked Clem whether nearby communities also reflected national heritages. "Danbury is mostly Catholic, Mapleton, too. All the towns in the area are Catholic, but the young kids don't go to church no more," he said. And that led him to tell me that it used to be that every family had a nun or a priest. And from there he went on to reminisce about the communities themselves. "Nobody went to the neighboring town to buy anything. When I was a kid, Danbury had four tractor dealerships—a town of seven hundred people. Most farms were one hundred sixty acres, some even as small as eighty acres. Danbury had four grocery stores. The Irish had a school, up to the sixth grade," Clem said.

The story Clem was telling reminded me of my small hometown of fewer than three hundred people—of the many businesses that used to thrive in a town where now there are less than half a dozen. And that led Clem to talk about his personal journey, of his own farming business, the help he had received from his father, and how his farm had grown over the years.

"My dad was giving us money all along, so over the years I probably got more than fifty thousand. I have five children, and I've given them a lot too. I always bought used cars. I once bought a brand new car—a Caravan. I also bought two new pickups in 1979. But the car I'm driving now is a 1983 Oldsmobile Cutlass—bought it from an old lady. I still got the Caravan." Clem told me reminding me of the frugality of other rich farmers I had known. Clem also told me of his accounts at Smith Barney, and of all the land he owns.

"I've made so many mistakes in my life, I shouldn't be wealthy, but I am. Money just keeps coming my way," Clem said, shaking his head. He didn't say how much money he had. But however much it was, he seemed more than content with it.

We had shared so much of our lives that I felt comfortable asking him, "Do your kids know that you're wealthy?"

He thought about it for a while before answering, "I don't know. I've given each of my kids a lot of money, so maybe they have some idea. I could live in a big house in town, but I just live in a regular farmhouse. I still like having land to putter on. This cowboy shirt I'm wearing, I got from my neighbor—it had a drip of paint on it somewhere, but I didn't mind. I have an older pickup—an '83."

As he was saying those things he realized he was sounding kind of eccentric, "You're going to think I'm crazy, all these stories I'm telling you." And that reminded him that just a few months earlier, while he was working on his corncrib, he had fallen off a ladder and broken a couple of ribs. But in the middle of the story about his recovery, Clem stopped and said, "Hey, you're not going to get to your destination if I keep talking."

"I'm in no hurry—got to let my lunch settle," I said. I'd been nibbling on some of last night's pizza while we talked.

And so Clem and I kept talking.

As we passed from our second and into our third hour of talking, I sensed that as much as Clem didn't want to, he was about to leave. He had tried three times already, yet each time another story popped into his mind as he turned to go. A man got out of his car right in front of us and nodded to me as he stepped onto the sidewalk. He was going, I was guessing, just like most of the other men who had walked by, to get a haircut.

"Would you mind taking a picture of us?" I asked. Clem had stood for a long time, but for the past hour, he had been sitting on the liar's bench right beside me as we told each other story after story.

"Sure," he said.

I handed him my phone and said, "Just touch the camera icon on the screen."

I'm glad that man needed a haircut that morning. I treasure that photo. It's a summation of all that I love about biking—and about small-town America too—sitting on a bench on Main Street USA sharing our lives. I hadn't asked for Clem's address, but I had learned enough about him and approximately where he lived that I was able to mail a copy of that photograph to Clem last Christmas. And as I had hoped, Clem wrote back. He thanked me and told me that he had put that photo on his mantle and that every time he looked at it he was reminded of that sunny morning we spent together and it makes him smile. And that photo does the same thing for me as well every time I see it—*the glucosamine dancer* that I shared stories with on the main street of Mapleton, Iowa one warm September morning.

I stayed in town another hour after Clem and I finally quit sharing stories. More people stopped by as I was packing up. I also walked into the barbershop to thank the man who had taken the photograph of Clem and me. We chatted—the man, the barber, and me. I wished I had needed a haircut or a shave.

As I was pedaling out of town, I noticed a young woman wearing an Iowa Hawkeyes sweatshirt standing in front of a store. She was looking at me with an intensity that told me she wanted to know more about me—or at least wanted to say hello. So I coasted up to her and stopped.

Glad I did, too. My GPS was telling me to head straight out of town, but I thought I should turn. The GPS was sending me northwest, but I wanted to head southwest. She assured me that the GPS was right— and that I was right too. The road, she explained, would resume its southwestward journey in a couple of blocks. She asked where I was going. I handed her a card and briefly told her my story. She told me she would track my progress on Facebook. I should be used to it by now, but I marvel at the potential the Internet gives us for connecting with people. Surely something good can come of this capability that we now have—maybe it can draw us together.

I certainly felt that Clem and I had been drawn together. Mapleton had the feel of a town that people loved to live in, that was still thriving—or if not thriving, then certainly surviving. It had withstood the destruction of a tornado and had done it in superb fashion. A resident, albeit a newcomer to town, assured me that even though she had recently arrived in Mapleton, she had been welcomed with loving arms. She attributed it to the strong Christian character of the town. When I was growing up, to call someone a fine Christian was to call him a caring gentleman or her a sweet gentle lady. It was refreshing to hear good associated with Christianity. It is rarely heard in this era of political correctness, when bashing Christianity is a talking point among secular progressives in the media.

I rode from Mapleton to Castana replaying in my mind the conversations I had enjoyed in Mapleton. In the three hours I had spent on its main street I talked with some two dozen residents, heard a little bit about each of their stories (in the case of Clem, learned a *lot* about his story), and also learned the story of the whole area, even its history— what nationalities had settled where and how the towns had developed. The nine miles to Castana passed quickly. I was following the gently flowing Maple River on a smooth, wide highway. Cars were giving me plenty of room when they passed. I rounded a curve and saw an old John Deere tractor pulling a silage wagon waiting at a stop sign. I sat up in the saddle and slowed my pace, hoping the driver would pull out in front of me. He did, and I took a few hard turns on the pedals and slipped comfortably into his slipstream.

And that is where I stayed for the next five miles, zipping along at eighteen miles an hour—four miles an hour faster than I had ridden into Castana, and doing it with a lot less effort. My heart rate dropped by twenty-five beats a minute. I barely had to push it over one hundred to float along behind the wagon. I kept expecting to lose my "pace car," kept expecting it to turn off at each farmstead driveway we passed, but it just kept trucking down the road, pulling me along with it. My mind went back to the gentle woman in the wheelchair who had prayed that I might receive "traveling mercies"—I don't know if this was what she had in mind, but I was sure thanking her for her thoughtfulness in praying for me as I was coasting merrily along.

That tractor didn't turn until near Turin—five miles down the road. It took a route leading toward high ground. I considered following it, but decided instead to head toward the bottomland lying along the Missouri River. At an intersection a couple of miles down the road I stopped by an old school that had been converted to a thrift store. I didn't see the owner when I walked in, so I walked around looking at all the stuff and found a fine collection of work produced by craftsmen and artisans from the area as well as an artistic flair for displaying all of the secondhand goods.

In the back of the store I discovered the owner and learned that this business had been her lifelong dream, but now that she had achieved it, she had changed her focus—she wanted to live in Italy. She had not seen my bike, nor did she know anything of my Italian story. It was but another reminder that in this country we have a strong longing for community. I told her I had been to Italy and had written of the experience. We talked of Italian food and Italian hospitality. She told me she hoped that when her husband retired from UPS he would be ready for a big adventure. I told her to keep her hopes alive—I had carried my Italian dream for years. And with that I said good-bye.

"May God bless you!" she called out as I was hopping on my bike. This was the second time I'd been prayed over, a short prayer to be sure, but nevertheless she had asked God to bless me just as the woman in the wheelchair had.

A mile down the road, I began hearing, but not yet seeing, a big engine that was slowly gaining on me. I wasn't certain what it was, so I slowed my pace and soon saw in my mirrors a monster of a combine coming around the corner with a corn head so wide that it completely covered the road. I knew I couldn't outrun it, so I began looking for a place with no obstructions on either side of the road so the combine could pass me. I didn't want to pull off the road and stop. I hoped once again to draft the "blessing" that had come my way. I slowed down to below ten miles an hour and moved over as far as I safely could. The driver slowed and maneuvered the combine's massive head around me, then punched the throttle—climbing quickly back up to twenty miles an hour.

I had hoped the farmer would climb slowly back to speed, but he hadn't, so I had to pedal furiously to double my speed. I was just about to slip out of the back of his slipstream so I summoned more resolve and rpms and pushed the bike back into the cushion of air boiling along behind the combine. Once I was in the slipstream, I was able to coast for a while as the energy of the burst slowly dissipated. The combine was so big and so fast that I was carried along at just over twenty miles an hour with barely any effort other than picking the swirling chaff out of my mouth. I was even able to keep up with the machine as it pulled over small hills along L-14. The combine carried me along to E-54, where the driver pulled up to the stop sign and dropped the corn head to the ground. I studied my map. I had followed the machine for four or five miles. If it turned left I could follow it to Moorhead, where I could turn right and follow the Soldier River to Pisgah through the Loess Hills. But that would involve climbing out of the Little Sioux River Valley, which I had been riding in since leaving the secondhand store. My other option was following the Little Sioux to the flat river bottomlands along the shores of the Missouri River.

I decided not to wait for the combine. I opted for the flat land run toward K-45 and a river road that I had been told would be a very pleasant ride south along the Missouri River and a crossing that would take me into Nebraska at Blair. That stretch of road along the Missouri became one of my favorite rides of the trip, but that didn't keep me from glancing at my map and wondering what the route through the Loess Hills to Pisgah would have been like. I contented myself with the thought that maybe on a RAGBRAI ride someday I would see what I had missed. I had never been to Pisgah but had always been curious about the name and wondered if it had a Biblical connection. I Googled it and found out that it did indeed. Pisgah was a mountain in the area where Moses received the Ten Commandments. The people who had settled this part of Iowa felt deep connections to the Bible and to Christianity, and apparently all these generations later the seeds that had been planted back then were still germinating.

Those three hours plus in Mapleton had not been recovered by the fast rides behind the silage wagon and the combine, and once again I was concerned about finding a motel before dark. Two choices presented themselves: Blair, Nebraska, and Missouri Valley, Iowa. Blair had the advantage of being on my route—no backtracking. A bit of the poetic also favored Blair. I liked the idea of crossing the Missouri River in the evening—a good way to end a beautiful day—and a good way to cross off my second state. If I could get to Nebraska before dark I would have crossed Iowa in seven days—six days of riding and one day just enjoying life with Jim and Cheryl in Forest City.

On the ride south along the Missouri the road was perfectly flat. I also picked up a bit of a tailwind. With the increased speed I was beginning to feel I had enough time before sundown to sit down for a meal. Since early morning I had been getting recommendations that I should eat at King's Crossing Restaurant in Mondamin. The twenty-some-mile ride south went by quickly. I reached Mondamin with the sun about three hours above the horizon. I pulled into the little town, about the size of my hometown, and rode down the main street. It didn't take long to find the restaurant—surrounded as it was by cars, and lots of people going in and out.

I was determined to eat what the regulars were eating, so as I was sitting down I asked the couple in the next booth what they were having. Turned out it was chicken fried steak, a favorite restaurant meal of mine when I was a kid, so in honor of my trip fifty years ago I ordered chicken fried steak, mashed potatoes, gravy, and corn. It was just as I remembered—very good and very filling—and eating that large meal gave me plenty of time to visit with the folks who had given me the friendly recommendation.

They turned out to be another of those Iowa couples who were blessed to be living within a few miles of all their kids and grandkids. As we shared our stories—of childhood, high school, and beyond—I learned that life for them was so stable they had attended the same church their whole lives. They told me with pride, and obvious pleasure, of the sporting events and school activities that fill just about every night of their week. Although I was almost certain of their answer, I nevertheless asked if they missed the amenities of larger cities. They told me they were close enough to enjoy city life when they wanted it, and they did in fact visit larger cities fairly often, but small-town life suited them just fine. If there was a better life for them to live, they didn't think they had heard of it. They were just where they wanted to be, doing exactly what they wanted to do.

That seemed to be true of everybody in the place. The restaurant was full; people coming and going—conversations flowing from table to table to table—most of the people in their sixties, seventies, eighties, and even nineties.

A frail man hooked to an oxygen tank announced to a man struggling by on two canes and weak legs, "I should know you."

"Well, you *do* know me! We're neighbors," the man with the weak legs shot back with a surprisingly strong voice that rang through the café. The whole place stopped eating, and everyone turned toward the two old men. The second man's quick retort brought a smile of recognition to many faces—probably most of all to those who had cared for elderly parents.

Over the years I had heard many such lacking-in-guile exchanges while my wife and I cared first for my mother and then later, for my wife's mother. The very young and the very old have no filters for their words—they say what they're thinking—with little or no thought to what anyone else might think. The conversations flowing through that room reminded me of the intergenerational exchanges that I have been missing since our parents died.

I didn't want to leave the camaraderie of that restaurant. But unless I started cranking my pedals, the sun—playing the part of the tortoise—was going to win the race to the horizon against me—playing the part of the hare.

From King's Crossing, the Missouri River was seventeen miles away and Blair was nineteen. The sun was about an hour and a half from the horizon. I had miles to go before I could rest, before I could sleep. But I also wanted to talk to the owner of the restaurant. I had heard she had an interesting story. As I understood it, she had a dream of returning to her hometown to open a restaurant, and Uncle Jimmy King had put up the start-up money—hence the name King's Crossing Restaurant. Whether Jimmy was the young woman's actual uncle or "uncle" was just an affectionate term for the generous man who had helped her realize her dream, I didn't know, but that was just one of the many questions I wanted to ask her. Unfortunately, she was far too busy that night to entertain my curiosity, so instead of peppering her with questions, I just thanked her for the delicious meal and told her how much fun it had been to eat in her restaurant.

I had just experienced small town living at its best. The young woman had created a true asset for her hometown—a place where people gathered and felt comfortable. I tried to imagine the joy it must give her. And what a gift Uncle Jimmy had given to the town as well, by using his money to shape the lives of his townspeople. I walked out that door reluctantly. If the town had had a motel I would have stayed right where I was—I would have ordered dessert and listened to more stories about small-town America.

But the town didn't have a motel, so I headed for the Missouri River and Nebraska. I had been in Iowa seven days. Five of those days the wind had been blowing stronger than twenty miles an hour—and most of the time it was on my nose or was a cross wind, with the exception of the wind that carried me into Forest City and the tailwind that I had just enjoyed on the way to King's Crossing.

On this, my final evening in Iowa, as I watched the sun work its way lower and lower, I was riding comfortably, but not hard. I had eaten a rather large dinner, but I had done it over the course of more than an hour, so I wasn't uncomfortable. I got to the river before the sun got to the horizon and had plenty of light to take a photo of Friday next to the Missouri River sign. I hopped back on my bike and climbed somewhat nostalgically up the gradient of the bridge while looking far below at the gently flowing river as I crossed into Nebraska—it had been quite a week. At the top of the bridge I watched the sun settle slowly into the distant trees—then I coasted down the slope into the traffic and busyness of Blair, Nebraska. I made my way through the commercial corridor, past all the chain stores and restaurants, to downtown Blair and pulled up in front of the Clifton Inn, a Victorian-era hotel exuding nineteenth-century character. But alas, I discovered that highway projects had brought construction workers to town and they had every room booked up. I rode back to a mom-and-pop motel along the riverbank I had noticed far below me as I coasted into town—the motel I had bypassed because I wanted to stay downtown in a hotel with character. But it too was full of construction workers.

I finally settled for a Super 8—one without an outdoor entrance. The owner was from India. His father, or possibly his grandfather, was assisting him. We *were* a nation of immigrants and we *are* a nation of immigrants—and immigrants once again are starting businesses when they get to America. The number of recent immigrants I've met on this trip has surprised me. America needs entrepreneurs, and I was encouraged to see that they are still finding reasons to come here.

As I cleaned my bike and washed my clothes, I thought back over the week I had spent in Iowa. I had not expected to meet so many people, and share in so many lives. Many of the discussions got into matters of the heart—things often not shared even with loved ones for fear of being judged or having to bear the consequences of sharing an opinion. It may be that Americans are becoming more willing to speak out, or maybe it is just that sharing opinions with a man on a bike that you most likely will never see again is easier than sharing opinions with neighbors and family—but I hoped it was the former. I hope we're becoming a people willing to speak up for what we believe.

Iowa surprised me in other ways too. The biking was better than I thought it would be. And the hospitality of the people far exceeded my expectations. The people of Iowa are what I will remember. Not the huge wind turbines, or the winds that almost beat me down, or the endless cornfields, or the rolling hills—no, my memory of Iowa will be the folks like Gene, who invited me to spend the night, and Clem, the eighty-year-old who squatted on his haunches to show me how good he was feeling now that he was taking glucosamine, or Jim, who showed me a business that is waiting to hire more people.

I can hope, but I can't expect my home state of Nebraska to treat me as kindly as the friendly rivals from Iowa. I can't imagine that Nebraska will welcome me with the open arms that Iowa threw around a wandering wonderer from Wisconsin. Steinbeck traveled through neither state on his journey with Charley, so any comparisons I make will be with the journey I took across Nebraska fifty years ago. I also graduated from the University of Nebraska, but it has been thirty-five years since I lived in the state. Can Nebraska possibly surprise me as much as Iowa has?

Chapter Ten

Nothing but heaven itself
is better than a friend who is really a friend.
PLAUTUS

Why Did I Not Know?

From the first pedal stroke in Nebraska I put my home state at a disadvantage. I began the day expecting that by nightfall I would be in Lincoln—seventy-five miles down the road—in the home of my best friend—the man who has had my back since we first met forty-three years ago in the summer of that very important year—1969—the year I met my wife—and the year I made up my mind about Vietnam: *I would finish college and take my chances with the lottery.* I wanted to get to Roger's home—I was worried about him. For weeks he had been enduring radiation treatments for prostate cancer. I didn't know what I could do, but I knew I wanted to be with him.

I regretted the control I was going to try to put on the day. But because my friend's days had been filled with structure—radiation treatments from nine to ten in the morning five days a week—I imposed structure on my day and told him I would arrive that afternoon.

I don't enjoy bicycling in large cities unless they have an efficient bike route through the heart of town. Even though I had lived in Omaha for three years just after my stint in the Army in the early seventies, I chose to avoid the city, bypassing it to the north and west. And were it not for Roger, I would have bypassed Lincoln as well, even though I had spent four years in the late sixties going to the University of Nebraska, where I received a degree in Architectural Construction.

From Blair I would have headed toward Kearney in the center of the state, one hundred seventy-five miles west, to find the grave of my great-grandfather. I had only recently learned that he was buried there, and I wanted to pay my respects. I wouldn't have cared what towns I passed through on the way. But because I was seeing Roger, I did care about which towns I would pass through. I wanted to travel efficiently, quickly, and safely to either Lincoln or Branched Oak Lake north of Lincoln because I knew Roger often spent afternoons there on his sailboat, THSLDO II. But I could hold off making that decision until I saw how quickly I was able to get from Blair to the outskirts of Omaha.

I hoped I'd get to meet some folks just like I had the day before, but I doubted I would—not just because I'd be rushed, but because the people in the restaurants and on the main streets along the way would probably be rushed too. I wasn't likely to find a Clem on my journey today or a kind woman in a wheelchair who would pray for me. No, on this day I would be a traveler with miles on his mind traveling among people who would not be curious about an old man riding a weird bike, or if they were, they would not let that curiosity rise to the level where they would engage him in conversation. I would be passing through towns that were bedroom communities for the jobs of the big city. I wouldn't be passing through the towns of independent people who farmed and operated the small businesses of the small towns of America.

At the Super 8 motel a truck dispatcher enjoying his continental breakfast recommended a route for me out of Blair. I let go of my desire to travel on quiet roads with wide shoulders and took his recommendation to ride Highway 30 because of its wide shoulders. It would be efficient. It would take me straight to Lincoln. I was no longer on a journey—I was just getting from place to place. I turned on the GPS to get me out of town. It led me down a street lined with trees and beautiful Victorian-era homes, blessed with character and personality, before dropping me off onto Highway 30. The traffic was heavy, but the shoulders were as advertised, very wide.

Twenty miles down that noisy road, in the western suburbs of Omaha, I stopped for biscuits and gravy at a franchise restaurant. I contrasted the experience to my biscuits-and-gravy morning at the Heartland Café in Britt, Iowa. The former dairy farmer's food was a lot better, and so was the feeling of community—Merv's was a gathering spot for the town. It welcomed me into its midst. In the franchise restaurant I was but one more person coming in and going out. No one took notice of me. At the Heartland Café three people had engaged me. Why is it that small town people take notice of folks? Is it just because of the size of the town? Or do small towns attract the kind of people who are more interested and curious about other people? Is it a good thing that I was approached by strangers, or was it a bad thing that I couldn't eat my breakfast without being bothered? The answer to that question probably goes to the heart of a person's decision about what community to call home.

I put in the miles and rode as quickly as I could through the hills west of Omaha looking for that last ridge that would carry me down into the Platte River Valley. I took a few photographs of the unspoiled countryside that is steadily being overrun by suburbanization. My first day in Nebraska was proving to be, as I suspected and demanded of it, a point-A-to-point-B day. Even the drivers seemed more aggressive. I wondered if it was just because I was near a large city or whether thousands of RAGBRAI riders crossing the state each year made the drivers of Iowa friendlier to bikers and less impatient. I stopped only a few times to take photos that morning, but I couldn't resist the adventitious lighthouse at Linoma on the Platte River. It marked the spot of a campground and swimming beach popular with college students in the 1960s. I was surprised that it was still there and that a relic so out of place and time was still so well maintained. Maybe Iowa was not going to be the only state with surprises.

While cooling off in the shade of the lighthouse, I pulled out my map to consider the benefits of the various routes into Lincoln. None of them looked good—all of them looked like busy thoroughfares. Thankfully Roger called at that moment to check on my progress. He suggested I bypass Lincoln to the north and ride straight to Branched Oak Lake on Malcolm Road. It felt good to be off heavily traveled Highway 30. Malcolm Road had little in the way of a shoulder, but it didn't need one—hardly anyone was driving it that afternoon. I had the road and what was left of the day to myself.

Suddenly I felt like I was back in Iowa—drivers were passing at a slower pace and giving me plenty of space. I began waving at drivers again—thanking them for their courtesy. My thoughts were those of a man on a journey once again. I no longer had to focus on avoiding the debris that collects on the side of a busy highway. The road was table-top smooth with not a pot hole in sight. I was riding over rolling hills, passing horse farms, beautiful ranch homes, and large SUVs, one of which caught my eye. It was sitting at a stop sign—too long, it seemed— it could easily have pulled out before I got to the intersection. As I got closer I realized I knew the driver—my good friend Roger was sitting there watching me pedal down the road.

I pulled up to the Range Rover, Roger got out, and we exchanged bear hugs. It was good to see him. The thrill may not have been the same for him, though—I had been riding pretty hard through a warm Nebraska day to get to this unexpected rendezvous. I'm sure I was a bit ripe. But Roger was a gentleman and didn't say anything. That too surprised me—I hoped the radiation treatments hadn't burned away any of his spunk.

Loading the bike into his car took me back to the last time I didn't bike all the way to my destination—near Cortona, Tuscany. Pietro had met me with a Fiat and I was only able to shoehorn my trailer and backpack into the tiny vehicle. But without the drag and the extra weight, I was able to bike twice as fast—fast enough to keep up with Pietro for all but the final few hundred meters to his mother's farm.

But Roger lived much farther away, on straight, high-speed roads, not the curvy, hilly roads of Italy, and we wanted to get to a birthday party, so we took the time to fit everything into the car. We skipped the lake and headed straight for Roger's home. I was a bit disappointed that I hadn't been able to bike all the way to Branched Oak Lake—I wanted to see Roger's new Hunter 335 in the water—but he promised that we would sleep on the boat the next night.

As we drove into Lincoln, we caught up on each other's lives. I shared with him the highlights of my journey and told him how much I enjoyed coming to the slow realization that it was him sitting at that intersection waiting for me to ride by. He told me of his battle against cancer—and how thankful he was that the radiation treatments had finally ended. He seemed hopeful and that really made me feel good. We changed our focus to the future and made plans for our time together.

After I got settled in and cleaned up, Bev, Roger's wife, joined us and we went to the birthday party of one of their friends at a downtown Lincoln restaurant. I got to see what a good life Roger was leading and came away from the experience thankful that he had so many good friends, and a good wife, to share it with. We left the party only a little early, came home, sat down in our favorite chairs, and talked late into the night as good friends do who have forty-some years of stories to share.

Roger is, among many things, a photographer, and has lots photos to remind us of our good times over the years. We have traveled the world together sharing our friendship and our professional lives. Our time together hasn't spanned the fifty years since I took my first bike journey, but it almost does—I was pretty wet behind the ears when I met Roger the summer of '69, just a few days before I brazenly, with much fear and trepidation, walked up to a girl I had never seen before and introduced myself to my future wife. Roger likes to tell the story that he too had been in the Union that morning on the campus of the University of Nebraska, and that he had spied her first. In fact, it was Roger who told me, when I excitedly called to tell him about her, that she was married. I told him no – she can't be—we've got a date.

"All I know is that when I saw her a half hour before you did, she was wearing a wedding ring, my friend," Roger shot back. And then he described her down to the earrings she was wearing just to show that he was a bit more observant than I was. But I thought he was just jerking my chain for only noticing her legs.

Turned out that Roger was right. But that part of the conversation about the girl with the long beautiful legs and warm smile I didn't even remember. I didn't find out that Roger was right for many weeks and by then it was way too late. We had long ago fallen in love with each other. Roger didn't even start telling that part of the story, the part that I had forgotten, until Mardi and I had been married ten years. But right from the start Roger began telling the story that he had seen her first that morning in the Union on the very last day of summer classes 1969.

Having a friend to look back over almost half a century keeps a person grounded and helps him focus on the important things—and nothing does that like almost dying. We have been through bypass surgery, cancer, and a car accident—any of which could have ended our lives on this earth. And recently, Bev sustained a major head injury in a freak accident. We all now look at life with an eye on eternity. When Roger and I met forty-some years ago, coming to the aid of a mutual friend who needed help moving furniture, our focus was, I think it is safe to say, on the next day, and the promising futures we hoped for—not on the fragility of life. But almost dying changes priorities. The feeling of invincibility that is common to young people is lost. We ended the night talking about seeing death as a transition, not an ending—and how deeply that change of emphasis impacted the lives we were now living.

As promised, before most people had started their day, Roger and I were out at the lake enjoying a beautiful morning cleaning his boat. I was spraying and Roger was rubbing, and Tim, a powerboat owner, was giving us a hard time about all the work entailed in owning a sailboat. All of sudden Roger grabbed the hose from me and began spraying the boat behind us. He motioned for me to grab a sponge for him. He handed the hose back to me and directed me to spray the side of the boat, which he began furiously scrubbing. After forty-three years of friendship, I knew Roger was up to something, but I hadn't figured out what it was yet.

"I suppose you been out here since sunup working on my boat." I turned in the direction of the voice and saw what looked like a seasoned sailor walking down the dock toward us with a big smile on his face.

"No, we've only been working on it a couple of hours. We had hoped to have it done before you got here, but your boat was kind of dirty," Roger deadpanned as he continued scrubbing.

"Yeah, right. I think I know you a little better than that."

"Oh, Jim, say hi to OJ," Roger said as he straightened up and went back to work cleaning his own boat. I reached out and shook his hand.

"How'd he talk you into this?" OJ asked.

"Roger's had my number since college," I said, pleased to know that Roger still had a healthy dose of playful mischievousness in him.

Both OJ and Tim were still smiling, obviously enjoying Roger's self-deprecating prank.

OJ hopped onto his boat and Tim began talking politics while he continued watching us work. He began by mentioning his distrust of AARP. Then he turned his attention to Obama and the liberal media, most specifically MSNBC—none of which he had anything good to say about—it's one lie after another, he said. When he learned that I was from Wisconsin, he told me how much he appreciated the fiscal policies of Wisconsinites Scott Walker and Paul Ryan. Another friend dropped by. Larry too expressed conservative values. Neither of these men seemed shy about sharing their views—no worry about being politically correct. They were instead worried about the future of America. If there were any liberal, Obama-supporting boat owners on that dock that morning, they kept quiet about it.

Lots of people stopped by—some, like Tim, for a long chat, and others for just a moment. I began to see how much like a small town this community of boat lovers was. They spend most weekends together during the summer and had grown quite comfortable with each other. Our little gathering was like a front porch get-together in the mid-twentieth century. The party the previous night had been to celebrate the sixtieth birthday of one the guys from the dock. And now this morning Archie, the fix-it guy, was fixing breakfast for whoever wanted it. He only asked that we bring our own plates.

They were an eclectic, fun-loving, generous bunch of folks of many stripes—salesmen, businessmen, artists, doctors, dentists—yet they all seemed to get along, sharing a love of the water and small-town living on that dock. They take care of each other and they also gather to raise money for the larger community—for the firefighters of the area and the young people too. The small-town atmosphere seemed at least as important to them as their love of boats and the water. Roger told me later that some of the boats hardly ever leave the dock—at least not until winter, when they go to dry dock.

Roger had the largest boat on the dock—and the largest cabin, with enough headroom for all but the tallest basketball player. Those features and his flair for hospitality and storytelling insured that his boat was the one on which people gathered. We enjoyed a constant stream of visitors the whole time we were there. When Roger and Bev are seeking peace and tranquility, they head out onto the lake.

We spent the rest of the day at the boat—Bev joined us for the evening. The next morning was one of those gorgeous, soft-light mornings that sailors live for as they watch the day come slowly alive. Bev fixed a tremendous breakfast of eggs, hash browns, sausage, and toast, topped off with a bowl of fruit. We talked about family, relationships, farms, and girlfriends (turns out we each had a former girl friend named Lynda). Roger had recently seen his Lynda at a high school reunion and came back with a story. After giving Roger a hug, she turned to her husband and introduced him. The man held out his hand and said, "Roger Morgan, Roger Morgan, Roger Morgan—I can't tell you how many times I've heard that name over the years, and now I finally get to meet the famous Roger Morgan."

The story of meeting *my* former girlfriend named Lynda and her husband, Phil, didn't have such an interesting punch line, but we had hit it off well, so much so that they had invited me to spend time with them the next time I was traveling through western Nebraska. This journey turned out to be the next time, and it also seemed to be the perfect time. Lynda had told me that Phil was just about as crazy about bicycling as I was, so I called and left a message to warn them that I was in the state and looking forward to a bike ride.

When it was time for me to leave after a few days of dockside living, Roger and I couldn't quite manage to say good-bye. He offered to drive me to Kearney, and I accepted. We couldn't bike together, but he could drive me to see the resting place of my great-grandfather. I was extremely grateful that he was willing to take the time to share that special moment with me. I knew I'd be miss meeting some interesting people in the small Nebraska towns I would have traveled through, but the experience of discovering my great-grandfather's headstone with my best friend more than made up for the "birds in the bush" I might or might not have encountered if I had biked from Lincoln to Kearney.

Finding the headstone of my great-grandfather within five miles of the highway that I had used to cross Nebraska going back and forth to the University of Nebraska was a bit of an embarrassment. Surely my father had told me where his grave was. Why did I not listen or retain that knowledge? Why did I not know there was a headstone right next my great-grandfather's with the name *JAMES SHAW* etched on it? Why did I not know of this James, who must surely have been related to me— possibly a great-uncle whose name I was given? He had died just three years after I was born. Why didn't I know of him? These questions were impossible to answer, but now that I knew where the graves were, I had a clearer picture of my history. I had known all my life that my father had been born in Kearney, but I knew nothing else about my family's history there.

Why did Dad not show me the house he lived in—or the farm where he was born? Did he think I was not interested? *Was* I not interested? Had he asked me and I declined? I could remember little mention of Kearney when I was growing up.

It seemed odd that I would first visit this gravesite with a friend and not with family, but here we were. Roger and I had shared a lot together over the years. Friendship is such a funny thing. I knew when I met Roger that I liked him, but did I know we would still be friends four decades later, and that we would share so many stories. They were just experiences at the time, but now they are precious memories, treasured in the context of having spent two-thirds of my life with Roger. He knows me as well as anyone and perhaps better than most members of my family.

As Roger has been doing for years, he took care of me that afternoon. And also as he has been doing for years, he took a photo of that moment— of me kneeling by the headstone of my great-grandfather, Owen Little Shaw—only one generation removed from County Cork, Ireland. Roger also found me a place to camp, along a creek running through a horse-boarding ranch. He's that kind of guy. It takes him about sixty seconds to make a lifelong friend—and sixty seconds after they met, the rancher offered me a place to sleep and asked if he could string an extension cord to the site.

Roger and I shared a quiet good-bye along that streambed. I shouldn't do it I suppose, but each time I say good-bye to Roger, I wonder if it will be the last time I see him. I hope I'm still wondering that as we pass our fiftieth, sixtieth, and seventieth years as friends. I want to walk again arm-in-arm with him down the streets of Nidri, Greece, just as we did when we had known each other only a short time and could not have imagined that we would still be enjoying our friendship so many decades later.

And now I was leaving Roger and heading across the rest of the state of Nebraska and part of Colorado to renew a friendship with Rossy, a friend I had grown up with, but had seen only once in the years since I had first met Roger. Would that relationship still be intact—that strange hard-to-define quality that is friendship—that feeling of just being comfortable in a person's presence? Would Rossy and I have changed so much over the years that we felt the need to please or entertain, rather than just enjoying our time together? Would we be able to talk about more than the past? Would we be able to talk about the future, and about the present?

This was the first time I had camped during the journey, and I had to think through the process of erecting the tent. I was also distracted by my thoughts. For much of the five days I spent in Roger's company I had been thinking—at least subliminally—of mortality. Roger's cancer had me concerned. Seeing my great-grandfather's grave and the headstone next to his with my name on it caused me to think in very concrete terms about my own death.

I couldn't help but notice that my great-uncle James Shaw's birthday was just one day after mine. I was sixty-five on the day I kneeled at my great-grandfather's grave. Owen Little Shaw had died when he was just sixty-six, just like John Steinbeck. I would turn sixty-six in two more months. My father, who was two years younger than Steinbeck, died when he was seventy-two. If that defines my span of years, I have only another half dozen years to enjoy my kids and grandkids. Only a few more years to take them camping, to teach them what I know about putting up a tent—of choosing which directions to orient the windows and door and where to place everything so that you can find it in the middle of the night, especially the flashlight.

I realized that even though I don't think of myself as old, my own kids do—and I'm sure my grandkids do. In spite of how young I feel, I have to admit that I am getting old. I have been on this earth—have been living this life—for a long time. It will soon be time for me to begin another life. Almost one-third of my high school classmates have already died. Am I ready for that? Are my loved ones ready? How does anyone prepare for that day? I was sure the subject would come up in the next few days. How can it not when you visit someone you have not seen for three or four decades?

Once I had the rain fly on the tent, the bike covered, and everything arranged just so inside the tent, I began writing in my journal. But I couldn't keep my eyes open, so I gave up, zipped the sleeping bag up to my chin, and went to sleep. I had managed to get only one thought on paper: *After so many years I'll probably look like my dad—and Rossy will look just like Ross.*

Chapter Eleven

*A friend is one who knows you
and loves you just the same.*
ELBERT HUBBARD

Looking Back

The morning started off chilly—maybe *cold* would be more accurate. I quickly dressed, pulling on enough layers for a winter ride. I wasted no time stuffing the tent and rainfly into the sack and packing the trailer. As I was pushing Friday to the highway, I programmed my former girlfriend's address into my GPS and discovered that I was right at one hundred miles from her home on Lake Maloney near North Platte. Bike Friday and I logged the first of those miles before the sun had cleared the horizon.

Within a few miles, though, my shadow suddenly stretched out in front of me and I began stopping to take photographs to give my body a chance to warm up—to absorb the warmth of the sun without the cooling effects of the wind I was generating as I pedaled along Highway 30. I photographed vestiges of the tourist route that 30 used to be—including a Conestoga wagon that had once been a souvenir shop but was now a slowly deteriorating anachronism. I even stopped to take pictures of a sign proclaiming this as the Lincoln Highway. I was looking for lots of excuses to stop that morning.

But eventually the sun climbed high enough to begin heating the world up. And I began stopping not to warm up, but to peel off layers of clothing, and stuff them in the trailer. I averaged about two miles between stops that morning. By the time I got to the second town, which was Elm Creek, I had stopped half a dozen times. At the edge of town I pulled off the last of my cold weather gear—my arm warmers and polypro gloves. I was once again in my summer biking uniform—chamois-lined biking shorts, short-sleeved jersey, padded biking gloves, and a helmet.

I didn't even get a mile down the road before I stopped again. I couldn't resist Mom's Kitchen. I was breaking a cardinal rule of the journey—stopping because of the name— with no consideration for the number of customers. I took a picture of Friday parked in front of the place—the only thing I could see in the parking lot was my long shadow. Wanda was my waitress. She was tall, wore a gold cross, and reminded me of the only other Wanda I had ever known—a high school classmate. She told me that not only did they serve biscuits and gravy she also highly recommended them. I'm glad she did. They were very good, and I was hungry enough that morning I didn't even need a doggie bag.

Besides her appearance, Wanda also reminded me of Wanda from high school in another way. She seemed a bit guarded—not unfriendly, but unwilling to express an opinion. She was a veteran waitress—she'd been working at Mom's Kitchen for more than ten years, I think she said, and probably knew it was best not to say too much—it can affect tips. I was chattier than normal that morning, wondering about the local economy, and I even asked her if people were talking about the election. Her response reminded me of what John Steinbeck had written in *Travels with Charley*—if people have opinions they keep them to themselves. "They don't talk much politics—they stick to farming in here," Wanda said as she filled my water glass for probably the fourth time.

I left her a generous tip. She was very professional. The food was good. She had been very attentive and even offered to fill my bottles with water and ice, an offer I gladly accepted. The day had started cold, but it was heading toward warm, maybe even hot, and I still had over eighty miles to ride if I was going to get to Lynda and Phil's place by dark.

Highway 30 runs parallel to the Union Pacific railroad tracks across much of Nebraska. Despite being offset by sometimes as much as thirty to forty yards, the long trains created a vortex—a wind tunnel—that bumped my speed up a bit. Every fifteen or twenty minutes I could count on seeing two or three big yellow locomotives gaining on me. I'd watch for them in my rearview mirror, knowing that when they got to me, they'd be pulling a massively long train.

I lost track of how many trains passed me that day, but between Cozad and Willow Island a train lumbered by going just twenty-one miles an hour, and for short bursts I was able to stay with it. But I could maintain only nineteen without going into cardiac overload—and so each car would pull slowly past my shoulder. But when you're talking about well over a hundred railroad cars that can take a long time. That train pulled me along at a pace five miles an hour faster than I had been riding. That doesn't seem like much if you are used to speeding along at seventy miles an hour, but when you're traveling by bike it can cut an hour's ride by fifteen or twenty minutes. And because of that train's enormous length I was able to stay with it for a full five miles.

I wasn't particularly hungry that morning because of the big plate of biscuits and gravy I started the day with, but I was stopping frequently, taking the time to go into each of the convenience stores I passed to grab a small bite to eat and a big drink. At the Get N Go in Brady, unlike at Mom's Kitchen, politics *were* being discussed. The place was also into hunting big time. I took a photo of the ammo display above the peanuts, nuts, and sausages counter, and just below the American flags, and right next to the tables where all the farmers and hunters were gathered. Hunting and guns were on their minds, especially "gun control." The men at the tables weren't really watching the TV, but occasionally I'd notice one of them glance at it. Whether it was to read the news ticker at the bottom of the screen or to take a look at Megyn Kelly, I couldn't say. But in the interest of full disclosure, I was doing a bit of each— news flashes about the investigation into the death of Ambassador Chris Stevens were sliding across the screen—and Fox News has never hired an on-air talent who was hard to look at. Megyn was muted—but the conversation in the room was animated—jumping from guns to second amendment rights to Obama to drought to farming and the price of grain and then it would start all over again—just not in the same order.

No one directly mentioned the death of Ambassador Stevens in Benghazi on the anniversary of 9/11, but these farmers were riled up by Obama's "way with words" and his unwillingness to ever "admit to doing anything wrong. He's always blaming somebody else"—digs that could have been set off by what happened in Libya. A fair assessment of the mood at the tables was that the men didn't like the way things were going in the country—and much of their displeasure was directed at President Obama. I didn't join in, but I sure did listen. I was definitely hearing what was on the minds of these guys—no need to guess how they felt. I wondered what Wanda would have thought.

I stopped briefly in every town I went through that day—to buy an apple in Overton, a Snickers bar in Gothenburg, or a Snickers Ice Cream Bar—which had become a favorite on this journey—in Maxwell. The place where I bought it is a favorite memory of the trip. It was a general store right out of my childhood, carrying a little bit of everything—and just like in my childhood, the place was run by a family member, a daughter of the owner, I guessed. Rachel was short, cute, and very Italian looking and had a friend helping her pass the time. It reminded me of the times I took over for my dad at his store. These girls seemed too comfortable with the place to have been employees. I liked the easy familiarity of the store. I began to feel right at home. I was within sixty miles of Hayes Center. These were people like the people I had grown up with—in towns where I had spent the first twenty or so years of my life—doing just what these girls were doing—hanging out, passing the time, and helping out at the same time.

Across the street from the general store was the smallest post office building I had ever seen—I didn't estimate the dimensions, but it looked like a building from a dollhouse collection. It was so small that I thought, *Thank God it's not closed.* But I'll bet it's on the chopping block. The United States Postal Service loses billions every year and is proving, like most bureaucracies, to be fairly inept. But better ways to improve the bottom line must exist than taking post offices away from small towns. Relax the regulations in small communities; change the pay and benefits structure; cut back on service; consider every alternative before forcing small towns to lose their identity.

The same thing happens when school districts become bloated with bureaucracy—instead of attacking the problem, the bureaucrats make the bureaucracy bigger and consolidate schools. They build a new school out in the country and give it hyphenated name. Identity and pride of place are lost and the communities wither soon after. Tough decisions need to be made, but community identity is a very precious thing. Considering how much money is wasted by the federal government, a lot of fraud and mismanagement could be eliminated before Maxwell, Nebraska, and other communities like it around America lose their post offices. Sometimes towns do have to die, but closing the schools and the post office is the death sentence to many towns.

South of Maxwell I stopped by the Fort McPherson National Cemetery. Even though it was not much more than an hour's drive from my childhood home, I had never been there. I was deeply moved—it was beautiful and felt very spiritual. Row upon row of perfectly spaced white crosses grabbed at my heart. It touched me to think of the sacrifices of all of these men. Fort McPherson was established as a military outpost in 1863 to protect settlers moving westward on the Oregon Trail. In 1873, additional acres were set aside to create a national cemetery. Over the years, twenty three cemeteries were moved from abandoned frontier forts to Fort McPherson, the last of which was Fort Robinson, which was abandoned in 1947. Veterans are still being buried at Fort McPherson. The total recently passed nine thousand.

I would have missed that beautiful experience if I had known that the GPS had chosen a route beyond the cemetery that I couldn't follow. What looked like a short cut to Lynda's place turned out to be a sandbur-infested dirt and sand road not fit for bicycle travel—at least not riding a Bike Friday and pulling a trailer.

Not being able to take that ranch trail forced me to stay on the stair-stepping river road that with every second turn took me north back toward Highway 30 and Interstate 80 and farther from Lynda's home. But this little-traveled route between the cemetery and Highway 83 was a welcome relief from the commercial corridor that has grown up along Highway 30 over the past one hundred years of automobile travel. The river road roughly followed the southeast-flowing Platte River and pulled me back to my childhood days of riding in the car with my dad, traveling through the Sandhills, where we often would drive for miles without seeing a ranch house. Interstate 80 was at times visible just across the river, but on the south side it was a completely different world—nothing was moving quickly—even the road was not made for speed. Every few miles it took an abrupt ninety-degree turn as it worked its way to the northwest.

On this road, which seemed so unlike the roads of the twenty-first century, I met the largest turtle I've ever seen. I stopped to watch it make its way across the road. At first I was concerned that it might get hit, but then I realized that this specimen was decades old, most likely older than I was, and had probably been crossing this lonely road its whole life. After leaving the turtle in peace to take its own sweet time I met a truck that I briefly considered flagging down. But then I realized there was a good chance that turtle would have been old news to the rancher driving that truck—my guess is that over his lifetime, which also appeared to have been even longer than mine, the rancher, as he traveled to and from his ranch, had probably seen that turtle dozens of times and had managed to avoid flattening it every time.

Even though the turtle had slowed my progress considerably, and it looked like the sun was going to win the race to the horizon, I nevertheless stopped to photograph a granite marker almost hidden from view by tall grass. It commemorated the Pony Express route across Nebraska. I was passing the site of the Cottonwood Springs station, which was in operation from April 3, 1860, to November 20, 1861—just a year and a half. I found it interesting to realize that the closing of the Pony Express station predated Fort McPherson by two years and that both of them had been built during the Civil War.

I also couldn't resist photographing a beautiful example of patriotic art adorning a ranch entrance. As I took a photo of the sign bearing flowing carved wooden images of a waving flag and the words "God Bless America," I noted that I had just passed the seven-hundred-fifty-mile mark of my journey and that in keeping with the image of a flowing flag, I was battling a strong wind out of the northwest.

When the miles for the day were a few south of one hundred, I was still stair-stepping toward the highway that would carry me six or seven miles south of North Platte to the south shore of Maloney Reservoir, where Lynda and Phil lived. I considered calling them, but the word I had left early that morning was that it would take me the whole day to get to their place—so no need yet to bother them. Even though it looked as if the final tally would be well north of one hundred for the day, I still had a chance to arrive in daylight, so I just kept trucking on, figuring I would call only if it looked certain I couldn't make it before dark.

I had plenty of water and plenty of snacks. I stopped frequently to make sure I stayed hydrated and full of fuel. Lake Maloney, I remembered from childhood, sat on a high plateau above the Platte River Valley, so I knew I had at least one major climb ahead of me. But first I had half a dozen miles of pleasant riding on a road lined with hayfields. I was enjoying the pleasant smell of freshly cut alfalfa. Pockets of cool air swept over me as I biked past center-pivot irrigation systems spraying thirsty cornfields—and over it all hung a big orange ball hurrying to the horizon.

When I finally arrived at Highway 83, which would carry me south, I made a bad decision. I saw a bike path crossing under the highway and decided to follow it. I didn't notice that it was getting very little use or maintenance or that it was infested with sandburs. I got off of the path as soon as I found a road that would carry me back to the intersection on 83 where I had gotten on the bike path. Once I was back on the highway I inspected my tires and found a couple of burs that hadn't worked in deep enough to cause a flat. I pulled them out and went to work climbing the hill. The road was wide and included a four-foot shoulder. The traffic was light. As I climbed the long hill, the sun reversed course and climbed too. Seeing sky between the sun and the horizon gave me hope that I could still get to Lynda and Phil's before dark.

I got to the top and discovered that the wind was blowing even harder up there. Just like in Iowa, on the final run to Jim and Cheryl's place in Forest City, I turned south ninety degrees and picked up a favorable wind that bumped my speed up into the mid-twenties. I covered the last half-dozen miles quickly and turned in to Lynda and Phil's driveway just as that big orange ball I had been chasing all day was settling onto the crests of the hills behind their house. I had ridden a century plus an additional eight miles and arrived only a few minutes before one of my trailer tires went flat. Even if I had noticed it was getting soft I wouldn't have stopped to change it. I'd told Phil early that morning I planned to arrive before dark, and I would have wanted to keep that promise.

Phil was waiting on the deck of his beautiful lakeside home enjoying the late summer evening light show. At our first meeting, a few months earlier, Phil and I had discovered that we both loved to talk bicycles. That evening we discovered that we shared another interest—restoring older homes. The gorgeous home Phil was showing me had only a few years earlier been an abandoned lakeside cabin—and Phil had done most of the work bringing the old place back to life. I thought, upon first seeing it, that he and Lynda must have paid a contractor a handsome sum to create their dream home—but instead it had been created by their vision, their willingness to endure years of hard work, and the dust and disorder of construction to end up with a home to share with family and friends.

Lynda was out for the evening, so Phil and I were on our own. I showered and we headed out to a lakeside café for dinner. We talked bicycles and home restorations and got to know each other better. Phil had promised me a bike ride, but he told me he was going to have to invite me back another day—he had been having trouble digesting food and hadn't been riding for a few weeks. I was disheartened to hear that he wasn't feeling in top shape, but I was glad he was inviting me back. I had already begun to get a taste of lakeside living, and I liked it.

When Lynda got home, I learned more about the conversion of the cottage to their dream home—of living in the basement for the first few weeks and having to crawl up and down a ladder through a hole in the bathroom floor to get to her kitchen. But she now has a house that betrays none of its humble beginnings—except in the stories she and Phil share of all those years of hard work, inconvenience, and sacrifice. I also got the Cliff's Notes version of Lynda's life since I last saw her. It was odd to realize that I knew nothing of forty years of her life— when I was fifteen, I couldn't stand not knowing what she had been doing for the last forty *minutes*! We spent hours each night talking on the phone—what about exactly, I'm not sure, but we talked. And we had no trouble getting a conversation going again—no trouble catching up on each other's lives. She, like many baby boomers, had been divorced, but unlike many in our generation, she had not switched careers. She had been an elementary teacher and had only recently retired. I was amazed at how easily and comfortably we began sharing our lives again. I hoped conversation would flow as easily with Rossy.

The next day Phil played the part perfectly of a hospitable host and took me to the local bike shop. He was certain that his friend Patty, who owned the store, would have a recommendation or two for dealing with the sandburs of Nebraska. It was great to see such a finely appointed shop in western Nebraska. Such a store could not even have been imagined in a small town like North Platte in the 1960s. The nearest bike shop to Hayes Center when I was a boy was in Denver. I was extremely surprised that Patty's store not only had lots of serious bikes for sale, but also heavy-duty tubes for the odd-sized wheels of my trailer.

Phil also took me to the Union Pacific Railroad museum, where all those trains I met on Highway 30 had been assembled. In the tower high above the museum we had a great view of the "hump," where cars were switched from one track to another to build the long trains that continuously cross the plains. The economy looked good from up there.

An older woman wearing a billowing dress was standing next to me watching the cars flowing off the hump. I made what I thought was an innocuous, just-being-friendly comment about the length of the coal trains being assembled, but it set her off. She was visiting Nebraska from back east—the Chesapeake Bay region. The sight of all those cars loaded with coal from Wyoming reminded her of all the coal companies in the east that had been shut down by the Obama administration. I assumed by the passion with which she spoke about coal that family members had lost jobs in the industry, but I didn't ask. I didn't want to risk opening any more wounds.

I tried to steer the conversation to less contentious grounds, telling her that I had once biked with my oldest son in the Chesapeake Bay area. But the conversation didn't stay on tourism or special trips with children very long. She moved it right back to America's wasteful ways. "We need to change the culture of Washington. I know people collecting big salaries from the government who do next to nothing to earn that money. We could shut down whole departments, and nobody would notice except the people collecting those bloated paychecks."

Had I been alone, I would have engaged her and tried to learn more about why she so distrusted Washington in general and the Obama administration in particular, but I felt Phil was probably eager to get going. I was sure he'd been up in the tower many times before with other guests. What this woman wanted to talk about was just what I had gone on the road to hear, but I also wanted to respect Phil's time and hospitality, so I told her I was glad to have met her and went to rejoin Phil on the downtown, downwind, North Platte side of the tower.

We had a chore to do in town—we had been charged with picking up wine for dinner. Lynda had invited two of our classmates to come to their house that night. Phil gave me the job of choosing the wine, so I looked through the local selections and discovered a full-bodied red from a vineyard just a few miles from Branched Oak Lake near Lincoln, appropriately named Nebraska Red. Phil agreed with my choice—"local" has a lot of enthusiasts—more so than when I was a kid. Back then homemade and homegrown didn't have quite the status they do now.

Dinner proved to be a surprising journey into the past. I discovered that I had not gotten to know Janet and Barb very well in high school. I had dated Janet briefly. She was pretty and always pleasant to be around but rather shy. Barb was more outgoing, but I had not gotten to know her very well at all. She told stories about her childhood that amazed me. I thought I had known her well enough that if she had grown up without running water in her house and had to take baths with water boiled on a stove that I would have known about it—but I didn't. As late as her freshman year, she told us, her family still used an outhouse.

Barb's story took on a romantic aura of the hardships that I associated more with my father's generation—not my own. I wished that I had gotten to know her better when I was in high school. She is a bit of an entrepreneur now—a porcelain-doll maker who dreams of opening her own shop. Her husband, Bruce, was also very outgoing. He told me that he had seen me sitting in front of the general store in Maxwell enjoying my Snickers Ice Cream Bar. He had recognized my bike from Facebook, but he was late getting his grandkids to a school function and couldn't take the time to introduce himself.

Janet was also married, but I didn't get to meet her husband. He goes out infrequently she said. I told her that I could relate—I didn't look forward to venturing out at night—especially when it involved over an hour of driving each way. I also told her I hoped she wouldn't have as much trouble staying awake driving home as I did on the nights I had dropped Lynda off after our dates. It was only ten miles back to Hayes Center, but I remember having to roll the windows down, even in the winter, turning the music up full blast, and pinching myself to stay awake on the drive to town. I had not yet learned of the powers of a mouthful of sunflower seeds in combating drowsiness.

Barb's story had been the biggest surprise of my evening, and it illustrated a point that has become, in the last fifty years, totally misconstrued. A child raised in what politicians like to call "poverty," is not necessarily condemned to a deprived life. But that is what pundits and politicians continually harp on—the supposed direct correlation between children raised in a low-income household and failure in life. That is absolute bunk. The correlation to failure in life is with children raised without accountability, ethics, or morals—and all too often without a responsible father.

Children raised in adversity have flourished in America since it was founded. In fact, some of the greatest people who have ever walked this earth were raised in households with little money. America abounds in Abraham Lincoln-type stories. Someone instilled in these people the conviction that what they became was up to them—that a productive life is not handed to you, you earn it. If children reared in affluence were the answer to creating a great society, we would be well on the way to it, but we're sliding the other way—we're raising a class of entitled young people who are devoid of responsibility to themselves or to others.

Talking with Barb convinced me yet again that the key to becoming a good kid—a productive member of society—is being born to a mother and a father who will raise you with the conviction that irresponsible behavior has predictable consequences and good behavior has pleasing rewards. Good kids are also raised with the conviction that they are loved, but even the burden of not feeling loved can be overcome if kids are raised to believe that what they do and how they treat people are better predictors of the kind of people they will become, than how much or how little money their parents made when they were children.

This journey across America had taken me, on this stop, deeper into my youth—into the 1960s—than I had expected. Talking with classmates reminded me of ideas I had lost touch with—ideas that must have been percolating but had not yet coalesced. That night we gathered glimpses of how others perceived us in our youth. It made me wonder how much we really change over our lifetime. I feel I have changed a lot—that I've grown—but I'm still, in many ways, the adventurous guy Lynda knew when I was fifteen. Was I too adventurous for her? Was she too settled for me? We enjoyed being with each other in high school, but not enough, I guess, to commit to each other. How much different would our lives have been if we had? A person never knows about the roads not taken—they remain among the great mysteries of life. It's a theme Steinbeck often visited in his books. He touched on it in his personal life as well. He returned, later in his life, to Salinas Valley to live. Whether he was trying to reclaim his youth or just wanted again that deep sense of connection to place, I can't say. I just know that I too feel a sense of place that I cannot ignore.

Chapter Twelve

I value the friend who for me finds time on his calendar,
But I cherish the friend who for me does not consult his calendar.
ROBERT BRAULT

In Time of Trouble

I spent one more day in North Platte than I had planned. When Sharon, the owner of A to Z Books, heard I was in town, she asked if I would stop by for *Open Mic* at the bookstore on Saturday night. Even though I always love the opportunity to get to know my readers better, I almost didn't accept the invitation. Saturday would have been a beautiful day to ride to Hayes Center—cool, calm, and sunny. Sunday's forecast was for a blustery day with a strong wind blowing out of the south—the exact direction I was heading. I had also been looking forward to spending a quiet Sunday with my aunt—going again with her to the Congregational Church I had attended when I was a kid.

But I had done that just four months earlier, when I traveled to Hayes Center to attend my high school reunion, so I opted to do something I had never done before and most likely would never get to do if I didn't do it on this trip. Staying the extra day also gave me the chance to walk down memory lane in North Platte. Lynda and Phil dropped me off downtown while they went to shop for a wedding gift. I discovered that North Platte now has art galleries and coffee shops to go along with the largest bookstore between Denver and Lincoln—the town, much to my surprise, is now filled with good art, good reading, and good coffee. I also discovered that the downtown area still had one business I remembered from my high school days—the photography studio that took our senior pictures. I remember the day quite well. We traveled to North Platte as a group and had the whole day off from school. I remember having trouble tying my tie. I also remember spending a good portion of the day hanging out in the bookstore. I still have the book I bought that day. I remember how long I agonized over the purchase. I didn't usually feel I could afford to buy hardbound copies, but I couldn't resist that book. It was beautifully crafted and very well written—a touching tale about the ironworkers who built the Verrazano-Narrows Bridge in New York City.

As memories of that day came back to me, I realized that book might have had more significance in my life than I realized at the time. I didn't totally understand my attraction to the book—I chalked it up to its relationship to architecture, which I planned to study in college. But now I think that what drew me in were the stories of the ironworkers— the Native Americans who specialized in bridgework and had become very good at it. I loved reading about their lives. I've also just realized that the book bears an uncanny resemblance to my first published book. I too chose to have my book illustrated with fine-line pen-and-ink art just like the drawings Gay Talese chose for *The Bridge*.

I didn't know then that I was destined to be a writer. I didn't even know that people *could* grow up to be writers. I didn't know any writers, but my love of reading should have told me more than it apparently did. I lost my desire to be an architect, but I never lost my love of reading—of being exposed to new ideas and new people.

And that is exactly what happened at Open Mic. Most of the people were interested in my stories of the Italian people, but a few were interested in writing—in learning what it takes to become a writer. They approached me after my talk and wanted to hear about the journey of my book to publication. And I told them. Had I been given the opportunity to ask Gay Talese about the journey of *The Bridge* I might have found the courage to become a writer much earlier in my life. But that was in the days before Sharon opened A to Z Books—before North Platte had a haven for writers, readers, and good books.

I sold some books that night, but as I learned the next day, those sales cost me rather dearly. On Sunday, September 23, I woke up early to try to get as many miles down the road as possible before the strong winds that were forecast for the day had a chance to begin blowing. As I had done at Jim and Cheryl's house, I said good-bye the night before. In Iowa I left early enough that I rode in the dark for half an half hour, but this time, even though I got up before the sun, by the time I took the first pedal strokes of the day, first light had come and gone. I could see the land around me, and it reminded me of the ocean—the distant ranch houses appearing as islands in a rolling sea of grass.

Less than an hour into my journey, my outside trailer tire went flat. I pulled onto the shoulder and quickly discovered the reason. The ditch was covered with goat head stickers—the kind with five extremely sharp points, one of which is invariably pointed straight up—and the wind, which had already begun blowing briskly, was driving the sandburs from the ditch onto the road. I was glad I had bought super thorn-resistant tubes for the trailer. But the rubber was so thick that it was almost like fitting a tire within a tire. But after a bit of struggling, the tube was inside the tire, pumped up, and ready for the road.

Half an hour later, I flatted again—this time it was the rear tire of Friday, making me wish I had picked up extra heavy-duty tubes for my bike as well. I didn't buy them because I was even more concerned that those tubes wouldn't fit inside the tires, but with two flats within the first hour and a half, I wished that I had given myself the chance to find out, even if the extra weight would have slowed me down. You can get a long way down the road in the time it takes to repair a puncture and get going again.

I had thought that I would be eating lunch with Aunt Lillian. But the headwinds and the flats were making me wonder if I'd even get to

Wallace, which was halfway to Hayes Center, by lunchtime. I noticed a vehicle making its way slowly down a long, sandy road connecting a distant ranch to the highway. I stopped at the intersection and waited for it. When at last the car had made it across the expanse, I told the driver I was headed to Hayes Center but wondered if I could get anything to eat in Wallace. She said there was no place to eat on Sunday, or maybe she said that they no longer even had a restaurant—I quit listening closely after I heard the word *no*. I'd have to get to Hayes Center eating energy bars, but the good news was that I wouldn't be riding half a dozen miles out of my way only to learn there was no place to eat. My third flat of the day, again on the rear wheel of Friday, stopped me about four miles short of Wallace, and a couple of miles short of the turnoff to Hayes Center.

While I was slapping a patch on the tube, a high-school-age boy stopped his car beside me.

"Can I give you a lift to town?" he asked.

I was a bit surprised by the question. Normally, the first question is *Do you need help?*

"No, I've just about got it fixed," I said.

"The store's going to be closing at one thirty. I don't think you can make it," he countered.

My quizzical look prompted him to tell me the rest of the story.

"My mom sent me," he said. That was a start, but I still wasn't up to speed. He saw that I was still perplexed. He continued, "My mom told you that you couldn't get anything to eat in Wallace. She forgot that the grocery store is open until one thirty. I can take you to town."

"Oh, okay, thanks a lot. But I wouldn't want to leave my bike here. I'll be fine." Now I understood.

"How 'bout I pick you up a sandwich or something?" he asked. "I've got to go anyway. My mom needs cream cheese."

And with that I gave the Good Samaritan some money, and asked him to pick me up a banana and a Pepsi as well. He sped off and I stood there watching him disappear while I marveled that a woman I had spoken to for less than thirty seconds had sent her son out to find me even though I never would have known she had failed to tell me about the grocery store. She knew I was unlikely to go into Wallace since it was a couple of miles off my route to Hayes Center, but still she sent her son out to help a stranger just passing through.

While I was putting the tube back in the tire, a ranch truck with Hayes County plates stopped to ask if I needed help. The driver introduced himself. I introduced myself. Jerry knew my family. I knew his but I didn't know him. He had graduated ten years after my younger brother and almost twenty years after me from Hayes County High School. I thanked him for stopping and went back to patching the tube. This part of the country, at least judging by the number of people offering help, seemed to have changed little in the past fifty years.

I had just finished putting the wheel back on and was stuffing the tools and repair kit in the little pouch that tucks up under my saddle when the young man pulled up and handed me a plastic bag. "They didn't have any bananas, so I got a couple of pears—and a big bottle of Pepsi and a ham and cheese sandwich. Hope that's okay."

"You bet. You need more money?" I asked.

"No, it was just a few pennies short."

I tried to give him more money, but he wouldn't take it. So I reached into my trailer and pulled out a gift. "What's your name and what's your mom's name? I'd like to give you a book I wrote about Italy."

"Thanks."

"The people of Italy are very friendly—and very helpful too—just like you and your mom." I finished inscribing it and handed it to him. "Thank you so much," I said. "That was really kind of you."

He smiled a shy teenager's smile and said, "You're welcome." He laid the book on the seat next to a plastic bag from the store, backed out, and drove toward the ranch road where I had first seen his mother about an hour before. He was driving slower now. He had his mom's cream cheese. I hoped it was for frosting on a cake for him and his friends.

I got to the turnoff to Wallace at 1:39. I would have been too late to get to town on time. Good thing the woman hadn't thought to tell me about the grocery store—I would have been frustrated that the flat tire had kept me from getting there before it closed—funny how things turn out.

I turned south, toward Hayes Center. Before I'd ridden much more than the length of a football field my bike was again feeling squirrelly. I stopped and reached down to feel the front tire. It was soft. I rode a bit farther to an intersection, a shortcut I had avoided because it wasn't paved, and pulled off the road, looking for a place with no stickers. Four flats in less than forty miles—this had to be my worst luck ever on the road. Sometimes I ride for a whole summer without flatting four times— many thousands of miles. The summer I was racing every week, and in training for Italy, I rode over six thousand miles—and I remember flatting only three times.

But I had more people to meet. A woman driving a big pickup pulling a horse trailer stopped before I had even pulled out my tools. Her daughter, who was riding shotgun, and was therefore right beside me, asked if I needed help. I leaned toward the truck and said, "No, it's just a flat, and I've got a repair kit." Her mom leaned forward so she could see me better. "Are you sure you don't need help?"

"No—thanks a lot for stopping to ask, though. Sure appreciate it."

"Well, if you're sure you're okay," she said.

I didn't bother to tell her how much practice I'd had that day fixing tubes—she would probably have insisted I throw my bike in the back. I just said, "Yeah, I've got it."

The full force of the wind hit me once the pickup was no longer shielding me. As I watched her pull onto the empty highway, I noticed that the truck was from a county to the south of Hayes Center. For a second I wished that I *had* asked for a ride. There was a very good chance she would have passed right through Hayes Center within the half hour—she would have had to drive only one block out of her way. But I wouldn't have felt right asking a woman and her teenage daughter to give a lift to a man they didn't know. I wouldn't want my wife to do that—even in Hayes Center—unless she knew the man and his family extremely well. But my thinking had been clouded by three decades of not living in this area. Although this woman looked slightly familiar, I couldn't say that I knew who she was, and I assumed she didn't know me, so I wouldn't have felt right asking for a lift. But I sure admired her thoughtfulness in stopping to ask if there was anything she could do to help.

In 1962 I wouldn't have given the woman's offer a second thought. I would have refused help back then as well, but I wouldn't have given any thought to the risk a mother and daughter were subjecting themselves to in asking a stranger if he needed help. They certainly had nothing to fear from me, but did they make that determination in the few seconds that they had to observe me before stopping to ask if I needed help? The woman had stopped the pickup so close that her daughter was less than an arm's length from me. I love being among people who are so trustworthy—and such good drivers that they know exactly where the edge of their truck is.

It's a shame that we are now living in a world where thoughts of violence and vulnerability come to mind when a stranger stops to offer help. But the exchange I'd had with that woman is one glaring difference between America 1962 and America 2012—between Nebraska 1962 and Nebraska 2012. America on the whole has changed a lot in those fifty years—Nebraska not so much. Unemployment is high in America as a whole—Nebraska not so much. Debt in America is disastrously unsustainable—but in Nebraska budgets are balanced.

The exchange with that kind woman brought to mind a unique quality of America—what sets America apart from other countries and other systems of government. Our states are still somewhat autonomous. If things get too bad in one state, you're free to move to another. And when the politicians in states like California and New York see that their policies have become so onerous that people are fleeing to Texas and North Dakota, those governments may be forced peacefully—without revolution—to change their ways. That's the beauty of America and the free market system. In America you can choose what kind of society you want to live in. If you value living among people where you can feel comfortable stopping to offer aid, you can move your family to a state like Nebraska.

By the time I'd finished the repair and had the wheel back on the bike, almost forty-five minutes had gone by. Had I thrown my bike in the woman's pickup and hopped in with her and her daughter, I would have been five or ten minutes into a conversation with my Aunt Lillian. But instead I was still gathering up my tools as a minivan went by. I noticed it because it was braking too early for the upcoming intersection. It stopped short of the stop sign, executed a one-eighty, and came back. A man whose clothing—a long-sleeved black shirt and a sweater on a hot day tipped me off that he might not be from the United States—leaned out of the car window and asked with an accent and phrasing that took away any doubt, "Can I help you?"

"No, I'm just about ready to go again. I had to fix a flat." I guessed that he was from Africa. But I couldn't get any closer than that. He parked his car on the side of the road and got out.

"It is really windy. You are not going south, are you?" he asked with great concern as he walked across the road.

"Matter of fact I am. I'm heading to Hayes Center," I told him.

He shook his head very deliberately as if to say, *You don't want to do that*. "Can I take you?" he asked.

"But you're going north," I said. "I'll be fine."

"But it would only take me half an hour to take you to Hayes Center," he implored.

"And half an hour back," I said. "No, I'll be okay."

"But how long is it going to take you?"

"I should be there in a few hours," I said. But as I made the mental calculations I realized that it might have been more accurate to say, *I should be able to get there before dark.*

"Oh, man! Are you sure you won't let me drive you?"

"No, I couldn't ask you do that. But if you had some water, I'd accept that."

"I don't have any water, but I have a Mountain Dew in the car. Do you want that?"

"Sure, if you can spare it."

And with that we began sharing. I learned that he was from Kenya, his name was Haran, and he had come to America only a few years earlier to be the pastor at the United Methodist Church in Wallace—a place he had never heard of before he got the job. He told me that he had grown to love the people of Nebraska—the people of these lonely high plains—and that he thought they had grown to love him too. I snapped a photo of him and me just before he reluctantly got into his van and turned around to drive into Wallace—I wanted to make sure I remembered his friendly smile and his warm gestures.

I had ridden barely half a dozen miles after saying good-bye to him when I began seriously rethinking my decision to refuse his offer. My rear tire was soft yet again. That flat brought the total to five for the day—four on the bike and one on the trailer. I had met a lot of people because of all the flats, but apparently there were more people I still needed to meet.

The first was a farmer heading north, who stopped to ask where I was going and if I needed help. I told him Hayes Center and that I thought I had it under control. But apparently my words didn't convey a lot of conviction. Maybe the wind was wearing down my resolve. He said he was running a few miles up the road to check on some things at one of his farms. "If you're still here when I get back, I'll run you to town," he assured me. I thanked him and off he went.

I finished the repair before he returned. I guess I got far enough down the road that I must have gotten south of his home farm—or maybe he too ran into problems that afternoon. As I struggled down the road about nine miles an hour, I saw a woman mowing grass near a machine shed. The door was open and I figured there would be an air compressor right at the entrance. There was also a standing spigot at the side of the concrete apron.

The woman seemed cautious as I approached, so I mentioned I was from Hayes Center, and she relaxed. She told me that yes indeed, air was just inside the door and that I was welcome to the water as well. I needed the air because I had been able to get the tire pressure up to only thirty-five pounds with my hand pump—my arms were feeling the effects of so many flats. I quickly bumped the pressure up to sixty-five pounds and topped off my water bottles. The woman had resumed mowing, so I just waved my appreciation to her and took off. Within a mile of that farm the rear tire picked up another sticker and went flat again. I didn't bother repairing the tube; even though the tire had lots of miles left on the tread, I put a brand-new tire and tube on the bike. That saved a little time, maybe ten minutes, and I was back on the road again before anyone stopped to offer aid.

Just across the Hayes County line I made an uncharacteristic stop for the day—not to fix a tire but to bump up my blood sugar level so I'd have the energy to make the final push into Hayes Center. The wind was still howling—blowing straight down the road at me. I had pulled off the highway and stopped in the lee of a windbreak. I was enjoying the Mountain Dew that Pastor Haran had given me when yet another farmer stopped to ask if I needed help. We dropped into an easy conversation, and I asked his name. The family name was familiar—turned out that I knew his dad, and he knew mine.

Mike was telling me he was getting ready to harvest the "Shaw ground" when a woman in a car slowed down to warn us that a semi was bearing down on us right behind her. We weren't exactly on the road, but we weren't exactly off it, either. When Mike heard the warning, he waved a quick good-bye and took off. I stepped off the road and turned to absorb the buffet of the windblast as the semi flew by.

As I watched the truck disappear in the distance, my thoughts went back to the interrupted conversation. When Mike mentioned "Shaw ground" I figured he was referring to the land that I used to farm as a kid. But when he motioned toward it, he pointed the wrong way—toward land that was at least half a dozen miles away (maybe more if the slight nodding of his head was meant to convey more than the mile or so I assumed) across a roadless canyon from the land I had farmed as a kid. Why, I wondered, was he calling land in this part of the county "Shaw ground"? I reached back in my memory bank to stories my dad had told me about his early history as a farmer, but nothing came to mind about land we might have owned or farmed at one time in the far northern part of Hayes County.

The day was getting away from me. I had begun the ride thinking I would be eating lunch in Hayes Center—now even supper was in doubt. Once again I was racing the sun to the horizon. Each flat was taking about an hour to repair, from the time I stopped until I had everything packed up and was again on the road. Within that hour average I was including the time I spent talking to the folks who stopped to ask if I needed help.

A few more miles down the road I could see the television tower that was nine miles north of town and it reminded me just how much television had changed our lives in the 1950s. That transmitter brought television to our community when I was nine years and was, in many ways, responsible for turning what had been a vibrant small town with lots of small businesses into a town that almost died. But it didn't. After a period of decline new and different businesses came to town.

One of the new businesses, a feedlot, was changing something else in Hayes County—the smell. Not only was the stench of the huge confinement operation attacking the air, it was also attacking the soil. A huge, thick cloud of yellow dust was rising from the denuded half-section where cattle were confined waiting to be fed and for their feces to be hauled away. But presumably this CAFO (concentrated animal feeding operation in the parlance of the USDA and EPA), which, ironically, was across the road from the television tower, was employing a lot of people and was good for the economy of Hayes County. At what cost, though, I'm sure some were asking. This is a question that can be dealt with on a local level and is but another example of why the American idea of local and state governance has proven to be so powerful and so effective.

The sight of that feedlot brought to mind another change that has occurred since my first bike ride. There was no Environmental Protection Agency in 1962; some local autonomy was lost when President Nixon established the EPA in 1970. If a general statement can be made about the differences between America 1962 and America 2012, it is certainly that the federal government has become bigger, more powerful, and more intrusive. Whether you see that as a good thing or a bad thing goes a long way toward defining your view of the role of government—and your view of what's best for America.

I'll remember the ride between North Platte and my hometown for many reasons—certainly for all the punctures. But I'll also remember it for the many offers of help—the sheer number pretty much defines where I'm from. I guess it should come as no surprise that among people willing to help a stranger would also be found a lot of people willing to stand up for the not yet born. Just as in Iowa, the farmers and ranchers of southwestern Nebraska were voicing their opposition to abortion by putting up signs on their land.

In the light of early morning I had noticed a billboard portraying a rather frail-looking ninety-some-year-old man cradling in his arms a newborn child—presumably his great-grandchild. Accompanying the photo were the words *Every life is worth living*. The photograph, the lettering, the mood of the billboard were just right, very touching. It stood at the edge of the highway right-of-way, a nice-looking farmstead a quarter mile behind it across a beautiful pasture.

Throughout the day I saw many signs reminding me of the preciousness of life. I stopped to take photos of most of them. There was something very moving about these lonely signs proclaiming the sanctity of life in a sea of grass stretching off to the horizon, broken only by fence posts, utility poles, and the occasional tree. I found especially beautiful a billboard with a very faint outline of a baby's profile, with just a hint of the features of the face—*Some Gifts Only GOD Can Give*.

Other signs caught my eye. On a dark background, a fetus in the womb was depicted next to the words of Jeremiah 1:5, *Before I formed you in the womb, I knew you. ~ God*. On the other side was a message in today's vernacular—on the left a Happy Face and on the right, *SMILE! Your MOM CHOSE LIFE*. When I was younger, I was ambivalent about sharing Christian ethics with the world, but the more years I get under my belt, and the closer I get to leaving this life, the stronger I feel that to not let people know what you think is to act cowardly.

I read a book a couple of years ago that cemented in my mind a sentiment that had been growing in me for many years—that I needed to not be afraid to stand up for the oppressed. While I was in Italy I became interested in the question of what life had been like for ordinary families in Italy and Germany during the rise of Fascism and Nazism. I did some research and discovered an eight-hundred-page book about the life of Dietrich Bonhoeffer that dealt with that question. I began reading it and couldn't stop. By the end of the week I had journeyed with him through the stages of recognizing, apparently before anyone else did, the evils of what the Nazis were doing—and the risk to his family for taking a stand, especially when he was threatened with prison for opposing his government. "Forget it, Dietrich," he was told by his friends in the government, "just because our laws are singling out the Jews, nothing will come of it—the Jews will not be harmed."

His was a lone voice in Germany, speaking against the evils of the Third Reich. To speak against abortion is not to be a lone voice in America, but it does take some courage. The good thing is that the voices speaking against abortion are making a difference. Each year for the past half dozen years, fewer and fewer people have been willing to acknowledge that they favor abortion.

I was surprised to be thinking about World War II Germany as I biked against the wind toward my childhood home, but the extremely slow trek had put me in a mood of reflection. I saw landscapes and farmsteads that took me all the way back to my earliest memories and made me think about my life's journey as well. I thought back forty years to my days in the US Army and the ambivalence I felt when *Roe v. Wade* was announced. I find it quite incredible that one person could hold such diametrically opposed opinions regarding questions of life within one lifetime.

I've read the stories of the Germans who took part in the slaughter of millions of Jews—who rounded them up, confiscated their belongings, and put them on trains bound for concentration camps. They didn't see themselves as evil. And neither do the people who favor "a woman's right to choose." I was in Vietnam when the Supreme Court announced its decision in *Roe v. Wade*. I remember little about how I reacted to the news except that I found it odd that the court found the "right to abortion" linked to a "right to privacy." I wondered about the rights of the man—the father—and his responsibilities. From what I knew of the court's decision, the rights and responsibilities of the father, as well as the future child, played no part whatsoever in the ruling. But I didn't dwell on the decision. I was worried about whether I would get out of Vietnam alive, and whether I would have a job waiting for me if I did.

The next time I remember thinking about *Roe v. Wade* was more than ten years later. I was riding in a car with coworkers who were expressing the opinion that people who voiced opposition to "choice" were Fascists. I said nothing. But that comment got me to thinking. It was obvious that the speaker assumed everyone in the car agreed with her, and except for me, apparently everyone did, for in one way or another they all chimed their assent. I said nothing and felt like a coward. I had been rendered silent by groupthink.

Our first child was born a year and a half after *Roe v. Wade*. Our second child was born in 1976. I witnessed the miracle of that first birth, and felt the miracle of the second when I held that child in my arms and sensed immediately just how different he was from our first baby. He came out of the womb already a unique person. When, I began asking, did he develop that unique personality? I doubted that it had been conferred on him at birth—so when was it that he became a "person"?

I began asking questions I couldn't answer. That incredible moment of witnessing the birth of your child is life-changing. I began asking "God questions"—questions not unlike those a young child asks his mother and father as he becomes aware of the strangeness of this world. *Where do babies come from? Why is the sky blue? How does a caterpillar turn into a butterfly?* Among the questions I began asking were, *Why does a mother have a right to kill her child? Why does a father not have a right to protect that child?* I asked *myself* those questions, but I didn't have the courage to ask them out loud among coworkers.

A few months after the birth of my second child I was back in Hayes Center to bury my father. The death of a loved one also leads to questions for God and about God. These momentous events are markers on our own journey from birth to death and back to life again. My bicycle journey in 2012 from North Platte to Hayes Center was going to carry me to within a few yards of where I stood that hot August day in 1976 saying good-bye to my father. I don't remember coming up with any answers that day, but losing my dad led me to ask questions I had never before thought to ask.

Today's ride was leading to lots of questions, too. I was biking through countryside I thought I knew well, but I was surprised at how different it looked—I was riding on a highway that was completed after I moved away from Hayes Center. But it wasn't just that the gravel road of fifty years ago was now asphalt—the biggest difference was that *I* had changed. I doubted that the canyons had gotten bigger in the years I had been away, but they sure looked deeper and wider. I had also forgotten just how far you can see from the cemetery on the hill where my parents are buried.

I parked my bike carefully on that hill to avoid picking up any more sandburs, and looked out at Hayes Center to the south, to the water tower that stands high above the trees and houses. I looked to the east and saw the pasture where I used to land my Cessna 182 Skylane when I was commuting between Omaha and Hayes Center—between my city job as a filmmaker and my country job as a mostly-weekend wheat farmer.

I walked first to see the headstones of my mother and father. Seeing them made me realize how long my mom lived without my dad. Mom died in 1997, more than twenty-one years after Dad died. Mom got to meet all five of my children—Dad got to meet only two. Seeing those dates in stone made me realize in a deeply personal way that I have been without my father for thirty-six years, more than half my life.

I thought of all the changes in my life during those years as I walked back across the highway and through a cornfield to the pasture where I would land my plane if there were no cows on the runway. The painted tires that marked the edge of the strip were still more or less in place. I continued walking down the runway, reliving some of the challenging takeoffs and landings—downwind, downhill takeoffs, and high-angle, uphill takeoffs over the electric transmission lines on the north end of the field, and even some departures on snowy days when the wheels of the plane and the whirring propeller made it look to observers as if a cloud was lifting off from the pasture.

I arrived back at my bike just as the sun was sitting like a big ball on the distant horizon—a phenomenon I had witnessed countless times either from a tractor seat or while driving back to our home in town after a long day in the fields. I was relieved to discover that all four of Friday's tires were still holding air.

The ride to town reminded me of the first time I had ever ridden to the cemetery. Rossy and I were probably eight and seven years old. We packed lunches for the mile-long trip. I brought along a minced ham and cheese sandwich—Rossy, I remember clearly, packed his favorite sandwich—white bread and mustard. I never did figure out why a guy who had access to all the good food in his mother's restaurant preferred mustard sandwiches. Other than that somewhat weird thought about my childhood, the final mile of the day passed without incident. I rode into town, past my parents' house, where I had lived from birth to almost age thirty, and down to my Aunt Lillian's house two blocks away, where I found her reading a book while she waited patiently for me. Lillian is the last living relative in my parents' generation on my mother's side. She is my source for stories about my parents that I forgot to ask while they were with us. I asked her what my parents' lives were like during the Depression and regretted that I had not thought to ask such questions on long drives with my father. What did we discuss that was more important? My guess is that we talked about nothing, so absorbed at the time was I in my own world.

It's the same with my kids. They are wrapped up in their own world. And with good reason—they're forging their way in it. They aren't looking back, just as I wasn't looking back as a kid, but if I *had* been looking back with my father, I might have learned a lot that would have helped me move forward.

Despite the fact that I then saw my father as old, my perspective now is that my father was not really that old. His lungs had just given out on him, and that made him old before his time. Also, he had lost his hair when he was very young—in his twenties, some twenty years before I was born. But I also vividly remember one of my high school teammates telling me that my father was movie star good-looking. Lee confided to me that he thought my dad looked just like Chuck Connors, *The Rifleman.* That elevated my father's stock considerably—*The Rifleman* was one of my favorite TV shows.

Lillian had prepared dinner, and while we ate, I told her about the people I had met on my journey and asked her about people I had failed to ask my parents about. I was especially curious about the James Shaw whose grave I had seen next to my great-grandfather's in Kearney, but she didn't know who he was. I called my sister to ask her about him. I figured since she was fifteen when he died that she might remember something about him. But she had never heard of him either. I was shocked.

The next morning Aunt Lillian blessed me with another down-home meal and more stories about my family. I pressed her memory about the farmland Mike had referred to as "Shaw ground," but she could remember nothing. After breakfast I went to see Dixie, a friend from high school who was now the editor of the *Times-Republican,* to look for information about my great-grandfather. I thought I would be searching through microfilms, but she took me to the archives and let me look through copies of newspapers more than one hundred years old.

And so began another journey—looking week by week through the yellowing papers hoping to find a mention of Owen Little Shaw. Such research is extremely time-consuming—even the ads are fascinating to read, for they too reveal just how different life was when we moved about the world by horse and buggy. A trip to town was worthy of a write-up— and that's how I came to learn that one James Shaw had traveled down from the northern part of the county on business. I found no mention of Owen Little Shaw or of my grandfather, Ellsworth Shaw, but here was the name James Shaw again—presumably the James Shaw who was buried in Kearney next to my great-grandfather Owen. I was stunned to discover that a James Shaw—a man no one in my family seemed to know—had set foot in Hayes County long before I did.

Armed with this fortuitous bit of information, I quit searching for my great-grandfather's name and headed to the courthouse. There I discovered a most interesting thing—even a shocking thing as I considered the implications: a land claim of 160 acres deeded from the federal government to James Shaw. And it was right where Mike had pointed when he mentioned where he was going to be picking corn—at the northernmost edge of Hayes County. The "Shaw ground" is exactly what the name implies—land first claimed from the US government and therefore named after the person who filed the claim. I also found the probate of James Shaw—detailed down to the hand chisels he owned, as well as each horse, wagon, and a whole lot more. I even learned that among his possessions were a watch and a violin.

I read through page after detailed page of what James Shaw owned when he died. But I was not able to determine why, if he died in Hayes Center, was he not buried in Hayes County? Why was he buried in Kearney? Then I realized what should have been immediately obvious. The James Shaw whose probate I was reading was not the man whose grave I saw in Kearney. The dates didn't add up. Could he be the father of the James Shaw who died in 1949? And if so, where is the James Shaw who homesteaded in Hayes County buried?

I stopped by the library hoping to find accounts of the early settlers of Hayes County. I found none that I had not already read, but I did find Aunt Lillian at the library doing some research herself. She too was looking back and wanted to read again about the early days of Mari Sandoz and learn more of the history of western Nebraska.

Lillian invited me to join her for lunch at the Senior Center. Even though a few of the folks dining with us that day had lived all their lives in Hayes County, none of them had heard of "Shaw ground" in the north part of the county. The memory of any James Shaw other than me in Hayes County had apparently been forgotten as well. My curiosity had definitely been whetted. I wanted to know who was the James Shaw who died February 22, 1918, in Hayes County, and who was the James Shaw who died November 18, 1949, and was buried in Kearney—and what was their relationship to me. And why the heck did no one in Hayes County have a story about either man?

The answers are out there somewhere, but with what was left of the day I wanted to visit with Lillian about her interest in early Nebraska history. At the library she had picked up *Old Jules*, the story of the Sandoz family homesteading in the Sandhills in the late 1800s. My family had connections to the Sandhills, to Arthur County, which lies just south of the heart of *Old Jules* country. In fact that is where Grandfather Ellsworth, a son of Owen Little Shaw, is buried and where my dad grew up, going to a country school not far from the family's ranch. My father didn't graduate from high school—he quit the year he would have been a ninth grader to begin his life as a cowboy.

All this information, and the questions that were swirling around in my mind, were helping me to realize that this town that spawned me has an intimate connection to the days of homesteading, is incredibly small, and is very remote. Yet it is home and still feels that way to me. I am closely linked to this land and these people.

Hayes Center is holding on, just as much of the rest of rural America seems to be holding on. Folks in small towns and rural areas of Nebraska are strongly conservative—they've got to be to survive. They're conservative of what little rain falls on these high plains, and they are strongly conservative of what little money falls upon their communities as well. But I hadn't come back just to see what Hayes Center was like; I wanted to see what all of America was like and how it had changed.

I had come to Hayes Center with the expectation that if I learned more about my family's history, especially that of my great-grandfather, Owen Little Shaw, I'd learn more about America. Instead, I learned that a man with the same name as mine homesteaded in my home county, and yet the knowledge of him, except within the ancient records of the courthouse, had been lost. Among other things, this points out the fragility of historical knowledge and family knowledge. How is knowledge lost so quickly? What does this say about history, and what does it say about any attempt to get a handle on our past? Without knowing exactly why, discovering the existence of a James Shaw buried next to my great-grandfather and learning that another James Shaw was one of the pioneers of Hayes County gave me hope that my quixotic adventure had not been in vain. Not only was I learning about my own family history, but I was also learning much about history itself, about knowledge—that on any given subject it can be woefully incomplete.

Steinbeck pondered whether he was learning anything on his journey, but his question seemed to be born of frustration, whereas mine seemed more related to amazement. If I was learning anything on this journey, it was just how much I didn't know. No wonder Proverbs cautions us that wisdom comes not from man's knowledge but from the *fear of the Lord*—which I had always understood to mean *a proper humility*. There's a very good chance that a lot of what we think we know will be shown to be wrong when we quit looking through a glass darkly and begin seeing face to face. I didn't ask these kinds of questions much when I was a kid, but now, regarding just about every subject that comes up, my first thought is to question if I, or we as a community, or a society, are taking the right view of things.

This may just be a sign that I'm getting old—that I've lived long enough to see man's knowledge fail too many times. But I now want to know how God sees this world. Many argue that such things can't be known—or that such knowledge is dangerous—especially when it is wrong or we interpret it incorrectly. If we learned nothing else on September 11, 2001, we learned that the perverted views about God held by radical Islamists could lead to disastrous consequences.

But having said that, I would come right back and say that until we're willing to ask the tough questions, and explore the possibility that mankind may have it wrong, it is unlikely that we will ever get an inkling of how God views us and this world. I've come to the realization that we can learn a lot coming to the realization of how little we know. People like Socrates, Einstein, and the writers of Proverbs, as well as Steinbeck, figured it out.

Chapter Thirteen

I believe that there is one story in the world, and only one …
Humans are caught—in their lives, in their thoughts,
in their hungers and ambitions, in their avarice and cruelty,
and in their kindness and generosity too—
in a net of good and evil …
There is no other story.
A man, after he has brushed off the dust and chops of his life,
will have left only the hard, clean questions:
Was it good or was it evil?
Have I done well—or ill?
JOHN STEINBECK, *East of Eden*

Another View of Life

I could have spent weeks in my hometown newspaper office researching my family's history and not learned as much as I did just stopping by the side of the road to take a drink of Mountain Dew. Through coincidence or fate, depending upon your view of the world, I gained a totally different perspective on my family's history in Nebraska. I now know stories of my connections to Hayes County that my folks had either neglected to tell me, had forgotten, or somehow didn't know themselves. History is like that. It must be remembered and passed on to be useful. And I'm still trying to figure out where the James Shaw who homesteaded in Hayes County is buried, but I do know he played the fiddle, something I've always wished I could do.

The monumental bestseller *East of Eden* was originally conceived by John Steinbeck as a family history for his children. But after researching and writing the story, he discovered that his family's story became the story of a valley, Salinas, and a state, California, and by extension much of America. That is the power of story. From another family's story it is possible to learn much about our own family's history.

Aunt Lillian told me she was reading *Old Jules* not just for what it told of the Sandoz family but also for what it told of her ancestors who had settled the high plains of western Nebraska during those same years. She felt that their story was her story. Lillian had not been born in Hayes County but had moved there when she was in high school. She was quite a bit younger than my mom. Lillian is eighty-eight. My mom, if she were still living, would have turned one hundred years old a few weeks after Lillian and I spent the evening talking about my parents' early days in Hayes County. But despite the age difference, Lillian is a great connection between my generation and that of my parents. She was able to tell me stories of my folks' early days in the county—of the difficulties my father and mother faced—what their fears and joys had been.

On Tuesday morning I bundled up, packed up, and paused at Lillian's front door to snap a photo of the two of us as the early morning sun lit up our faces. She was happy, I think, and I know I was. I was thankful to be doing something I enjoy and thankful I had a relative to share the moment with. I hopped on Friday, waved one last time to Lillian, glanced two blocks north to my family's home where fifty years I had begun my teenage ride, and joined the exact route I had ridden those many years ago.

As I pulled out of town on Highway 25, I traveled in my mind's eye up and down the streets of my hometown. So firmly planted is Hayes

Center in my mind that I can conjure images of just what the town looked like when I was a paperboy carrying the *Omaha World Herald*, to each of my customers. I also got to know the people too. Each week, on Saturday, I knocked on their doors to collect the "paper" money. At some homes, it was a quick transaction, at others, it could take quite a while, depending upon how long it took to find enough coins or how much a customer might want to talk.

I was heading south toward the canyons I had ridden through many times as a young boy. The traffic was light, and except for one trucker who apparently thought that only he should be on that lonesome road, the ride that morning was uneventful. The trucker I remembered, though. When he was over a mile away, on the other side of Government Canyon, he began blasting his horn—for what reason I never determined. Except for that minute-long attack on the peace and quiet of the morning, he passed without further assault.

The first town on my route, just as it had been fifty years ago, was Palisade—a town that had a certain attraction to it when I was a child— for it had the nearest swimming pool. I didn't stop in Palisade on that first trip, but this time I opted to bypass the bypass of Palisade. I rode down the main street and noticed a restaurant. I looked inside to see if I recognized anyone, but I saw no one familiar. I wasn't hungry enough to sit down for a full breakfast, so I walked across the street to the grocery store to get some fruit and candy bars.

I also picked up a bit of conversation in the grocery store. As I was choosing an apple I heard a voice near the front of the store that I recognized. The low pitch was so distinctive I was even able to put a face with the deeply resonant sound, as well as the family name, but I couldn't put a first name with the video playing in my mind. He noticed me as I stepped up to the counter to pay for my Snickers and apple and banana. "You look just like your dad," he said.

"I know you too, but I can't pull out your first name," I said.

"It's Bill," he said.

That released a flood of memories and associations. I even remembered a tractor the man had bought from my dad. I was embarrassed and didn't admit that I did not recognize the storekeeper, but he knew me—and somehow he also knew I'd be passing through Palisade that morning. Rural communities are like that—information travels quickly and efficiently. We talked briefly—mostly about the tractors I delivered all over the county for my dad—then I took off with promises to both men that I would ride safely.

The highway from Palisade to Wauneta was much as I remembered it—light traffic with a narrow shoulder—and with the exception of one trucker, the drivers were courteous and safety conscious. Apparently I had passed that air-horn-blowing trucker somewhere along the route, and now he was passing me again. And once again he began blasting his horn a mile before he got to me. And again he pulled around me without further incident, but the experience was unique—in my decades of riding I have never encountered a driver who used his horn so aggressively.

The morning passed quickly. The day was beautiful, and memories of childhood colored the route. I arrived in Wauneta at lunchtime and, as I had done in Palisade, took a detour into town along the main street. This time I was hungry. I had food in my pack, but I was looking for a place to sit down and take a break. I chose a busy bar and wrote notes and sipped on a big Pepsi while I waited for my pizza. A lot of farmers and ranchers came in to eat, too. The place was pretty lively except for two cowboys who ambled in and sat down in the booth next to me.

"He doesn't talk much" would have been an apt blind date description of either of them. They said but one word to each other the whole meal. And that one word they saved until they were ready to go. The one nearest me, the one with a kerchief around his neck, said, "Ready?" The other cowboy nodded his big hat once. Then they both stood at the same time and walked out. I gathered it wasn't their first quiet meal together, and from the looks of their well-worn boots I'd bet that they had spent quite a few silent days in the saddle together as well. These guys were real cowboys. I wouldn't have been surprised to find out they had horses tied up in front of the place.

Again, just as in the restaurant in Palisade I peeked into, I saw no one I recognized, even though I was still less than fifty miles from my childhood home. Not one person was curious either. No one, including the waitress, asked where I was heading. I asked for a doggie bag, got Styrofoam cartons, and took six slices of sausage-and-mushroom pizza with me.

Before heading out of town, I posed my bike in front of the Chateau Theater, where Lynda and I used to go see her favorite Elvis Presley movies. I was happy to see a current film, *The Odd Life of Timothy Green*, listed on the marquee—and glad to see that main street Wauneta didn't have a boarded-up movie theater dragging it down. A couple of miles north of Wauneta I stopped to take photos of an intersection where Lynda and I could have been seriously hurt on one of our cross-country back-road trips to the movie theater. We were on a county road I had never driven before—one without amenities like "Stop Ahead" signs. We came up over a hill going way too fast and I saw in front of me a T-intersection with a canyon bank beyond. I was going downhill. I was on sand. There was hardly any chance to slow down, let alone stop, and at the bottom of the hill was a highway. My only hope was to set the car up in a slide that would get us around the corner without flipping over—and pray that no one was coming. I shuddered at the memory of it—in those days there were no seatbelts, cars had bench seats, and girls sat in the middle, right next to their dates. How different our lives would have been if either of us had been seriously hurt that day. But like that "soundless" tree falling in the forest, no one saw us fly through that stop sign and slide onto the highway. The car wasn't damaged. No harm, no foul. We coasted slowly into Wauneta and went to see *Kid Galahad*.

During one of our wide-ranging conversations over the weekend, I had asked Lynda about that close call, and she had absolutely no memory of it. I was shocked. That fearful moment was seared into my brain. That night I lost a bit of my youthful conviction that I was invincible. Nothing had happened, but the "what ifs" scared the hell out of me.

I chose to ride to Imperial on Old Highway 6. It was a long climb to the top of the plateau above the Frenchman River Valley. At the top the vista opened up to a scene very Grand Canyon-like—and that is the exact thing local promoters noticed. They call it the Little Grand Canyon. And just as it does at the other Grand Canyon, the vista humbles a person. Between thoughts of *What if Lynda had been hurt,* and the humility that a grand vista inspires, I was feeling quite thankful.

Imperial was at the fifty-mile mark for the day. On my first ride, fifty years ago, I had thought it might take me all day to get to Imperial, but I arrived in town in the early afternoon. Even after I had eaten it was still early afternoon, since I had gained an hour passing from the Central Time Zone to Mountain Time. I went swimming at the local pool, and like a typical teenager I got bored, so I hopped back on my Raleigh Sports to press onward toward Colorado. But on this stop in Imperial, I didn't go swimming, and I didn't get bored. I decided to seek out the author of a book I had read a couple of years earlier that had deeply impressed me. You may have heard of it or even read it. It's been on the *New York Times* Bestseller List for many months, has sold about ten million copies worldwide, and was written by a first-time author who also happens to be a pastor from Imperial, Nebraska.

I read it before it became popular, so I felt a kinship to it—not just because I felt I had *discovered* it but because I knew what these people were like—I had grown up playing basketball against kids who lived in Imperial. When I read it I wondered why the whole world wasn't talking about the book—the story was that good. Within a few weeks the whole world *was* talking about it. Todd Burpo, his wife Cassie, and their son Colton began appearing on the early morning television shows talking about Colton's discovery that *Heaven is for Real.*

I wanted to meet the author and thank him for writing about Colton's encounter with a sister of whom he could have known nothing—a sister who had died before she was born and before Colton was born. My wife had suffered two miscarriages, and I believed that we had seven children despite the fact that we had been able to raise only five. I loved the encouraging implications of what Colton had told his father, and I wanted to ask Todd if that aspect of Colton's story had affected other readers deeply as well.

But I couldn't recall the name of Todd's church. I doubted that I would have trouble finding it though. I asked the first person I saw on

Main Street the name of Todd Burpo's church. The man didn't know the name either, but he was able to direct me to it—not by an address, or even a street name, but by the number of blocks and whether to turn left or right. That's how directions are given in small-town Nebraska. The man also gave me directions to a bed-and-breakfast, but I didn't find anyone home. I did find a hunter and her husband who were also looking for the owner of the B&B. Neither of us knew how many rooms were available, but that couple had clearly gotten there first. So I moved on to the church.

Things were pretty quiet there too. While waiting for someone to show up, I journaled. Before I had finished one page, I was greeted by a winsome, friendly man who introduced himself as the executive pastor. He had recently joined the church staff as Todd Burpo's assistant—to help Todd deal with the increased demands on his time since penning a worldwide best seller.

Phil told me that Todd was out giving a speech, but was expected back at any moment. He encouraged me to wait. While I waited, we chatted, and I discovered that Phil had only recently moved to Imperial from Colorado Springs and that he had a connection to Hayes Center— his father had been a pastor in a small church there many years ago. Phil had even been born in Hayes Center, but he left before he started school, so we never met. He also told me that I was welcome to pitch my tent on the church grounds. When Todd showed up half an hour later, he pegged the hospitality meter. He told me I could accept Phil's offer, or I could find a place to throw my sleeping bag inside the church, or if I preferred he would put me up at a local motel. Now that is Hebrews hospitality! Hebrews 13:2 to be exact.

Todd and I flowed into a relaxed conversation. He was wearing a ball cap with the logo of a film company on it. I asked him about it and discovered that he had recently been meeting with studio executives and was at that moment wrestling with all the decisions inherent in turning a book into a movie while maintaining control so that the film would be true to the message of *Heaven is for Real*.

Todd struck me as being a humble man overwhelmed by what God had done with the story of his son's experience of almost dying—of passing from one life to a very different life and then back again. I was surprised to discover that a book that has now been translated into more than thirty-seven languages and has sold ten million copies worldwide received a very chilly reception from the publishing industry at first. Christian bookstores wouldn't have anything to do with it. Within a few months that changed as readers across America began talking about *Heaven is for Real*. Todd told me the book was such a phenomenon that even Walmart changed its policy against stocking the book of a first-time author.

Everyone assumes they would love to suddenly be given the success that has come Todd Burpo's way. But those dreams of fame rarely consider all the demands on a person's time. Many years ago my small film company and a movie production corporation from New Zealand were collaborating on the creation of a thirteen-part documentary television series. I couldn't believe the stack of documents generated by the lawyers over that little deal. The decisions and documents accompanying the conversion of a book selling millions of copies into a movie must be beyond imagining. I asked Todd if he was surprised by it all. He said he was. I also pried a bit and found out the name of the producer he was working with. Turned out Todd has some good people in his camp—people who know their way around the big business of Hollywood—who should be able to give him the control he wants over the final product.

I commented on the work clothes Todd was wearing and asked if he needed help. He explained that he is also a soccer coach. While we talked I helped Todd, Colton's younger brother, Colby, and Phil spray-paint goalposts that would soon be erected on a playing field next to the church. I liked the easy manner of the way Colby, who I guessed was about eight, was working with his dad—it reminded me of all the work I did with my father when I was young. Even the familiar way they parted brought back memories. The exchange was short, simple, direct, and with no complications of big city life.

"Dad, I'm going back to the house."

"See you later, Colby."

That was it. No need for Colby to wait for his dad to finish to get a ride home. Life had been like that for me. From the time I was five years old I had been able to roam freely around my hometown.

Later that evening Todd stopped by the church to see how I was doing and to give me signed copies of *Heaven is for Real* and his new book, *Heaven Changes Everything*, which was scheduled for release a few weeks later. His inscription in the first book, just like the exchange that I had witnessed between him and Colby, was short and to the point: *To James Shaw, Heaven is for Real, and you're going to like it! Todd Burpo Hebrews 12:2*

Todd confirmed that other readers too had reacted strongly to the passages about Colton meeting his sister who had died before she was born. In that thought is what I'm sure for many people is a complete paradigm shift. The Bible backs up such a view, but when it is presented in the unsophisticated words of a little boy, it is a game changer. His words carry a level of authenticity and believability that touch people. Todd also shared with me that Colton's words had also been a great source of comfort to those who have suffered through an abortion or a miscarriage.

The book has made it possible for Todd to speak with thousands more people than he thought he would ever connect with. But that opportunity has put great strains on his time with his family. He receives far more requests to speak than he can possibly accept. And now, because of the movie, even more demands are being placed on his time and his family. But Todd has a demeanor about him that seems capable of calming the storms around him. He seems singularly suited to the task of bringing to an increasingly secular but spiritually hungry world a touching story that connects people to eternal truths. The phenomenal success of *Heaven is for Real* speaks of that hunger.

During the summer I trained for my American journey by riding two thousand miles. I also got ready for the trip by rereading *Travels with Charley.* I was struck that Steinbeck assumed his readers were Christian or at least were familiar with Biblical stories. Steinbeck's life could be interpreted as evidence of the growing secularism in this world—and the conflict with deeply held Christian beliefs. Late in his life, in a letter to his doctor about the care he wished to receive as he was dying, Steinbeck wrote that he had no hope of reward or fear of punishment, and no fear of death. He also mentioned in that letter that he was not religious. But his life and his writings tell a very different story, especially his directions to his wife, Elaine, regarding his last rites: "I want the Church of England funeral service—I want the 'I am the resurrection and the life, saith the Lord.' I don't want a bunch of people getting together for a memorial telling yarns about me." Steinbeck died in 1968 on December 20, a few hours before the official onset of winter. His funeral was held a few days later at Saint James Episcopal Church on Madison Avenue in New York City.

I'm not sure what motivated Steinbeck to offer to his physician thoughts that seem to directly conflict with his lifetime body of work as well as the way he lived his life. He wrote in *Travels with Charley* that he attended church each Sunday during his twelve-week journey. It may be that Steinbeck's assertion to his physician was merely giving voice to the worldview that was at that time beginning to dominate education and the media in America. But life—and death—has a way of intruding upon a secular progressive worldview.

The book that Todd Burpo wrote presents a very different view from that of the materialist. How much does our view of God and Heaven affect the kind of lives we lead here on earth? This is a question that fascinates me, and despite his momentary assertion that he had no expectation of an afterlife, it was a question that fascinated Steinbeck as well.

As I analyze my fascination with Steinbeck, as well as his reception among readers and critics of his work (primarily *The New York Times* and *Time* magazine), I am struck by the power of his convictions and his willingness to include in his books what secularists today consider to be moralizing, even preaching, but fifty years ago was seen as delving into character—what makes a person tick, why does one son turn out to be good, the other evil? For that is exactly the theme of *East of Eden*—a *Steinbeckian* retelling of Genesis, the story of Cain and Abel.

Steinbeck's last novel, *The Winter of Our Discontent*, which was released the year before *Travels with Charley*, portrayed what happens to people when they lose their moral underpinnings—when they sell out for easy money and lose sight of the importance of character in shaping their family and the character of their country. Steinbeck may have flirted with a materialistic view of the world (matter is all there is—there is no afterlife, no God, no Heaven), but the stories he told are of a very different world. In the worlds that Steinbeck created there exists a strong reliance upon a code of ethics—a conscience written on the heart of man that did not come from man.

Steinbeck wrote of the inner world of faith that informs our lives. I think that is why just about every book he wrote is still in print. He wrote of timeless matters—especially of man's yearning to be free. America represented for Steinbeck, the land of the free, and he told that story almost perfectly in *The Grapes of Wrath*. And that's what I saw and heard as I rode across the heart of America—people yearning to be free.

When I was young, I saw the phrase *yearning to be free* as a platitude. I had not yet been in a country or even in a situation where people weren't free—where they were not in charge of their destiny or even their daily activities. Now I've lived long enough to have been exposed to people who aren't free. I've seen what living under suppression and oppression is like, and I've talked with people yearning to be free. Freedom is a powerful force—and Americans must be mindful of the dangers that lurk in compromising freedom in the quest of security. That is the choice that may come closest to defining America's future. Which path will we choose?

Freedom is a theme Steinbeck returned to again and again in his books. That we have a choice is a denial of the materialism that Steinbeck momentarily professed. The more I learn about Steinbeck's personal life, the easier it is for me to see that the choices we make in life are often paradoxical, even inexplicable. That's why it's best to approach life with a healthy dose of humility. I may think I understand the works of Steinbeck, because of all the books I've read about Steinbeck, but I cannot say that I truly do. I would never have supposed that late in his life, Steinbeck would call himself an agnostic, even an atheist—his books reveal the questioning of an agnostic, but never the convictions of an atheist. A study of the writings from his forty years as an author might indicate that he was at times a conflicted man, but for Steinbeck to assert that he was not religious, is to me nonsensical. He may have only been trying to make the banal distinction often offered by non-believers that he was spiritual, not religious, but I think not. I recognize that the word *religious* carries a lot of baggage—I feel it should carry even more, for I assert that everyone is religious, including the atheist, because religion's purpose is to try to get a handle on life's big questions, and we're all trying to do that—but I doubt that Steinbeck was thinking in that vein. That letter conveying his final wishes, if it represented what he felt at the time, was an aberration. It was in conflict with the themes of the books he wrote, even the letters he wrote just before and just after the letter to his doctor, as well as how he lived and died.

Three years before I took my journey across America, I traveled to Italy to pick olives for Tuscan farmers. I had been exposed to Italian hospitality and friendliness and I wanted to see if by sitting down to eat at the tables of Italian farmers I might figure out just why Italians are so much fun to be around, and why they are so welcoming to strangers.

I spent seven weeks picking olives, and almost fifty days eating with Italians in their kitchens, but I left the country without coming up with a plausible reason for their singular devotion to living a life dedicated to the service and the enjoyment of others. For that is what I felt in Italy: Italians want to make the lives of those they come into contact with better and more enjoyable. I became the recipient of their compassion one evening in a small hilltop town when I arrived searching for a farm I had heard about through the Internet. In *An Italian Journey* I wrote of being taken under the wings of half a dozen people in that town. They were not able to put me in touch with the farmer I was looking for, but they made sure I had a place to spend the night. They put me in touch with the local priest, and he threw open the doors to the church, invited me in, and let me unroll my sleeping bag in a Sunday school room.

But I left Italy without seeing what I had come to discover. I was too close to it to see what was right before my eyes. I left Italy saying that such behavior was just tradition for Italians—like the instinct that makes birds fly south for the winter. It's just what they do. It took a year for me to finally *see* what I was looking for. I was watching a film by Roberto Rossellini, *Era Notte a Roma*. Rossellini's film told the story of farmers who hid Allied soldiers on their farms at the risk of being shot by the Nazis if their efforts were discovered.

Rossellini wondered why these farmers would risk their lives for strangers—people their government classified as enemies. Rossellini, a self-proclaimed atheist, came to the conclusion that they did it because of their commitment to Christian principles—to Christian charity. It was such a surprising statement, but it was an eye-opener for me, especially since it was coming from an avowed atheist. Was Rossellini saying that only Christians are charitable? I doubt that. But he was clearly stating that a defining characteristic of a Christian is charity.

Consider Steinbeck. Many of his friends saw him as charitable and extremely generous with the money he made from his best-selling books. But if you asked him if he was charitable because of his Christian beliefs, he might very well have said that he was not. It is hard to know with certainty why anyone does anything. It may even be hard for the person himself to know exactly why he acts as he does.

On my trip across America I have so far been invited into people's homes four times, and each time it was Christians who opened their doors and their lives to me. On my trip to Colorado when I was a boy I showed up in a small town wondering where I might throw my sleeping bag. A man in a pool hall, a tobacco-chewing, rather foul-mouthed character who appeared to be the town's pool shark, directed me to a local pastor. As I made my way to the pastor's house, I wondered about my initial assessment of the man—there seemed little doubt that he was an extremely good pool player—the double bank shot I saw him make to win the game confirmed that, but because of his *colorful* language, I was surprised that he was the one, out of all the people in the pool hall, to suggest that I go see the pastor. It wasn't just that I was surprised that it was *the foul-mouthed pool shark* who suggested that I go see the pastor, it was that *he* was the one, of all the people in the pool hall, who seemed most concerned about helping a stranger. I wanted to ask the pastor more about the pool shark—to ask if he really was as kind-hearted as he *didn't* appear—but I didn't get the courage to ask. The pastor asked me a few questions and when he had heard enough of my story he invited me to sleep on his open-air front porch for the night. I wished that one of those questions had been, *Who sent you to me?*—but he didn't ask that question, so I never did learn any more about the kind-hearted man in the pool hall. But his act of generosity and hospitality sure got me thinking. And I still think about the implications of that encounter—a man who I didn't know and who didn't know me—directing me to a Christian pastor.

What kind of country would America be if it weren't populated by Christians? To me it is an interesting question—a question that I hope stays in the abstract. Many people express a fear of Christians, even a hatred of Christianity and Christians. Certainly an anti-Christian sentiment exists in much of the media, so we may continue to see a country that is less and less under the influence of Christianity. What then?

What of the questions that *Heaven is for Real* brings to mind? I was profoundly moved by the implications of what little Colton Burpo said about his journey to Heaven. But as I reflected on my conversation with Todd about people's reactions to the book—the praise was not universal—I realized that the response to Colton's story strongly emphasizes a theme running throughout the Bible. Matters like Heaven must be taken on faith. Even if a child returns from Heaven, or Lazarus returns from Hell, if our faith tells us not to believe Colton or Lazarus, we won't.

We don't know of such matters as Heaven with absolute certainty, and for that we can be thankful. Life would be a whole lot less interesting if we knew all the answers we so diligently seek. We don't know for certain if we'll be welcomed to Heaven by children we lost on this earth through miscarriage or abortion. We may be convinced that God exists, and that we understand him correctly, but because we are *looking through a glass darkly,* we cannot say exactly what God is like, and to me, that makes life eternally interesting.

Ponder for a moment how different life would be without mysteries. I'm quite convinced that life would be pretty boring if people didn't have to live by faith in this world. And if someone counters that he doesn't live by faith, ask him why everyone doesn't believe what he believes—that forces the issue—some things we *know* only by faith.

I also discovered in writing about my search for the "why" of Italian life, that we have developed in this country a thin skin when it comes to opinions that veer off the secular progressive reservation—the politically correct ideology that is taught on the campuses of America and is promulgated in what has come to be known as the liberal mainstream media. I studied Italy thoroughly for years. I read books by its many famous authors, and equally famous non-Italians who wrote about Italy, and I lived and worked and dined among Italians for a season—the season of the olive harvest. I in no way proclaim myself an expert, but I did come up with a well-reasoned view about the reason for the Italian emphasis on hospitality—one that I had never before seen offered about the reason Italians are so beloved in the world—why they are so friendly and willing, if need be, to lay down their lives for friends, acquaintances, and even strangers as they did during World War II.

I came to the conclusion, as I wrote earlier, that it was the Christian influence on Italy—the Roman Catholic traditions—that influence the lives of Italians to such an extent that they are just good people to be around. And since I did not come to that conclusion—did not see the light until Rossellini opened my eyes long after I had returned from Italy—I did not write of that revelation until the final chapter of the book. That led a number of reviewers to write something similar to this review, "I loved your book, your descriptions of Italy and its people. I was going to give your book a rating of five stars, which it deserved, until you started writing about religion. Keep your opinions to yourself." The writer of that review, instead of the five stars he had planned to give the book, gave it two stars.

I had been offering opinions about everything I encountered in Italy throughout the whole book—and that reader had apparently been enjoying reading those opinions, whether he agreed with them or not until I attributed the hospitality and friendliness of Italians to traditions informed by Christianity. It had finally occurred to me that the reason Italian farmers were willing to die for strangers is the same reason that Italians are willing to extend the hand of hospitality to strangers and tourists still today—and for that Italians are almost universally loved.

I am quite certain that the writer, from the many other things he wrote in the review, would have been pleased if I had attributed the friendliness and hospitality of Italians to climate, or food, or who knows what (he offered no rebuttal or alternative explanation)—but to attribute their concern for their fellow man to the Italian people's understanding of their responsibilities before God was not permissible. My book, my search, was a mystery that he was happy to follow along with until a solution was offered that brought Christianity into the picture.

I would have been thrilled if this reviewer had offered an alternative explanation to what I had proposed—that would have represented a healthy interchange of ideas. But ridicule, intimidation, and an attempt to silence are all too often the strategies of those whose ideology is political correctness—off-the-reservation thoughts and expressions are not allowed by the PC police. It is a tendency in our society that portends of bad endings.

Chapter Fourteen

If there is no God, no devil, no heaven, no hell
then therefore there are no rules.
JOHN STEINBECK

Roots Still Run Deep

I left Imperial at sunrise knowing I had a long day in the saddle to get to Sterling, Colorado—the only town on my route where I could be certain of finding a motel room. Between Imperial and Sterling lay almost ninety miles of a steady climb fighting a brisk breeze. Traffic was light; only a few farmers were on the road.

Memories flooded back as I worked my way west. Farms, businesses, even windbreaks triggered memories of my ride of fifty years earlier. The sight of a country schoolyard brought back the memory of rushing to an outhouse only to discover too late that toilet paper was not in good supply during the summer months. I had to use pages from the copy of *Travels with Charley* I was carrying. I tore them out sparingly, front and back, fearing I would get to the story itself before the job was done.

The Colorado state line arrived mid-morning—earlier than I expected. The "Welcome to Colorful Colorado" sign had been moved since I had last traveled this road. The sign now had a huge grain elevator for a backdrop instead of the wide-open prairie. Fifty years ago the sign was located just past the curve where Highway 6 turns directly west, at a point half a mile into Colorado. Back then its placement had poetry to it, even grace. The sign's placement now, while technically correct, was born of a bureaucrat's decision and not an artist's.

With the crossing of my third state line behind me, my next goal was to get to Holyoke, where I had spent the first night of my journey fifty years ago. I had arrived late Sunday evening and had been told by the owner of a local gas station to throw my sleeping bag on the floor of the men's room in the town park rather than risk sleeping outside. He assured me that no one would be using the bathroom, but just in case, I should lock the door.

Just after midnight I was awakened by a carload of boys who had been out drinking and needed a place to relieve themselves. I chose to remain silent, despite their pounding on the door. After a few minutes of loud threats to "whoever is in there," they drifted away, perturbed and mystified as to why the door was locked. The fact that they were underage saved me—they couldn't very well ask the local sheriff or a police officer to investigate. I lay awake for a while fearing they or someone else might come back, but no one disturbed me the rest of the night.

On this journey I was behind my schedule of fifty years ago. I arrived in Holyoke mid-morning of the second day out of Hayes Center with forty miles already registered for the day's leg—the last five of which had been fast and easy. I had been taking a water break by the side of the road when I heard a combine approaching—I looked up and saw that it was almost to me. I jammed my water bottle into its cage, jumped on the bike and began pedaling as fast as I could. I wanted to time it so that I would be up to speed but still have power in my legs when the combine caught me. I'd be in my top gear ready to push the bike and trailer another four or five miles an hour faster down the road once the combine was breaking the wind.

I got up to fifteen miles an hour in a burst of energy. The timing was good. Nothing was coming. I checked the mirrors; the combine was pulling around me. I pushed harder—once the combine was alongside I ducked behind it and the speed of the bike jumped from fifteen miles an hour to twenty. I checked the mirrors again and saw that a pickup truck was following a good distance behind the two of us. Maintaining that speed required only light pressure on the pedals. My heart rate settled down from the high one-fifties to a comfortable one hundred thirty-six beats a minute.

And that is where it stayed for the next six miles as I rode along in the chaff and cornstalks blowing off the machine. I followed that header-less combine all the way to town, to the east side of Holyoke, where it turned off at the local John Deere dealer, presumably for repairs. The pickup also turned off. I gave both drivers a hearty wave and continued into town. I had not eaten breakfast in Imperial, choosing instead to snack on the slices of pizza I had been carrying since the Good Times Bar in Wauneta. But now I was ready to fill up my tank. I chose a main street café and ordered a big meal—a Rancher's Breakfast—knowing that I had fifty miles of pedaling to get to Sterling.

I wrote notes while I ate. Until the last few minutes of my almost hour-long breakfast I was the only customer. A young couple with their child still strapped into a car seat came in, but their focus was on their napping son and keeping him asleep so we exchanged only muted greetings and a tipping of our heads and smiles as I left the restaurant.

Each time I return to my bike I reach down and squeeze my tires—the front tire was firm, however the rear tire seemed a little soft so I took a tour of town and found an Ace Hardware. But their tubes were filled with goop. The "helpful hardware" man told me that I should be able to find heavy-duty tubes at a bike store near the viaduct in Sterling. To confirm my squeeze test I stopped by the Cenex station on the west side of town. I wheeled my bike up to the large open door where a young man was repairing a truck tire. I asked him if I could borrow a tire pressure gauge. He reached into his shirt pocket and handed one to me.

I tested all four tires and discovered that indeed, my rear tire was not holding air, but it was an extremely slow leak—it was only a couple of pounds low and felt the same as it had twenty minutes earlier. I slowly rotated the wheel, but found no stickers working their way into the tire, so I decided to wait until evening to repair the tube. I walked back over to the young man and handed him the gauge. He took it, but immediately offered it back to me. I said, "No," and shook my head.

He held his hand even closer to me and motioned for me to take it. "When you need to check your tires you will have a gauge," he said.

I shook my head again.

He smiled, offered it again, and said, "Go on—take it."

His manner was so respectful and earnest I decided I had to accept it. It truly would make a lot of sense to be carrying a gauge. I thanked him for his thoughtfulness and generosity. We exchanged names. His was Gomaro, "rhymes with tomorrow," he told me. We shook hands. I tucked the gauge in my handlebar pack and waved good-bye. His mention of the word "tomorrow" made me realize I was close to the end of my journey. As early as the next day I might get to Loveland. After weeks on the road and over a thousand miles I might be meeting the friend I had not seen for decades.

Outside of Holyoke the topography turned from ranch land to a bit of farmland. The road was as I remembered it—long, wide, and unrelenting. The road was climbing higher. Since leaving Hayes Center I had climbed almost a thousand feet. The town of Paoli, which consists mostly of a massive concrete elevator, proclaimed, on its city limits sign, that its elevation was 3898 feet. I stopped to take a shot of the stark beauty of the white elevators reaching into the dark of a Colorado blue sky. Next stop was Haxtun—nine miles down that never-ending ribbon of concrete.

I was looking forward to getting to Haxtun to discover whether one of my favorite restaurants when I traveled this route with my dad was still in operation. I couldn't pull the name out of my memory bank, but I certainly remembered the location. I pulled up, parked my bike and trailer in the same spot my dad always chose, and went inside. The place didn't look the same at all, but it *was* a restaurant. Back then it was mostly counter, with just a couple of tables. Now the room was huge. What I remembered as the kitchen was now a large dining room. But despite all the changes, I was certain I was in the same building.

I told the young waitress that I remembered eating coconut cream pies here and wondered if she knew the history of the place. She smiled. She not only knew a bit of the history, she was able to show me photos taken in the old café that showed her as a young girl. Her grandmother, she informed me, had baked all those pies I remembered so fondly from my own childhood.

Those pictures confirmed that roots still run deep on the plains. She showed me more photos that captured the long history of the café and its importance to the community and then she introduced me to some longtime customers. They too recalled that the place used to be one long counter and that her grandmother had indeed served some of the best pies in all of eastern Colorado. Over the years the restaurant had various names, but when they mentioned Home Café that brought even more memories flooding back—of all the cinnamon rolls my family had bought here on our trips to and from the Rocky Mountains.

I could easily have stayed longer but again the sun and I were doing battle, and the sun had the wind on its side. The next town, the next elevator down the road was Fleming, twelve miles distant. It took most of an hour to get there. In the twenty-one miles since Paoli, I had climbed three hundred forty-two feet—a grade that is barely perceptible, but still we were climbing.

On the other side of Fleming, I saw a sight you don't expect anymore, anywhere. But I suppose if you are going to see it, the high plain of Colorado is a good place. I kept looking away and looking back thinking my eyes were playing tricks on me in the shimmering heat. Heading toward me on the empty highway with its very wide shoulder appeared a team of four mules pulling a covered wagon, and behind that a supply wagon, and behind that a two-wheeled garden cart flying a huge American flag—perfectly filled out in the strong crosswind.

Walking alongside the caravan was one more mule—what I presumed was a reserve animal so that the duty of pulling could be rotated.

I stopped before the convoy got to me so I could take photos. I wanted a picture to prove to myself, and others if they thought I was pulling their leg a bit, that there really is a man out driving a team of mules across America, and has been for a long time, ever since he left his home in Tennessee six years ago. He told me that he would soon be turning south, on Highway 385 when he got to Holyoke—winter was coming on and he was heading to Texas at three miles an hour.

I asked about his typical day and he told me that taking care of the animals—especially finding enough hay—was almost a full-time job. His only helper was another animal, Shep, his dog. He loves seeing America, but his main goal is to tell people about the Bible—about "the good news of Jesus," he said. "I want to spend the rest of what's left of my life evangelizing," he told me and to his mules he sang out, "Walk on." As the train pulled away I took one last photo. The huge flag almost filled the frame. The line of wagons pulled my eye to the horizon. In the distance I was just able to make out the grain elevator where he planned to turn south toward Texas.

I had not expected to meet someone traveling across America at a pace even slower than mine. For the second day in a row I was going to win the race to the horizon with plenty of daylight to spare unless I had lots of flats in the final miles. I figured I had ridden eight of the twenty miles between Fleming and Sterling, but I had one long climb to get to the big downhill that would carry me into the Platte River Valley again— the valley I had been following through Nebraska until I turned south to climb up to the high plains of Hayes Center.

Fifty years ago I made the long run into the valley weaving and bobbing around the yellow dashes on the highway as though I were an Olympic racer carving through the gates on a slalom course. I was listening to *Hit the Road Jack* by Ray Charles, I had the wind at my back, not another soul on the road, and a long, empty highway in front of me pointing right at the Rocky Mountains. I was feeling good.

This time I didn't weave. I wasn't playing music. The road wasn't quite as empty and I was battling a fierce crosswind. Other than that things looked pretty much the same—surprisingly so.

Fifty years ago I didn't ride into the town of Sterling. On this trip I planned to. Fifty years ago I turned southwest and followed Highway 6 and the Platte River toward Denver and the turnoff to Brighton. This time I was going to keep on a westerly heading and climb once more out of the Platte River Valley. I planned to follow Colorado 14 and head across a very desolate part of Colorado. I wanted to ride though some new country—to experience a part of Colorado I had never been through before. My wife has a small interest in the mineral rights to some land in Weld County and I thought it might be fun to give her a firsthand report on the oil boom reported in that part of the state. It would cost me nothing in miles—the GPS assured me that Colorado 14 was the shortest route to Loveland.

I dropped into Sterling looking for the bike store by the viaduct that the helpful hardware man told me I'd find. It turned out not to be so easy. The search, however, put me in touch with a woman who moved, with nary a transition sentence, from telling me she didn't know if there even *was* a bike store in Sterling to telling me her life story. Maybe it was my weird-looking bicycle, but Mary (not her real name) opened right up to me. She told me she was sixty-six years old and getting disability checks, but that she hadn't cashed any. She wanted retirement checks instead. She then switched gears and mentioned that she was the black sheep of a prominent family in town, but soon she would be homeless—the woman she was living with hadn't paid her mortgage in six months.

"They're going to foreclose on her," she said and then she leaned in close to add, "The people of this town hate Obama."

"Why?" I asked.

"They just do," she said. I wondered why she had brought it up. And then I wondered why she didn't want to say more. I assumed that what she perceived as a hatred of Obama had something to do with the foreclosure.

Instead she said, "The only good thing about America are the men and women who have fought for our country."

And then conversation got even stranger. She looked up and down the sidewalk before she whispered, "There are warlocks in Sterling."

She seemed to be confirming what many advocates for the displaced report—the homeless often need more than just a place to live. She didn't say what a warlock was and I didn't ask—but I sensed from the way she said it that it was something she feared and thought that I should fear as well.

She carried about her a fearful countenance—about many things. I wanted to help her. The system didn't seem to be serving her well. Compared to fifty years ago, we are reticent to label people, but she knew she needed help—she *knew* she deserved a label. When I asked her what I could do for her she quietly said, "You can pray for me." The look on her face told me that she knew her problems were complex—that the solutions, if they were to be found, would not be easy. As we parted she seemed a little less agitated, a little less fearful. And if my perception was more hope than reality, my prayer was that she would soon find more peace, someone willing to put a label on her, willing to discriminate enough to diagnose her problems, and help her find a place among good people who would love her and help her find the road to recovery.

At the stoplight, half a block from where I had said good-bye to Mary, a man pulled up beside me. He too was on a bicycle. He asked why I was flying an Italian flag.

I gave him the Cliff notes version and then asked, "How did you know it was Italian?"

"My wife was stationed in France," he said, and then he steered the conversation to the politics of Europe. From there it was a short trip to the politics of America.

"I'm afraid of what Obama is doing to this country," he said. The way he said it made me think he too was a veteran. I asked and he told me about his tour of duty in Vietnam—it almost overlapped mine. We had, by that time, sat through quite a few light changes. I had learned that his name was Steve and he was in his early sixties. Once again he brought the conversation back to America.

His distrust of Obama was visceral. His countenance changed as he talked about Obama's abuses of power. He seemed to be a student of history, especially European history—of World War II and Germany— he saw many parallels to what was now happening in America. I noticed half a block from us a movie theater with *2016* on the marquee and asked if he had seen it. He said he hadn't, which surprised me. It didn't surprise me, however, that he said he wanted to see it.

The fears Steve was expressing about Obama were similar to the themes of *2016*—what the year 2016 would be like if President Obama were elected to serve another four years. Hyperinflation was just one of his fears. He had others no less deeply felt. He felt Obama was lying about Benghazi, that the decision to blame the attack on a video had been approved by Obama, maybe even conceived by Obama. "What bureaucrat is going to take the risk of going out on their own and lying about what happened that night if it isn't coming down from on high?" he asked rhetorically. I didn't answer, but I had to admit it was a perceptive thought—one I hadn't considered. He also felt that Obama and Attorney General Eric Holder were covering up the truth about gunrunning in Mexico. He didn't trust Obama at all.

I had been in Sterling an hour. I hadn't found the bike shop the helpful hardware man told me that I'd find, but I had talked at length to two people. I was grateful that people were sharing their opinions about the state of America with me, but even though that was exactly what I had gone in search of, at that moment I needed to make sure I had time to find a room before dark, so I asked Steve if I was heading toward a motel. He told me that indeed I was, "Three blocks on the left, you can't miss it."

I have always hated the expression, *You can't miss it*, for indeed I have missed places when told that such a thing is not possible. But in this case, I did find it. However I did not find a room. The place was full, once because of construction workers taking the rooms on a monthly basis. But the owner, who looked like she had stepped from the set of a 1960s movie—too much makeup and hair too big, directed me to another motel. In fact, she called ahead and vouched for me. "No he's not one of those," she said in response to a question just after she mentioned that I didn't have a car. She hung up and told me that the owner of the motel was rather particular about her clientele. I was afraid to ask her what "those" was, fearing that I might have to confess—that I was indeed "one of those."

She directed me back to where I had come from, near the railroad tracks. It was a classic 1950s motor court motel. The kind of place I liked, just the basics, a bed and a shower, and a price as near to fifty dollars as possible. Fifty years ago the price was nearer to five dollars, but what you got was just about the same—a good, safe place to sleep. And just like fifty years ago, lots of the people were hanging around outside the rooms, in the courtyard, sitting on springy metal chairs—the place had a sense of small-town community.

I found the same thing the next morning, but not where I expected it. I looked for a mom-and-pop restaurant to match the motel I had just spent the night in, but I didn't find anything matching that description. So when I came to the McDonald's on the highway I opted for expediency. I had a lot of miles to travel—at the very least ninety to get to Greeley—and more like one hundred ten or twenty if I decided to stretch it out and go for Loveland. I felt like riding fifty or sixty, but on this route finding a restaurant might even be hard. Finding a motel short of Greeley seemed extremely unlikely.

I ordered a breakfast burrito and met Bill and Kay. They were curious about my travels—they too had spent time in Iowa and had similar stories about the hospitality of Iowans. Norm stopped by to talk—he was interested in Friday. He rides another brand of folding bike—a Dahon. He wanted to know where he could buy a Bike Friday. I told him about Campus Cycles in Denver. It was that kind of morning. In many towns, McDonald's is where senior citizens now gather. I scratched my plan for a quick pit stop—too many good folks to talk with—and again the future of America came up. Debt was on the minds of the folks in McDonald's. The distrust of Obama was less vehement than Steve had expressed the night before, but the concern over the economy was no less strongly voiced. *It's immoral, the debt we're leaving our children and grandchildren* summed up the outrage I heard that morning in Sterling.

The conversations were informed and stimulating, and the food was surprisingly good and cheap, so I ordered another round of burritos and fresh-squeezed orange juice before hitting the road. I checked my computer and discovered I would be hitting the thousand-mile point of my journey somewhere west of Sterling and I wanted to be prepared. For the first time in all those miles I used a two-pound weight I had been carrying since Wisconsin. I stopped by Walmart on the edge of town and remembered the kick in the gut I had suffered in West Bend, Iowa, when I thought that Friday had been stolen . In that huge store I'd be farther from my bike than I had yet been on this trip so I decided to use the lock I had carried all those miles. But I needn't have stopped. The tubes I found in Walmart were filled with slime, so again I passed on them, and came out of the store carrying only a couple of bananas and a handful of candy bars.

On the edge of Sterling near Pioneer Park, just as I was about to complete the climb out of the valley I looked up to see an ominous warning: "No Fuel Next 60 Miles." That also most likely meant that I would find no fuel for my body either. The sign should have made me backtrack five miles to Highway 6 and head toward Fort Morgan along the I-76 corridor, as I had done fifty years ago when that section of the Interstate was called I-80 South. But I rationalized that I had Snickers, I had apples, and I had bananas. I felt I could ride sixty miles even if the winds weren't favorable.

But the winds were favorable, so I pushed on and the miles passed quickly. The road was smooth, little traveled, and had a shoulder almost five feet wide. But still I became concerned as I pedaled across the high plain. The land was very sparsely populated. I traveled over an hour and saw almost nothing but grass and sage—very few ranches even—in fact so few that when at last I came to one I took a photo of it. Hardly even saw any billboards.

About twenty miles into the day's ride I entered the Pawnee National Grasslands—it was full of stark beauty and little else—an occasional ranch and a few trees; otherwise, just grass, sky, and a ribbon of a road.

So barren was the land that I was a bit shocked when a small town materialized a couple of miles ahead of me. When at last I got to it I saw a billboard advertising a café. There was no indication where this café was to be found. I could see nothing on the road ahead and the town itself was about a mile off the highway down what I assumed was a sticker-laden gravel and soft-sand road. I'm still not sure why I ventured down that lonely road. I guess I was getting a little spooked by riding so far and seeing so little evidence of civilization. I also had cut into my reserves a bit on the morning's ride and had no assurance I wouldn't be riding another thirty-five miles to get to "fuel." I squinted into the distance trying to see if there was anyone near the cars parked at the far end of that dusty little town.

I didn't find a café at the far end of that road but I was welcomed to Stoneham by Forrest and Johnny Jack—lifetime residents enjoying a beautiful morning in the warm Colorado sun. I joined them. Johnny was on a four-wheeler and was showing off a tire iron that he had forged that morning. He was dressed like a cowboy in a Sergio Leone Spaghetti Western and had the good-looking but slightly sinister face of a Clint Eastwood nemesis, and a misshapen black hat to top it all off.

Forrest was the owner of a repair shop that used to be a filling station but was no longer. He was a big solid man dressed like the mechanic that he was, in rugged blue jeans and a gray mechanic shirt, and a ready smile. Forrest also had the solid grip of a man who had been clasping large wrenches all his life—and the scarred knuckles to boot.

Forrest was Irish and Native American out of Orange, Virginia. "My dad was born in 88. He died at eighty-four and Mom at ninety-three. I'll be seventy-three in November," he said. And it was a healthy seventy-three that Forrest looked.

"My dad came out here from Virginia and homesteaded in 1911— my mother came up from Oklahoma territory—that's how I come to be here," he said. He told me that he keeps the farmers running with his repair shop and that he also runs some cows too—twenty-some head. "Farmers are doing real good," Forrest added and then asked, "You got protection for rain?" I should have taken that as a warning from an old-timer but instead I told him about how little rain I had run into on my trip.

Johnny Jack looked and sounded more Indian, more like a man of the land, than Forrest, but he told me he was German as he pocketed some beautiful geodes he had been showing us and took off. Standing there, as the sound of Johnny's four-wheeler faded into the distance, I got a sense of the loneliness of the plains as I said good-bye to Forrest. This is big country. Stoneham could easily be used for a movie set, especially the white church standing like a lone sentinel on the plains. I took a photo of it. Big cumulus clouds were gathering in the sky above. The beauty of the scene kept me from thinking about what those big clouds would in time be bringing to the high plains—at that moment they were just a gorgeous backdrop to a pretty photo.

I should have kept right on moving down the highway when I got back to Colorado 14, but instead I pulled into the parking area of another filling station that was no longer operating to see if any sandburs were lodged in my tires from my off-road adventure. I found nothing and was getting ready to hop back on Friday and take off, but my curiosity got the better of me. I could hear someone working inside the open doors of the abandoned filling station. I guessed that it was whoever had built the wildly colorful lawn ornaments that were on display in the parking lot. I walked in through the big doors and smelled paint. I followed the smell and discovered a solidly built man wearing a ball cap, bib overalls and a white T-shirt in the back of the building applying a coat of green paint to a propeller-driven yard ornament.

I asked about the Jeep I had walked past to get to him—an old Willys Wagon just like the one my father had when I was a kid—the first car I remember getting behind the wheel of. The man began a story about that Willys that didn't end until I had discovered that he had at one time been a rancher not far from where I used to live in the Roaring Fork Valley of Colorado more than thirty years ago. We shared our names and then the names of some of the people we both knew and the places we had lived—Carbondale, Basalt, Aspen, Snowmass, El Jebel. Ted at one time owned the liquor store there. He mentioned Crawford's Trailer Park—I had almost bought a trailer from Floyd back in the '70s. Ted had built homes around the golf courses that I had flown over on final approach to the Glenwood Springs Airport. We found we had a lot to talk about. We didn't know yet how much.

Ted left the valley in '76 and bought a ranch near Silt, Colorado. I had moved to the Roaring Fork Valley in 1977. He later left Colorado and moved to Michigan, but his kids didn't like it, so he moved his family back to Silt, and then to McCoy and Burns—before moving to Stoneham where he had been for twenty years. He was still ranching, but over his lifetime he'd done lots of things, including running a truck stop.

He walked me next door to show me what had at one time been a café—most likely the café that I had seen advertised on the billboard when I had first pulled into Stoneham two hours earlier. He told me that his late wife had run that café—that she was known throughout northern Colorado for her food and good nature. And I believed it, looking at the press notices and photos hanging on the walls—it looked like the place was pretty lively back then. Those photos reminded me that even though this part of the country still looked the same in many ways, life was really different not all that long ago—at least in this one town, because of that one woman.

He told me about his four kids—the stories sounded very typical of what is happening to the American family. He mentioned first the youngest and the oldest, the two he was most concerned about. "My youngest lives in Michigan. Seems like she could find every bum in the world," he said, "and now they've all left her and she's alone with her boy. I wish he could live here where everybody could be his grandpa and grandma. He could live like a boy should."

He knew it was not likely the boy would ever live here on these high, lonely plains, but still he carried that dream—he wanted his grandson to grow up as he did, hunting and fishing, free to roam wherever his curiosity led him.

"My oldest lives in Florida—two children by two different men. Not sure how she got so messed up. She was raised in the church, but it didn't take," he said. "My two kids who are living here are doing real well. One is with Ace Hardware. The other is ranching not far from here."

By that time our conversation had developed a deeply philosophical tone so I told him I thought that there were mysteries we were never going to be able to solve about why things turn out the way they do for our kids. He had brought up a profound mystery—why some kids rebel and some don't. I doubt he expected an answer, but I think he did appreciate that I had heard his question. And so I *walked with him* for a while before turning the conversation to the yard ornament he was painting.

"How did you get started making these?" I asked.

"It was my grandfather's fault. He made miniature windmills in Germany. I've carried those patterns all over—and whenever I had a chance I built some of them and I guess I got good at it," Ted said. "I kept building them. Eventually I had chicken houses full of them, and everything else. I'd give 'em to anybody that wanted 'em."

The counters and tables in the café were covered with hundreds of brightly painted yard ornaments, many of them playful flowers.

"I was showing them to a friend one day and she said, 'You ever gone to a flea market?' I said no, and she told me I should give the Mile High Market in Denver a try. So I boxed up enough to fill an old pickup truck and away I went—got over there, and set up. I don't know if it was even four hours 'fore I was completely sold out—over a thousand dollars of windmills. Sold them at forty dollars, fifty dollars."

I was surprised by the low price. The windmills and yard ornaments were amazingly complex—and a whole lot of fun to watch move.

"An old guy who had been going to flea markets all his life had been watching me and said he'd never seen anything like it. I knew right then that maybe this could turn into something. That was thirty-some years ago. I've been blessed with it. I put the kids through college with this. State fairs—Christmas shows. At one time I was setting up booths that cost two or three thousand dollars and selling life-sized Christmas and holiday displays. I'd make fifteen or twenty thousand dollars a show. I had two guys working for me. Sold things in forty-some countries around the world," Ted added.

"You advertise on the Internet?" I asked.

"No," Ted said, "I can't keep up with what I've got."

"You need one of your kids to come work with you."

"The kids don't want anything to do with it."

"That's too bad—bet you miss your wife," I said.

"I do. We were together forty-eight years. She helped me so much. I miss her in so many ways. She was a heck of an artist," Ted said as he showed me a Conestoga wagon sculpture. "It was perfect hanging here in The Prairie Café—it fit right in."

It did indeed. "Bet some museums would love to have that hanging in their Early American displays," I said, "That is beautiful—look at that dog underneath the wagon. Wow. She was really talented."

"Yes she was. I miss her so much. My wife never knew a stranger. People liked her. I still get calls." And Ted went on to tell me about that day that he can't get out of his mind.

"I had been out here working. I heard her drive in. I went in the house and I could see she was laying on the floor. I'm looking at her as I'm walking around—we had a round table in the kitchen. I said 'What the hell you doing down there?' Then it hit me. Her tongue was hanging out. 'No,' I cried … She'd died just like that—a massive heart attack."

I shook my head slowly side to side. Ted looked down at his hands, remembering.

"Took me a long year or two to get over it. I don't know if I've really ever gotten over it. It was terrible. Now I look back, this has been four, four and a half years and I think '*What a way to go, if you're gonna go, never have to be in a doctor's office.*' "

"Never have to be in a hospital," I added.

"What a blessing to go that way. Go quick. I had no idea how much I would miss her. She did all the office work. I never even knew where the checkbook was. I'd never washed clothes. She was it, and I had to learn everything. I'd never cooked anything."

"You take care of yourself now?" I asked.

"I just got done canning pickles and beans."

"Is that right?"

"Oh yeah, I eat a good meal every day. A steak, a lot of stir-fry. I bake. Cakes and pies."

"You turned real domestic. Any place close by where I can buy you lunch?" I asked.

"No there's not. I'm okay. I've got a package of Johnsonville brats," he said. "I gotta bunch a guys coming out from the city shooting prairie dogs. These guys are gunsmiths. They camp out here overnight. No motel in Briggsdale. Kimball, Nebraska is forty-some miles. The nearest motel is Greeley."

"Well, I'd better let you get ready for them and get on the road then," I said even though I sensed that neither of us was really ready to let go of what had come our way that morning.

I was fascinated by his business, by how successful it was, and how he had built it up into an enterprise that was ensuring him a comfortable retirement—and doing it making lawn ornaments. He was obviously a talented craftsman—and a dedicated one. His designs were colorful, playful, and well executed—and extremely low-priced. I had watched him work while we talked. What he did, he did well, and quickly.

He had work to do to get ready for his friends and I had lots of miles to cover but still we kept talking—he mentioned that he had also done commissions. Ted pulled a white sheet off a beautiful piece of work—a replica of a Cessna 210 that he had crafted for a friend. It was about three feet long. Next he uncovered a gorgeous eighteen-wheeler—perfectly detailed, perfectly crafted—a bargain at over one thousand dollars considering how many hours of work had gone into it.

What a tale of American entrepreneurship. Here was a guy in a desolate part of Colorado on a very lonely stretch of highway making a good living. I'm not sure he thought his story was all that special. He said that just about everybody he knows is self-employed, and that most of his friends are like-minded—they find a way to survive, to make a living, and take care of themselves and their families. I was learning a lot from Ted, about the way things used to be, the way they are now, and the way they can be if you work hard. I would have liked to keep talking to him—but the sun was moving through the sky and I wasn't moving at all. I did have the wind was on my team for once, but I was still a long way from a motel and a long way from where I had told Ross I would be at the end of the day.

Raymer was ten miles down the road. Ted told me I would be able to eat there and that I would be able to eat well, but I would find no motels until I got to Greeley—at least another sixty miles. It was well after one o'clock when I resumed my ride through the Pawnee National Grassland. I was in an area so sparsely populated and a county so large that I would still be in Weld County when and if I got to Greeley. I had already been riding in the county since just after nine that morning—it was beginning to look like I'd be spending the whole day in one county. With so many miles ahead of me it didn't make sense that I was taking so much time talking with people. I guess I was realizing my trip was getting close to ending, and I didn't want to let go.

I got to Raymer rather quickly. The wind had shifted a little more and was now kicking right at my back. I didn't rush lunch at all. I chatted with truckers. I chatted with farmers. I especially chatted with the waitress, Andrea. She was friendly, gorgeous, and witty. She also drove the local school bus—I spent so much time eating lunch that she left to go pick up the kids on her route while I was still polishing off the piece of coconut cream pie I had reserved when I first walked in the door and spied it all by itself on the shelf.

I left Andrea's tip with her husband who worked in the kitchen and began talking with Paul, a long-haul trucker. He also was very local, knew everybody, had eleven grandkids, and told me about all the oil trucks that were traveling up and down the highway. He advised me not to take the shortcut to Greeley—he said the road was full of trucks and had no shoulder. He suggested I stay on Colorado 14, and just keep going west. But this made the whereabouts of food and motel a big question mark.

Those big, white, fluffy cumulus clouds that had been but a beautiful backdrop to the photos I had taken in Stoneham were an ominous bank of black clouds as I set out from Raymer bound for Briggsdale and the Highway 392/Highway 14 decision. Between me and that decision was an exciting blustery ride. I was riding toward that dark sky at twenty-some miles an hour. Every few miles I stopped to take a photo—dramatic shots of oil wells set off against the thunderheads on the horizon. And at each stop I tried to reach Rossy but the signal was never strong enough. I kept watching the sky—hoping that the rain would stay in the foothills, but late in the afternoon it boiled out over the plains and hung for the longest time right on top of me. Just as the first drops began falling I found myself at a driveway leading to a big storage tank—the whole sky had turned black in an instant. I knew without a doubt that the clouds were just about ready to open up and drench me. I was not wearing my rain gear so I pulled onto the gravel road to ride the fifty yards or so to the oil facility. I hoped that somewhere within the facility I would find something to duck under that would protect me from the wind and the rain.

When I got on the other side of the tank I saw a young man reading gauges and taking notes. I rode up to him asked if I could step inside a small building I had noticed among all the pipes and valves. He said, "No, I can't let you do that."

I looked at him for an explanation. After a rather unpleasantly long delay, he said, "Regs won't let us—insurance and lawyers, you know."

The rain was by then getting serious—I asked if I could at least take shelter on the other side of the building, out of the wind so I could put on my rain gear.

"Guess I could let you do that," he said.

I pushed Friday past the pipes, and even had to lift the trailer over the last one. The building wasn't big enough to give me much protection, but I was able to stand in the lee of it and open the suitcase without the rain falling directly in. But putting the gear on while standing in mud and fighting the wind was a clumsy ordeal that threatened to cover all my gear in thick gooey clay.

The young man continued to work and take readings. I lost track of him but not of time. It took me over twenty minutes to get my rain gear on and my suitcase buttoned back up. I tried my phone—still nothing. I stuffed it into an inside pocket and looked up to see that the young man had pulled his pickup around to the side of the building where I was now standing, and he was motioning out of the driver's side window for me to get into the truck with him. I maneuvered the bike and trailer closer to the building, into the spot where I had been standing, and sloshed through the rain and mud to the other side of the truck and jumped in.

"Thought maybe you'd like to dry out a little. By the way, my name's Jeff."

"Hey, thanks a lot. My name's James—OSHA makes your life a little complicated, does it?" I said.

"Oh they usually do, don't they?" said Jeff.

I pulled off my jacket and put my gloves on the dashboard to dry and asked Jeff about his job.

"I'm a pumper. I go around and make sure everything is running. We need to physically look at these wells. I run up about thirty miles north. Eighteen to twenty-nine wells. Sometimes as much as two hundred miles a day—a thousand miles a week," Jeff said.

"Sounds like they keep you moving. Are things as crazy around here as they are in North Dakota?

"North Dakota is a lot different—we're just not taking off here. Nobody's getting the big gushers," he told me and went on to explain that there was a lot of oil coming out of this area but life hadn't changed a lot yet. No boomtowns—people are commuting from Greeley. We don't even have cell towers around here.

"Yeah, I've noticed that," I said.

We talked of his opportunities for advancement and his plans for the future and where I might find a motel. By that time the rain had changed from a downpour back to the big drops and the sky was less black. I thanked Jeff and hopped out of the truck, walked through the muck to the bike and trailer, maneuvered both around the puddles that had formed and worked my way back to the highway. I rode very slowly at first so that I wouldn't throw mud from the wheels.

Eventually the puddles in the road cleaned off the tires and I began pushing harder on the pedals. But the effort no longer yielded twenty-some miles an hour; the wind had shifted and was once again pushing against me. As I struggled along I kept checking my mirrors, expecting Jeff to pass me, but he never did. Guess he had other wells to check.

I did see lots of sheriffs' cars though. They'd appear in my rearview mirror and then scream past me. Something had happened in the vicinity and the cars were making their way back toward Greeley one by one. They were rejoining Highway 14 from the south. One of the sheriff's cars got to a stop sign just as I was riding by, but something kept me from asking for help. By that time I was worried about getting in touch with Rossy, and the sheriff probably could have gotten through to him. But getting cops involved when you don't absolutely need to is rarely a good idea—unless you know them and they know you. Otherwise, it can be a formula for lots of unintended consequences. They're paid to be suspicious.

On my ride toward Briggsdale I was passed by no fewer than half a dozen sheriffs' cars. I never did learn what had happened in that remote part of Weld County on that cold, windy, wet afternoon but it was something that unleashed a lot of manpower into the area. Each sheriffs' car that passed me was going faster than the last—they seemed to be responding to a breaking situation. My situation wasn't an emergency— at least not yet.

So I rode slowly on toward Briggsdale. I had not yet decided whether to bypass Greeley, but I was leaning toward committing to getting all the way to Ault or to a motel along the I-25 corridor in case Rossy couldn't pick me up. I was also committing to getting closer to Loveland. Each mile I was riding was two miles that Rossy would not have to drive. Jeff had already told me that I wouldn't find a motel in Briggsdale and the convenience store there was pretty small so when at last it appeared I rode right on through town, even though it would have been good to warm up a bit. On the other hand, I rationalized that getting started again would be hard. Better to just keep going—besides the ten or fifteen minutes I might spend there could be very precious. It would soon be dark. So I just kept going west on 14. I lost some of the wide shoulder I had been enjoying, but I also lost a lot of traffic—it had turned toward Greeley on 392, the road that Paul, the trucker, had told me would be a bad idea on a bike.

I didn't take any more photos the rest of that day—hardly stopped at all—except to make repeated calls to Rossy to try to get a message through to him. The land was desolate—I don't think a dozen cars or trucks passed me that evening. I was afraid that Rossy was worried about me. I was overdue and had not made contact with him for more than six hours. The worst part was that I had not realized until late in the day that my messages weren't getting through. Rossy was probably in Greeley waiting for me and I had no way to tell him that not only wouldn't I be there at five—I was no longer even heading toward Greeley.

Had I known this desolate country had no cell phone coverage, I would have planned my day differently. But because I didn't know, I now had another story to tell my kids and grandkids about *why the earth is round*. The day treated me to dramatic skies, beautiful photographs, memorable conversations, and a deep sense that the land shapes a person. The people I met that day seemed much like the people I had grown up with on the plains—the people of Hayes County—who had been shaped by the wind and the sky just as these people had. Stoneham, Colorado was separated from Hayes Center, Nebraska by two hundred miles of high-country plains. But the wind and the lack of rain that shaped my country also shaped this country and the people who lived here. I felt at home. It was funny to me how familiar it felt even though it was the first time in my life I had traveled in Weld County. That land was isolated and so was Hayes Center. The interstate ran fifty miles north of Hayes Center. Stoneham was between interstates—I-80 was fifty to the north and I-76 (old I-80S) was fifty to the south.

The traffic wasn't heavy. I did have a bit of a shoulder, but not enough to be truly comfortable being on that lonely highway in fading light. I still had Snickers bars and I still had water. But I would have loved to see a convenience store, but I saw nothing—even the intersections had nothing but stop signs. I was again relying on getting to a certain mileage on my bike computer. I could no longer make out the squiggles on my maps as the sun moved lower and lower. I would soon have to turn on my lights and my strobe and I wanted to just keep moving until I did. I knew I was on the right road and I would eventually get to something.

Each time I crested a rise I expected it would put me within range of a cell tower. I'd look off into the distance hoping to see signs of civilization, but each time all I saw was an unbroken sea of grass. The pattern was getting old—climb, crest, look, and see nothing. But this time my phone started beeping as I reached the top of the hill—my phone began confirming the delivery of the messages I thought had been sent hours earlier—and it started receiving messages as well. But still I couldn't reach directly Rossy by phone.

Darkness overtook me on the diagonal road that lies between Briggsdale and Ault, down near where the highway turned west again. I turned all my lights on and kept on pedaling in the dark. My headlamp was not strong enough to fully light the roadway, but my lights, both front and back were strong enough to ensure that people could see me. Even so, whenever it was possible I pulled completely off the road when being overtaken from behind. This slowed my progress considerably, but so would getting clipped by a car or getting hit by something extending from a trailer that an inattentive driver might be pulling.

I was worried. I wanted to be off that highway. I stopped to check reception again and was surprised to see a strong signal. But before I could punch in Rossy's number, my phone began ringing. I was thrilled to hear Rossy's voice. I apologized to him. He was, as I had feared, in Greeley, and had been waiting since five. I asked if he knew where Ault was. He said he didn't, but he was sure that his GPS did. I didn't ask if he had gotten my text messages—just said that I was coming in on Colorado 14 and told him I would stop at the first gas station I saw in Ault.

If I had had more battery power on both my GPS and phone I would have attempted to pinpoint for Rossy exactly where I was and would have asked him to meet me out in the country, but without battery power I opted for the simplest instructions I could give. I told him that if he didn't see me in Ault he should head east on 14. I didn't think there was any way we could miss each other if we stuck to that plan.

I hung up, shut my phone off so that in an emergency I'd have enough battery left to get through to Rossy, and took off—figuring I would get to Ault in about thirty minutes. But thirty minutes came and went and so did the eighty-seven mile mark that I had calculated for Ault.

I kept riding. What looked like the outskirts of a town just kept rolling past—but no town—no place to get warm and wait for Rossy. I thought that maybe I was reading my computer wrong—in the dark I couldn't see it very well. Just as I was beginning to question my calculations a pickup pulled up behind me and didn't pass—I assumed it was Rossy—the road was straight and there was not another car in sight for miles. I turned off at the nearest intersection. The truck followed me. I was guessing that Ross must have met me, but couldn't find a place to pull off so he had to go down the road and turn around. I couldn't see him very well with the headlights shining in my eyes, but I recognized his voice. My assumption was correct—behind the wheel of that truck was the friend I had not seen for over a quarter of a century.

We greeted each other with hugs and "How are you's" and "It's good to see you's" and "I was beginning to get worried about you" and quickly settled into our old friendship as we tried to figure out how to pack Friday into his mid-sized, crew cab pickup. The trailer went into the back seat, the bike into the bed of the truck. The wind that had been blowing across my wet clothes all afternoon was taking its toll now that my body was no longer generating heat. In the short time it took to figure out how best to load the trailer and the bike I got thoroughly chilled. As Ross was closing the tail gate I hopped into the front seat. My core temperature was down. My body began shaking as I peeled off the wet layers. The decision to not stop anywhere along the road long enough to get chilled had been a good one. I'm sure the cab was plenty warm for someone in dry clothes, but I asked Ross if he would mind turning up the heat.

A couple of miles down the road we came to the gas station I had been expecting to see for so long. Ault would have been only the fourth town I had passed through on my eighty-some-mile ride. As my body slowly warmed and Ross and I talked about the lack of cell phone coverage in the area, I tried to assimilate the impact of what had turned into a very difficult day. I had been more than ready to call it a day at 4:25 when that massive thundercloud swept over me darkening the sky and obliterating the mountains.

Evaluating the wisdom of the choices I had made that day was difficult. I had arrived safely, but at what cost—will I soon have a cold to deal with or worse? How would the day have turned out had I ignored the trucker's advice not to take Highway 392 to Greeley? I'll never know. I do know that Ross didn't seem to mind picking me up—to rescue me as it were—and the short road trip gave Ross and me some time to catch up on each other's lives. I'm not sure whether he said anything, or whether I just quit doing it, but on that drive to his house, it no longer felt right to call him Rossy.

When we got to his suburban ranchette, Ross showed me to a comfortable room where I was able to spread out, analyze, and organize. As I unpacked I noticed that I had carried very little with me that I had not used. And even though I had used the tent, mattress, and sleeping bag, I felt that those items might not make the list for the next trip.

While Ross and his wife Jan made the final preparations for dinner, we continued catching up with stories from the decades since last we had seen each other. The meal was pure Italian delight—delicious food, time to enjoy it, a great wine from Chianti, and conversation that ranged not just over the lost years but over our whole lives. Ross delighted me with stories of people I had forgotten and even told stories about himself and my dad that I had never heard. He prefaced one story by telling me that the statute of limitations had passed so he felt he could safely tell me about the time he pushed all of my dad's tractors out onto Main Street. He even admitted to watching the next morning as my dad climbed up on each one to start it and drive it back into line in front of the store. I hadn't realized there were so many stories about Rossy I had never heard—like the one about dropping into the high school through an access door in the roof and chaining all the outside doors shut—then clambering back out of the building to await the arrival of the startled and soon-to-be-frustrated principal.

I wanted to hear more of Ross's exploits and he wanted to hear of mine. He wanted to hear about Machu Picchu and Alaska and Greece and India, but mostly we talked about Italy. Jan and Ross told me that they would soon be leaving on a walking tour of Tuscany. Despite the fact that his family was from Italy this would be Ross's first trip to the land of his ancestors. They showed me their itinerary. They were delighted to discover that they would soon be walking through some of the same hilltop towns I had biked through three years earlier.

The meal was Italian length, but we still had more to talk about, so we moved our celebration to the hot tub, turning our attention to the characters of Hayes Center. We wondered whether other small towns had so many characters per capita—we made lists and attached anecdotes to each in our minds. As we told our stories we began wondering if the fact that Hayes Center was not connected to the rest of the world by a paved highway until the mid-fifties had something to do with the long list of characters we had come up with. I told Ross about the interesting people I had met on my journey—how easily I could see Clem, Ted, Forrest, or Johnnie Jack fitting right in to our Hayes Center cast of characters. We also wondered if America could long survive if it quit producing the kind of people we had grown up with.

Chapter Fifteen

In a time of universal deceit—
telling the truth is a revolutionary act.
GEORGE ORWELL

With No Frustration, Apology, or Embarrassment

The next morning Ross and I got the day off to a good start by walking four miles along the Little Thompson River that runs through the heart of Loveland. Ross maintains a pace of eighteen-minute miles and walks twenty miles a week. I asked about his regimen and learned that he had undergone bypass surgery, has multiple stents in his coronary arteries, and takes medicine to control the Parkinson's disease that occasionally affects his motor control. He shared with me that he feels Lipitor may have caused him to get Parkinson's, and that he is now firmly against the tendency of the medical profession to push drugs.

I offered him no argument. In fact my response was a hearty *Amen*. The list of warnings accompanying the pharmaceuticals pushed on television should be fair warning that the drugs are dangerous enough to attack the body in myriad ways. My favorite among the long list of euphemisms is *may cause death* rather than *this stuff can kill you.*

As I've watched Ross occasionally struggle to complete what used to be simple movements, I have been struck by his apparent lack of frustration, apology, or embarrassment. He exhibits no evidence of a pity party. He has altered his life as necessary and is doing what he can to minimize the effects of Parkinson's disease by staying active and following his regimen of daily hikes—forcing his muscles to work again—and forging new pathways for the neurons in his brain.

We completed our four-mile loop right on pace and Ross asked if I was up to more walking. I told him I was and he took me to the Benson Sculpture Garden. He enjoyed showing me Loveland's strong connection to the arts. I vowed to bring my grandkids someday—to let them experience the fun of seeing art outdoors—of being able to walk right up to it, interact with it, and even sit on it.

As we walked around the pond marveling at the size and creativity of the sculptures Ross and I found lots of time to talk. We reached back to those years when we lost contact with each other. I learned that only a few days after he found out he was losing the job he had enjoyed for decades, he got hit with another blow—his first wife ran away with her boss—moving out lock, stock, and barrel. In one sentence Ross had told me the condensed version of life in twenty-first century America—layoffs and divorce.

Ross also told me of happier times—of meeting Jan and marrying her and the good times they've enjoyed since they brought their two families together. Jan is a few years younger than Ross and is very gracious, and Ross is extremely gentle and loving with her. They met at a dance and hit it off at once. They discovered they were both from small towns in Nebraska and found they had a lot to talk about—it didn't hurt that they both enjoyed dancing.

Ross and his family were among the very few practicing Catholics I knew growing up. But he isn't a practicing Catholic any more. I asked him about that. There was a story there too. A coworker had asked him if his relationship with Jesus was personal. A few nights later Ross heard an evangelical preacher deliver a Gospel message that he had never heard—and before the evening was over Ross had seen his life in a new light and had committed his life to Christ.

The story of his conversion helped me understand why Ross wasn't feeling sorry for himself about his Parkinson's disease. He told me his faith was giving him the strength and the understanding to deal with his loss of motor skills. Our conversations ranged over a lifetime of ups and downs for both of us—job losses and deaths, successes and marriages. We even talked of all the people who are moving to Texas to escape burdensome taxes and regulations—and to find jobs. Ross had considered moving, but he is surrounded by family in Colorado, and like Jim, he knows the good thing that he has.

On the Sunday I spent with Ross and Jan they shared with me the good in their lives. We went to church, met up with children and grandchildren, and then took over a large portion of a favorite historic restaurant for Sunday dinner. And if they hadn't hiked taken me hiking through Rocky Mountain National Park to the gorgeous Bridal Veil Falls and later a chance meeting in Jamestown with Julien of Julien's Cliffhouse Kombucha they would most likely have spent Saturday with at least some of their kids and grandkids as well. Which is just what we did after lunch, heading out to play Frisbee golf with one of Jan's daughters and her husband.

Seeing Ross and Jan surrounded by so much family and hearing of all the family I didn't get to meet convinced me that John Steinbeck would have judged Ross's life a success. Steinbeck offered in *East of Eden* a vision of the failed life—a life that tried to accomplish too much, yet failed the crucial test: "When a man comes to die, no matter what his talents and influence and genius, if he dies unloved his life must be a failure to him and his dying a cold horror."

As we talked, I began comparing our lives now with the way we had lived in Hayes Center. I was struck by how much more comfortable life was for both my former girlfriend Lynda and for Ross than it had been for their parents. But the improvement of their financial condition was not the most striking thing I learned while spending time with them. What gave me the greatest sense of hope for America was that both were extremely focused on the importance of family and friends in their lives. Sure it's just two families, but to me that bodes well for America. Each had been divorced, yet neither had given up on marriage and family. Maybe they were now more appreciative of the value of a strong family because they had for a while been without it. And I think the same may be true of the social engineering experiment that began in the sixties when those championing a so-called *free love* attitude began denigrating the family unit. But America, at least from what I had seen in the heart of this country, is once again strongly celebrating family. It may not yet be evident on the coasts—and you certainly don't see it in primetime network television, but I'm not sure who watches that stuff anymore.

On my American journey I had the privilege of being a guest in the homes of seven families, and I don't think any of them would accuse me of hyperbole if I said that none of them value anything on this earth more than family. We baby boomers are once again recognizing the importance of family, and that makes me optimistic for America's future. We have of necessity matured, and my hope is that because there are so many of us, we will be able to bring much of America along with us for the ride.

I'm optimistic, but I can't overlook the comments I've heard on my journey that make me fear for America's future. We are at a crossroads on our journey as a nation—it may even be said more accurately and ominously that we are at a tipping point. Many nations before us have prospered, and then failed for one reason or another—disease, famine, war—but it may be the great philosopher Pogo who most clearly summed up America's greatest problem: *"YEP, SON, WE HAVE MET THE ENEMY AND HE IS US."* Cartoonist Walt Kelly penned that iconic comic strip aphorism in celebration of Earth Day 1971, but its message need not be limited to our dishonoring of creation—it applies equally well to the preservation of the American idea as it does to the American continent.

Chapter Sixteen

My mamma always said life was like a box of chocolates.
You never know what you're gonna get.
FORREST GUMP

A Giant Blue Bear

I woke up on Tuesday, October 2, planning to split firewood all morning and leave for Denver about noon. But a power outage at his plant gave Ross and me the gift of one more day together. We drove into town to enjoy a leisurely breakfast at The Egg and I, a Loveland landmark, and then we walked for a while among the tasteful displays of fresh food at a nearby farmers' market. I picked up half a loaf of cinnamon/apple bread for the road and Ross picked up a large supply of natural joint cream for his upcoming walking tour of Tuscany.

As we strolled about I became concerned about getting a late start, but I didn't tell Ross. Even though we didn't get back to his house until noon, I still wanted to help lay up as much firewood for Ross and Jan as I could. By delaying my departure I was cutting into my "what if" time, but if problems were few and if I didn't stop to eat, I felt I could still get to Denver by dark. The bread I'd picked up at the farmers' market would have to be my supper.

We began splitting firewood about the time I had planned on leaving for Denver. Ross used a mechanical splitter and I grabbed a monster maul, just like the one I had at Rock Ridge Farm, to split the big chunks that his electric splitter couldn't handle. It felt good to be swinging a heavy maul. My legs had been getting plenty of exercise—my arms and upper body not so much. I wasn't sure how long Ross would want to work, but I hoped it would be long enough to justify taking a few moments to create a half-circle of massive stump ends piled two high surrounding my chopping block to prevent the wedges from flying across the corral. It takes a bit of effort to build it, but the fence keeps the chunk I'm splitting standing upright on the chopping block ready for my next swing. It's much more satisfying to be splitting chunks than chasing them.

While I worked I occasionally glanced at Ross. My admiration for him was deepening. Despite the loss of motor control that made this work more difficult, he showed no signs of frustration. He just did what he could at a pace he could handle.

I was watching the time, too. I figured three o'clock was the very latest I could get on the road. My brother's place near Downtown Denver was almost sixty miles away, and a rather stiff crosswind was blowing off the mountains. On the plus side was the knowledge that there would be few temptations to stop along the way. I would be riding in commuter traffic through suburbs almost all the way to Denver.

Ross and I kept at it. Our rick of firewood was growing at a nice pace—we were making a significant contribution to the size of his woodpile. Just as I was beginning to resign myself to arriving in Denver after dark, Ross walked over to check out the wall of logs I had built around my splitting stump and to tell me that he thought we had split enough to call it a day. I was glad *he* had made the call; I couldn't bring myself to do it. Most of the wood in his pile was beyond the capability of his little electric splitter, and turning those logs into firewood was the best way I knew to let him know I appreciated both his friendship and his hospitality. As we were putting our tools away the thought hit me that I wished I could stop by regularly to split wood for Ross and Jan— and to get another fix of stories about the characters of Hayes County.

Saying good-bye to Ross touched me. I knew it probably would. He had refreshed memories of childhood that had dimmed and in some cases completely faded. Many of my childhood memories are bright, and I have often written about them, but Ross had put an extra glow even on those stories. While we shared our last anecdotes about the town's many memorable people we checked around the house for stuff I might have left behind, and then he walked me to my bike. We hugged, said our good-byes, and I hopped on Friday and rode away. At the corner I looked back—Ross was watching. We waved to each other. I vowed to myself to stay in touch with him, and if at all possible find a way to get together with him at least once a year, maybe even talk him into visiting us in Wisconsin. Who knows what story he would remember to tell me next time! Though I wouldn't really expect him to be able to top the one about pushing my dad's tractors into the street. Next time I see Dad I just may ask him if he suspected that it might have been Rossy who had pulled that prank—a prank that I don't remember Dad ever sharing with me.

The roads to Denver were multi-lane and filled with traffic, but they had wide shoulders. The main downside was the noise—the sound of cars whizzing by. Even though I was riding hard I wasn't making great time because of the crosswind, but for most of the afternoon it looked like I would be able to get to Denver before the sun settled behind the Rocky Mountains some forty to fifty miles off my right shoulder.

To conserve the GPS battery I used it only at interchanges and in the hearts of the towns I passed through, like Longmont, Lafayette, and Broomfield. I was nervous about making a wrong turn—I feared biking into Denver after dark. My estimate of arriving in Downtown Denver at dusk was based on riding the shortest distance possible between Rossy's country acreage and my brother's city apartment. I had no idea what awaited me in Denver. It had been a long time since I had spent much time in Downtown Denver, and I had never biked in the heart of the city.

As the sun disappeared behind the peaks, I turned the GPS on and left it on. It led me through the crowded streets of Westminster, down the angle of Speer Boulevard, and across the Platte River. The last time I crossed the Platte, just outside of Sterling, the tallest structure I saw, besides the ubiquitous concrete grain elevators was the viaduct that carried me over the train tracks. This time I rode over the bridge just as the daylight was fading and was ushered into a canyon of lights stretching up into the air at least forty stories above me. This was the part of the ride that I had most dreaded because I didn't want to be riding in the city after dark—but now that I was here I couldn't imagine a better time or a better entrance into the city—or a better ending to my thousand-plus-mile journey than to ride from a small town in Wisconsin across two mighty rivers, then crisscross another as I worked my way across the high plains of Nebraska and Colorado battling winds that at times were blowing fifty miles an hour to arrive in the heart of a major American city just as the lights were coming on and the sky straight above me was growing black.

What I had feared only minutes earlier as I made my way down crowded and pothole-laden suburban streets now felt like the perfect ending to my journey. A few hours earlier I had thought I wanted to travel beyond Denver, but somehow the feeling that came over me as I pedaled through the bright lights of 14th Street had a momentousness to it that spoke more of an ending than a transition. I had no idea why it felt so right, but I had no doubt in my heart that it did. It felt so good that I had to strongly resist the urge to let out a loud whoop of triumph as I pedaled alongside the people milling about the glass walls of the Colorado Convention Center.

But instead of yelling at the top of my lungs I pulled to the curb to take a picture of a giant blue bear that appeared in front of me peering into the windows of the Convention Center. I don't know whose fanciful idea that four-story bear was, but it sure grabbed my attention as I bicycled up the tree- and flower-lined street toward the State Capitol. The bear looked friendly and so did all the people nearby.

It was a relief to be among pedestrians. In the suburbs you find plenty of cars but very few people without a covering shield of steel, plastic, and glass. I was among people and I loved the feeling. I was once again reminded of why I had so loved biking around Italy—your fellow travelers weren't always confined to automobiles and you had a chance to talk with them or just listen to their conversations—many of them were walking or biking. It wasn't eavesdropping as much as it was like listening to music as I biked along.

I could not logically know what my future held in store for me that night, but nevertheless I felt at home at the moment—I had arrived—but I didn't know why I should have had that feeling. For years I had hated Denver. During the ten years in the seventies and eighties when I traveled to the city on business from the Roaring Fork Valley I would get on I-80 heading west just as soon as I could complete my list of city chores. Back then I wanted to be back in the mountains as soon as I could. But on this night the city felt great—the rhythm was right, the pace had slowed, the traffic was moving at bicycle speed or just above—the people were walking, queuing up for theaters, coming out of restaurants, enjoying themselves where they were, not hurrying and scurrying somewhere else. I liked that.

I had no way of knowing when I pulled over to the curb to take a picture of that huge blue bear looking into the lobby of the Denver Convention Bureau, that in just a few short months my oldest son would buy a condo in the towers of the Spire, rising some forty stories behind me on the other side of the street. I also didn't know how much I would enjoy being in Denver. I thought I would spend a couple of days with my brother and son, then head up into the mountains, to the Roaring Fork Valley and Aspen just as I had done so often three decades ago.

But in the succeeding years Denver had changed greatly and so had I. That night I was sensing it at an unconscious level. On the conscious level I had just ridden fifty-some miles through suburbia on heavily traveled roads with multiple lanes of cars whizzing by at highway speeds. I had enjoyed wide shoulders during the ride from Loveland to Denver, but the moment I crossed the South Platte River on Speer Boulevard and turned onto 14th Street, everything changed. I found myself riding in a dedicated bike lane all by myself, and the few cars with me on that street were traveling along at a pace only slightly faster than mine.

My GPS was directing me to bike around the Civic Center and climb the hill on which the Colorado State Capitol Building sits. Once I was on the backside of the Capitol I noticed that I was now on 14th Avenue heading toward Clarkson Street where my brother had been living for a number of years. I had not been to Denver during that time, so I was not sure exactly where I was going. I lost my sense of direction as I made my way around the State House. It felt like I was riding in a circle, but I was determined to relax and follow the lead of the GPS even though I was convinced it was taking me back downtown. I had ridden across four states in six weeks, and the worst that had happened to me was a hard-fought day of riding against the wind and suffering through six flats—no mechanical breakdowns, no one had robbed me, no one had run me off the road, and my derriere, as the French call that weak link in the cyclist's arsenal, hadn't even gotten sore.

But the trip had not been uneventful—far from it. I had met dozens of interesting people. I had been exposed to the thoughts of folks from many different backgrounds and even foreign countries. I was ending the trip confident in the character of the American people, but nonetheless still fearful for our future. I had talked to enough people who were concerned about the directions that our country was headed that it would not be overstating the situation to assert that about half the folks I had talked to were deeply concerned about the integrity of the people who are working for us in Washington.

I hadn't planned it, but I was arriving in Denver just as the eyes of the world were turning to the city for the first of the presidential debates. Maybe it was just the drama of the moment, but I had begun my ride solo, searching for America, and now it felt like the rest of the country was taking up my quest and had descended with me on Denver full of anticipation and with the same questions on their minds. *Where is our country headed in the next four years, and who is going to take us there?* The politicians were not the only ones who were, with deep solemnity, saying that this election would be the most important election of their lifetimes. The sentiment seemed universal that evening as I rode along the streets of Downtown Denver. The newspaper headlines were proclaiming it and so were all the television screens ablaze in the city that night.

I had never before imagined that someday I might live in Denver, but I now see in looking back that a willingness to give downtown living a try had its genesis that night on 14th Street riding past all the bars and restaurants and theatres and museums and then up the hill and around the Capitol and past all the beautiful old Victorian houses and mansions. The GPS took me right to my brother's apartment where I found his roommate, Danise, waiting outside for me because each of us now carries a "doorbell" for the home of every one of our friends right in our pocket.

The cell phone, among other devices, is one of those inventions that lead me to question Steinbeck's quip: *Why is it that progress always looks so much like destruction?* I agree with that sentiment more often than not, especially when I see the changes wrought on our families, out-of-wedlock births, fatherless homes, the size and intrusiveness of our government, and of course things like violent video games, and our seemingly inexhaustible desire for things. But that desire and man's curiosity led to the cell phone—and as a parent, I love it. I love being able to be in constant contact with my kids if need be. And on this night I felt much safer knowing that even though I was only half a block from the notorious underworld of Colfax Avenue, I had to wait not one second to be let into the steel-gated enclosure surrounding my brother's apartment building. No one had time to even approach me, let alone the time to mug me or panhandle me.

I unhooked Friday's trailer and hefted it up the steep open-air stairs—then hustled back down the steps to grab Friday. I grabbed it low, by the pedals and hoisted the almost forty pounds of bike and lights and batteries and water and spare tubes and tools up two flights to the deck at the back of my brother's apartment. I did not yet know that I would not bike out of Denver, but just the act of carrying Friday high over my shoulders while glancing out at the skyscrapers of Denver had an air of finality and triumph that hinted at what was to come.

I received no welcome to Denver from my brother or from my son to Denver; both were out of town the day I arrived. But it didn't matter. I had been welcomed by Denver even though no one except Danise had spoken to me directly since I had entered the city. Downtown Denver had sung out to me—the brightly lit buildings, the pace of the traffic, the dedicated bike lane, the people out on the streets just enjoying themselves. I wasn't biking down a street filled with nefarious people making furtive moves in and out of shadows and doorways. I was among happy people and that made me feel welcome. No one shouted obscenities at me, or made gestures, or even took much notice of me. I was not an oddity. I felt at home biking those streets just as I have felt at home biking in other cities of the world. I know what it is to not feel welcomed—and on this night I felt welcomed as darkness fell and a full moon rose over the city.

It felt like Denver had much to share with me. I was looking forward to what the next day would tell me about Obama and Romney—and about America and Americans. At that moment things looked a lot better than I had expected them to. A full moon has power not just over the tides, but over thought as well. Life for the moment looked good—very good.

Chapter Seventeen

As societies grow decadent, the language grows decadent too.
Words are used to disguise, not to illuminate, action:
You liberate a city by destroying it.
Words are to confuse, so that at election time
People will solemnly vote against their own interests.
GORE VIDAL

The Eyes of the World

The next morning the mood of Denver pulled me into thinking nationally—I felt like I do every time I set foot in Washington, DC—that the world is taking notice of what is happening here. The headlines of the Denver Post screamed of the importance of the event that would take place on the Denver University campus in about twelve hours. I walked around Downtown Denver marveling at its transformation and absorbing the energy of a revitalized city. Very little looked familiar until

I happened to walk by the Brown Palace Hotel. That historic Denver icon has been in the heart of the city since 1892 and will always carry a significant spot in my heart. It was the first hotel I paid one hundred dollars a night for a room. My wife and kids were with me many decades ago, and we wanted to splurge and feel like we were partaking of luxury. We knew that the hotel had hosted the likes of the unsinkable Molly Brown, the Beatles, and every U.S. President, except one, since Teddy Roosevelt—and that it was the place to see and be seen. I'm just guessing, but if that same urge had come over me as I walked past the hotel that morning, with the media of the nation and the world in town, the tab would have been more like five hundred dollars or maybe more—if I could even get a room.

I jogged over one block to the 16th Street Mall, the epicenter of the new Downtown Denver, and began catching snippets of conversation influenced more by mainstream media than Main Street. I even overheard the phrases "war on women" and "reproductive health care" while waiting to cross Larimer Street—jargon that I had yet not heard on this journey except while watching the purveyors of groupthink on television. I kept walking until I had covered the length of the Downtown Mall—to Wynkoop Street—and then I crossed over to the southwest side of the mall and ducked into one of my favorite booksellers, the Tattered Cover Bookstore, where I spent what was left of the morning absorbed in the pleasurable task of discovering books not yet on my must-read list.

I spent the early afternoon near the opposite end of the mall at the Denver Public Library, researching books that were already on my list but that I had not been able to find in used bookstores. The mood on the mall that day was decidedly political. I had traveled the length of it both directions, and just about every conversation I overheard that day had something to do, even if only tangentially, with the fact that in just a few hours President Obama and Governor Romney would be facing off a few miles away on the campus of Denver University.

I circled back to my brother's apartment to get Friday so I could bike to Campus Cycles, the shop where I had bought my folding bike a few months before my trip to Italy. I wanted to check out their supply of heavy-duty tubes and test-ride some bikes, but my main reason for biking down there was because the store was only a few blocks from Denver University. I wanted to get a feel for the mood of the people waiting to attend the debate in person. Once I arrived at DU, I found that the debate was going to be shown outdoors. The campus was rocking. I was surprised to discover that I could join the celebration of music and food and political theater from the other side of a temporary fence—and if I could find a local homeowner who had been given a "we're sorry for all the disruption caused by this debate" ticket who was willing to part with it, I could get through the gate and participate up close and personal.

The sense of anticipation was palpable—the supporters on both sides knew this was going to be big. I saw no major confrontations; only a bit of what might be called sign heckling by a few young Obama supporters who were thrusting their placards aggressively toward people walking by whose ideas they didn't like. With that exception, the *DebateFest* was packed with enthusiastic, respectful supporters across the political spectrum. The largest and most noticeable group was a gathering of Women For Romney supporters wearing red T-shirts, and gathered in a circle praying in support of religious freedom and for the protection of the not-yet-born.

I stayed near the entrance gate for an hour listening to the energetic music of the warm-up band—they were quite good—they were playing music that was finding favor among all age groups. Because I was on a campus, I had expected the crowd to be overwhelmingly in support of Obama, but a closer look at the variety of signs displayed by the people didn't support that assumption. I was also surprised when a chant that began during a break by the band started off weak and within thirty seconds had faded out completely. Maybe the crowd just wanted the music back, but the chant "four more years" got off to an anemic start —and never seemed to have a chance of gathering enthusiasm.

The eclectic bunch on the outside of the fence kept milling about— listening, watching, and hoping that we would find tickets. But in the hour-plus that I hung around I saw but two people part with their tickets, and I wasn't even close to being in the right place at the right time. So when clouds blocked the sun and a stiff wind blew in, dropping the temperature fifteen degrees within a few minutes, I got the message. I hopped on Friday to bike the fifty-some blocks back to Downtown Denver.

Crossing over I-25 on the way to my brother's apartment was eerie. All the lanes were closed—not one car was on the interstate. Folks from the neighborhood were out taking photos of the abandoned freeway and feeling the weirdness of walking above a highway completely devoid of cars. It was obviously a scene they had never before witnessed, and they wanted pictures to back up their stories and to help them remember this special day when the presidential debate totally disrupted their normal routine. The only thing moving in that surreal concrete trough was a commuter train.

The ride north of I-25 through stately Washington Park started out enjoyable, then turned memorable. The park, although designed many years ago with wide boulevards for automobile traffic, was now dedicated only to people-powered vehicles, runners, and walkers. Pulling into the park from the busy surrounding streets was like being dropped onto a green sea of silence. As I pedaled along absorbing the quiet, a young man on a sleek road bike pulled past me as we were rounding a circular drive. I picked up my pace, hopped on his wheel, and drafted him. I was testing the fitness I had attained on my thousand-plus-mile ride pulling fifty pounds across half of the country. He was less than half my age, and two thirds of my weight. The fit young man was riding an expensive Trek Madone, and from his rock-solid, efficient riding position and the colorful kit he was wearing I could tell he was a serious cyclist. He was riding hard, and so was I—much harder than I would have been were I on the New World Tourist that I had taken for a test ride at Campus Cycles a few hours earlier. That bike was outfitted with high-pressure one-hundred-psi tires and flew down the wide roads with minimal pressure on the pedals. But even on Friday, with its front tire at forty-five psi and the rear at sixty-five I was keeping up with this young man riding Trek's Tour de France bike with one-hundred-thirty-psi tires. Of course he was the one breaking the wind—but it still felt good to be flying through the park so fast.

We got to the north edge of the park still hooked together in a small *peloton*. He headed west. I would have liked to follow him, but the GPS was suggesting that I continue riding north, so I reluctantly let him go. The route north led me through a neighborhood of well-kept classic homes dating back to the early twentieth century. The ride was much more sedate, not only because I wasn't racing, but also because I was checking out the beautiful yards in the neighborhood and yielding to traffic at cross streets.

The GPS, despite my slowed pace, still indicated I'd get to Jerome's apartment twenty minutes before the debate was scheduled to start. But by the time I had negotiated the traffic and climbed the stairs with Friday, Danise and I had only fifteen minutes to make it to the neighborhood bar where we had decided to watch the debate while feasting on all-you-can-eat chicken wings. We got there just as Governor Romney and President Obama were being introduced and found that the place was packed and full of raucous energy. We worked our way into the room, and after a bit of jostling found seats with a clear view of the television, but soon realized we could hear nothing except the blended voices of a couple of hundred pumped-up people. So we made our way out of the bar and across the street to a sub shop that also had its television tuned to the debate. Our hurriedly made decision worked out. We could hear—and not just the television. We could also catch the reactions to the debate from the other folks in the room. We settled in. The name of the place was Subculture, and seemed entirely appropriate.

Students and young professionals predominated—an Obama crowd, we assumed. The general tone of the comments in the early part of the debate confirmed our assumption, but we were surprised at how quiet the room became as the debate wore on. When the television was shut off at the end of the debate I was shocked to hear no one saying that Obama had won. I thought Romney had done well, but I hadn't realized it was such a decisive win that political spin, except from one drunkenly boisterous individual, would be absent in that room.

To me Governor Romney looked and sounded presidential. I wasn't sure what to make of President Obama's performance—he didn't look comfortable, he sounded petulant, and he had spent an awful lot of time looking down at his notes. But I didn't realize how deeply disappointed his supporters were until the debate was over. The consensus of the hubbub in Subculture was that Obama had been abysmal—that maybe as President he had forgotten how to handle opposition—or maybe he was just lost without his teleprompter.

A young man sitting at a nearby table struck up a conversation with us. His name was Zach. We learned he was a Subculture regular, a chef at a nearby restaurant, and a strong supporter of President Obama. We asked how he thought his man had done. "Romney won—he clearly outperformed Obama." He was uncomfortable saying it, but he said it and immediately gained my respect. He wasn't a spinner. Zach also noted that Obama looked angry much of the time. From the things he said about Romney, I gathered that this was the first time he had seen him in a sound bite lasting more than ten seconds. He was surprised that Governor Romney was gracious and in command of the facts and the situation, but I didn't get the feeling that Zach's awareness of Romney's strengths was going to affect his vote.

I didn't listen to any pundits that night—I was more interested in digesting what we had seen, what we had overheard in the restaurant, and the opinions of Zach. I also had my own impressions to mull over—and Danise's as well. I didn't know her well enough to know which candidate she favored, although before the debate started I would have guessed Obama, but that could have been for no more solid of a reason than I knew she had only recently arrived in Denver from Washington State—and that would give the odds to Obama if polls were accurate. Her immediate post-debate thoughts didn't reveal who she favored either. She felt Romney appeared to be in command, not just of the facts but also of his emotions, and Obama not so much. She had obviously been impressed with Romney, but I wouldn't have bet money on her vote.

Not until the next morning did I see or hear the opinions of the "experts." And again I was surprised. The Denver Post headline was blunt—"Round One Romney." The consensus seemed to be that the debate might be remembered as one of the most decisive wins in presidential debate history.

But the biggest surprise was that NBC and MSNBC had not found a way to "spin" Obama's performance. Even Chris "Obama puts a thrill up my leg" Matthews couldn't put a happy face on Obama's lackluster performance. "What was he thinking?" was Matthews' lament. I don't think anyone had seen this coming—a performance so anemic that even the most animated of the Obama cheerleaders did not try to paint white as black and black as white. The emperor that morning was wearing no clothes.

My thoughts went to the people I had met on this trip. Most of them would be encouraged that Romney had performed so well. At that moment I was feeling just how out of touch the media is, especially with those people who live in the heartland of America. The media, in all of its pre-debate buildup, had been focused on how bad Mitt Romney was, but what Americans had just seen, was how good Romney was.

I thought also about my journey, and at that moment I realized that it would be anticlimactic to travel beyond Denver. I had set out to take the nation's temperature, and I had taken it. I had spent the past six weeks talking to people, and what I had heard did not match what I would have known about America were I only watching television. The election wasn't over, but the debate, the lead-up to it, and the coverage of the debate, exposed America's weakness—objective reporting, reporting without cheerleading, is done by very few reporters in America any more. But for the first time in a very long time the liberal media did not stand by their man—he had failed too miserably and too many people had seen it for themselves—the truth could not be spun. The debate revealed that a crack might be forming in the monolithic structure of the American media.

I began listing the pros and cons of ending my journey in Denver. The "pros" were winning. At that moment I was feeling good about the future of our country—not because of who had won, but because I had seen the glimmer of a possibility that truth might be gaining some traction in the media. Obama had done poorly, and the media could not, did not spin it otherwise. I had not, until that moment, even seen a hint that such a thing was possible. That was encouraging—a harbinger, I hoped, of things to come. A return of the national press to a useful function—a free press capable of holding the powerful in government— as well as themselves—to standards of truth and honesty. Either would be a game-changer in America, but if forced to choose, I'd go for the honest press.

I was also encouraged by the memory of all the good people who had crossed my path on the journey, and those who had selflessly invited me into their homes reassured my belief in the goodness of Americans. I also thought of the kindness of all the people who had paused in their daily tasks to give me directions or recommend a good place to eat. I had gone in search of the people of America and I had found them.

When I travel around the world I love seeing the differences in cultures and customs, but what I most enjoy discovering is our shared humanity—and learning from others how to attain the highest and best manifestation of that humanity. To me nothing expresses it so well as being either the benefactor or the bestower of hospitality. I like the intensity of life shared with relative strangers. The stories we tell each other often carry an extra dose of fervor because our time together is limited.

The next day I was reminded of Tuscany, and of Italy, on the 16th Street Mall. People were walking and enjoying themselves—the only mechanical sounds I heard were the relatively quiet electric buses. Otherwise people were moving under their own power—including a few who were biking. A street musician was performing in the sun on the mall. A short, solid young man wearing a bowler and blousy shirt was juggling balls and performing magic tricks a few feet away. A strange looking, very intense girl with piercing, almost iridescent, eyes was standing nearby assisting him with props. The scene was similar to those I often saw in the quiet heart of Florence, Italy where people are encouraged and cars are banned. I was sitting on a bench absorbing the sun just a couple of blocks from where I had entered the city less than forty-eight hours earlier —on a night when it seemed Denver was lit up just for me. I had not expected to be met with such joy and light. And whimsy too—the big blue bear peering into a window was just plain fun. I felt drawn to that monstrous bear as though it were me peering into the window of Denver, a new city and a new way of life.

In *Fresh Air Fiend: Travel Writings,* Paul Theroux maintains that *True travel is launching oneself into the unknown.* I had launched myself into the unknown, and for the past forty days the unknown had had its way with me. And now despite my earlier conviction that I would travel beyond Denver, I no longer felt like doing it. My journey was ending, at least the physical part of it. But like all true journeys, I had much more yet to discover about the miles I had traveled and the people I had met.

Like Steinbeck I too had recognized that my journey was over before I had expected it to be. But unlike Steinbeck I would not have to suffer though hundreds of miles of travel without engagement. I had gotten the first hint when I bicycled down the canyons of 14th Street, but I said nothing to anyone. I wanted to see if I would feel differently after I had spent a few days with my oldest son, Matt, a pilot for Southwest Airlines.

On Friday he flew into Denver to join me for the weekend. Denver will soon be his home base, but at the time he was training in Albuquerque with his Air National Guard unit. I walked down to the 16th Street Mall terminal to meet his bus from Denver International Airport. Like him, I love the fact that travel is possible between downtown and the airport without using a private car. He and I both love living in the country, but we also both love the convenience of living where it is possible to not be dependent on a car for getting around.

Our timing was good. As Matt was walking out of the bus terminal pulling his carry-on suitcase, I was walking in. We spent the next three hours eating, catching up with each other's lives, and walking all over the city while he showed me his favorite haunts, and I began imagining what it would be like to live in the heart of a major city. Matt was telling me, as we walked around Downtown Denver, that he thought he would not buy a home for another year—and that if he did, it most likely would be out in the foothills, maybe near Golden or Evergreen, so that he would have easier access to the snowmobiling that he loves so much. But that afternoon I planted seeds within Matt that I hoped would grow. I told him about my new feelings about Denver as he showed me all things he loved about the city. One of those favorite things was Yogurtland, a weigh-it-yourself yogurt shop with all the fixins and plenty of exotic flavors from all over the world. And that is what he saved until last.

We were selling each other on Denver. I'm not sure Matt realized at the time that I was already sold on it. I was being subtle; at least I hoped I was. I didn't want him to think it was my idea for him to do what he did less than a hundred days after we walked all over the city together. I wanted him to buy a place right in the heart of downtown—I'm not sure he had yet considered such a move. But a few months later, on the thirty-first of December, he closed on a beautiful condominium with views of the mountains to the west that he loves to snowmobile in as well as a view straight down of that big blue bear thirty-four stories below that I stopped to photograph the night I first biked into Denver.

I had unwittingly followed Theroux's advice. My journey had taken me into the unknown. I had discovered on my American journey that I liked city life—that I liked Downtown Denver. That realization took me back to the first time I had seen Denver back in the sixties, and I remembered that my first impressions of the Mile High City when I was a teenager had been very positive. The first bike race I had ever seen was on a closed-off circuit of the East 7th Avenue Parkway, and that memory reminded me of something I had forgotten—I hadn't always disliked Denver. I also realized that this journey had carried me into another unknown—a place that I had not expected to find—I had found a renewed faith in the American people, the American spirit, and the unique idea that is America. I don't think I would have seen it if I had not gone on the road. I would have remained stuck in that view of America that the mainstream media paints.

Chapter Eighteen

I am a firm believer in the people. If given the truth,
They can be depended upon to meet any national crisis.
The great point is to bring them the real facts.
ABRAHAM LINCOLN

Reflection

Sunday morning Danise and my brother Jerome, a professional photographer, who had returned from his own travels, drove me to the station. Matt met me and we rode together on the bus. I got to DIA, Denver International Airport, for half price because I'm sixty-five. Matt got there for free because he's active military. We both got there happy because we were dropped off at Southwest's terminal and had neither the worry nor expense of parking a car. I said good-bye to Matt quickly; he was rushing to a plane that he hoped to be able to fly jump seat back to Albuquerque. I had plenty of time, but since my flight was within a few seats of being sold out I headed to the gate as early as possible to increase my chances of getting a boarding pass. And it worked, I was the third from last to be called, but Friday and I both got on.

The trip home was quick and uneventful—just like Steinbeck's return to Long Island—all those miles yielded so few memories. All of a sudden, with no fanfare, the adventure that I had dreamed about for so long was over. I was back in Wisconsin. My journey had been more than I expected. I had learned much about the mood of the heartland. I was gratified to learn that in America strangers are still welcomed, hard work is still lauded, and I need not be as cynical about Americans as a person might become if his principal contact with America is through the television set.

I loved the feeling of being home—of hugging my wife and returning to my favorite routines—drinking tea from my cherished mug and stretching out in my La-Z-Boy, a remote nearby with a mute button I can find. And I loved watching the patches of sunlight follow their familiar paths across the floor as they warmed up the room where I write.

I sipped my Lady Grey tea and dunked my ginger snaps. I opened my journal, made notes, and jotted down calculations. Friday's odometer at the end of the journey registered 3094 miles. When we left this house forty-two days ago it read 1918 miles. We had ridden 1176 miles in six weeks. But during that time away the house I thought was going to be taken off the market for the winter suddenly had an accepted offer and we had only a few weeks to find a new home. I had lost the comfortable room filled with early-morning sunlight where I had planned to write the stories of the people I had met on my American journey. But a few days later—thanks to the realtor who had sold the house and knew of a family looking for good renters—we had a place that we liked even more than the house we had just lost. I had not thought that possible—the place on Leonard Street had seemed perfect. But the home on Patriot Place was more perfect, and in ten days we were moved in and I had an even better place to write An American Journey and my wife had another house where she could turn loose her talent for presenting a house to its fullest potential.

Even the toil of moving aided the process of writing—the physical effort involved was helpful. While I packed our things I reflected on the journey and fleshed out my journal entries while my memory of all that had happened was vivid. Some writers dread that first blank page, but I love writing—I even love the process and challenge of writing and before October had ended I was well on the way to completing the first draft. One of the most marvelous things I've discovered about the process of writing is that it has an almost mystical power to take me places I did not expect to go—you expect it in fiction—the characters take over and insist that the story is theirs. I have found that the same thing happens in nonfiction. In writing that first draft, I discovered an America I didn't know was still out there. During the writing and research for that first draft I came across a dare that Steinbeck had issued to writers that challenged, motivated, and shaped the completion of my first draft and every revision since. I mustered the courage to accept what Steinbeck had said was the biggest challenge for a writer—to write the truth. After sifting my odyssey across America through the sieve of Steinbeck's challenge I saw that political correctness was the greatest enemy America and Americans face. And the only way I know to wage war against that enemy is to use words and ideas that benefit truth no matter how passionately truth is resisted by the collective cloud of the thought police.

While I wrote, and re-wrote, the campaigns made their final cases for support of their candidates. In the second debate, Candy Crowley of CNN aided and abetted a statement by President Obama about Benghazi that was worthy of five "Pinocchio's" that left Romney stammering in disbelief, not knowing what to say. Romney thought Obama's lies about Benghazi would sink him, but despite the optimism I had felt in Denver that things had changed, the *elite media* rallied around Obama and said, "What lies?"

Then Hurricane Sandy ravaged the East Coast, silencing Romney for five critical days and completing the resurrection of Barack Obama, as the natural disaster allowed him to appear presidential rather than petulant and petty. The third debate, focusing on foreign policy, featured a neutered Mitt Romney, who inexplicably did not even mention

Obama's lies. He was fearful of what the media would do to him if he called out Obama on Benghazi. He had done it before and the press had ravaged him. Romney thought he could coast to victory on the strength of his first debate performance without taking on the tag team of President Obama and the media. He had plenty of material with which to go on the offensive, including the Benghazi murders, the lack of a military response in the ongoing attack on our consulate in Libya, the bungled cover-up, the gunrunning in Mexico known as "Fast and Furious," Obama's failed economic policies, the crony capitalism of the green energy stimulus money, and looming over it all, the disastrous effects of Obamacare on jobs as well as healthcare, but Romney's advisers convinced him to play it safe, thereby setting the stage for what was to come.

Epilogue

Nearly all men can stand adversity,
but if you want to test a man's character,
give him power.
ABRAHAM LINCOLN

The Responsibilities of Freedom and Free Will

The presidential election of 2012 is over. Barack Obama received fifty percent of the votes cast. Mitt Romney received forty-nine. The Electoral College count, however, was not close. Obama won the swing states of Ohio, Florida, and Pennsylvania. Of the four states I biked through, only Nebraska chose Romney. Despite the heartfelt pleas of Americans, President Obama is following the failed model of European socialism, pushing for higher taxes and unlimited debt, which is a recipe for Greece-like insurrection in the streets.

I went in search of America and felt the pulse of the American people. I was following in the footsteps of John Steinbeck's *Travels with Charley,* but what I learned reminded me of another book by Steinbeck that came out when I was in high school, *The Winter of Our Discontent.* The discontent of America is, I predict, going to grow. President Obama is aware that the majority of the American people have finally realized the disastrous consequences of our national debt, but he is not changing course. Despite his promise to "not increase debt by one dime," Obama is on his way to increasing the burden on the American taxpayers by some five trillion dollars, to a total of twenty-one trillion dollars, which would be a doubling of the nation's debt and not the promised halving of the burden on our children and grandchildren. The difference between the promise—five trillion—and what we are likely to get—twenty-one trillion—is staggering to contemplate—and that doesn't even include the confounding costs of Obamacare to the American taxpayer and the American economy. And should Obama be successful in granting amnesty—and therefore eventually welfare and benefits for the millions of illegal immigrants, their families, and their descendents—we will soon be insolvent.

If you voted for Romney, you most likely are already discontent. If you voted for Obama, you may not yet be discontent. The shoe has not yet fully dropped on the Benghazi debacle because most of the media refuses to let it drop. Romney never challenged Obama on the convoluted lies that he and his administration told the American people and the families of the four murdered Americans. Except for a few reporters like Jennifer Griffin and Catherine Herridge of Fox News, commentators like Sean Hannity on Fox, Glenn Beck on the Blaze, a few folks on talk radio, and one brave soul at CBS, Sharyl Attkisson, the media never demanded that Obama quit stonewalling and tell the truth about Benghazi. The mainstream media never demanded to know what happened before the attack, during the attack in which men died needlessly, or what has happened since in covering up the truth about the way the White House and the State Department handled Benghazi. The big news, when it finally breaks, will be the revelations of what the Obama administration was doing in Benghazi in the days and weeks before the attack, as well as its cowardly decision to leave the men to fight and die alone. But that will not happen until whistleblowers (truth-tellers) get the safeguards they need to protect themselves, their jobs, and their families.

Steinbeck issued his warnings about loss of character in 1961. He won the Nobel Prize in 1962 for his body of work, but *The Winter of Our Discontent* was prominently mentioned as being the catalyst for the award. Steinbeck was calling out America—issuing warnings about what will happen if we accept as normal a world in which we lie to each other and in which we allow ourselves to be lied to. Steinbeck did it by telling the story of a scrupulously honest storekeeper, and the path of destruction his family went down when he began compromising on his good name. Steinbeck knew that the politics of a person were not as important as a person's willingness be truthful in both word and deed. Steinbeck was, as was my mother, an Adlai Stevenson Democrat, but honesty was the characteristic Steinbeck most strongly sought in those he wanted governing him. My memory of Stevenson was that he was so honest and unassuming that he even allowed himself to be photographed with a hole in the sole of his shoe.

Much more than shoes in need of resoling is wrong with most of our leaders in Washington today, but I am going to posit that nothing will bring us down quicker, or more decisively than accepting lies from our leaders, especially when the misrepresentations are coming from the President of the United States. Once a leader finds that he is able to lie to the American public and get away with it—and that the press will even provide cover for him—there is no end to the damage he can unleash on the people that he is sworn to protect. The death and destruction that Hitler brought to Germany began quietly with lies—lies that no one called him on.

Lord Acton's warning has become an oft-misquoted cliché, but like most clichés, it became one because it packs truth and understanding within it: *Power tends to corrupt and absolute power corrupts absolutely.* Because of that tendency the framers of our Constitution gave us the First Amendment. They knew we needed a press that would ferret out the truth. But when that First Amendment protection is abrogated by a majority of the media, America's future is in doubt. People in power must be held accountable to the truth, not to ideology. The court system is too slow in discovering the misdeeds of people in power; even when they perjure themselves, nothing comes of it in today's divided political climate. Lawyers align to make the lying words meaningless and the liar limps away to lie another day. Attorney General Eric Holder is a perfect case in point. Only a press acting as a watchdog, not a lapdog, can get the truth to the American people. Politics, and people drunk on power who think only they know what is best for the American people will not save us—only the truth will.

Our founders recognized the corruptibility of human behavior, and that concept stands at the core of our American Republic. Our forefathers instituted a system of checks and balances—and that includes the press—to combat the evil that man is capable of. They knew the dangers of power because they had suffered under it. And they knew that the intoxicating allure of power would entice the ethically weak across the whole of the political spectrum. They also were prescient enough to know that a government of the people, by the people, and for the people is held in check from tyranny only by a people whose concern is for their neighbors—E Pluribus Unum—Out of Many, One.

I will mention just a few of the more visible signs that I see as representative of the great dangers that America faces—signs that get at the heart of why such a large proportion of our society now seems to find coercion and lying acceptable. Just today I learned that a six-year-old girl from West Marion Elementary School in Marion, North Carolina, is at the center of a controversy after educators ordered her to remove the word "God" from a poem she was slated to deliver at a Veteran's Day event. The first grader intended to use the opportunity to honor her grandfathers, who had served during the Vietnam War.

But a parent of one of her classmates got wind of the little girl's audacious poem and complained. The deeply offensive part of the poem that led this protector of sensitive ears to take action was this line: "He prayed to God for peace, he prayed to God for strength " That this little girl was honoring her grandfathers did not matter to the folks who bow down to the god of political correctness. They humiliated her. *How can it be fair for that insensitive little girl to mention God,* they asked? *Might someone be in that class who doesn't believe in God, what then? What of that disbelieving child's rights to be protected from thoughts of God?* they implored.

The school, apparently fearing the Gestapo of the thought police, told the child to remove the line. The superintendent justified her actions; "We wanted to make sure we were upholding the school district's responsibility of separation of church and state from the Establishment Clause." She went on to say that after consulting with advisors, the school decided that allowing the line would constitute an endorsement of "one single religion over another." What that religion was, was not stated, nor did the school board seem concerned about the "free exercise thereof" provision of the First Amendment. They were also taking away the little girl's "freedom of speech." It seems worth pointing out as well that very few religions, with the obvious exception of the religion of atheism, do not worship God—the name may be different, but God is God.

There was, however, a dissenting opinion. One school district employee had apparently been educated somewhere outside of the secular progressive educational establishment and had the courage to speak up for the Constitution of the United States at the hearing and say that the school was guilty of "hushing the voice of a six-year-old girl." He contended that she was not trying to pray or coerce others to engage in a conversation with God, she was simply explaining what her grandfathers had done in their time of need—in short she was just telling the truth about her grandfathers. But the purveyors of political correctness didn't see it that way. The word *God* cannot be uttered in the public square they maintained. The school administrators, cowed by the *purveyors of political coercion,* were less concerned about the first grader's rights to freedom of speech and expression, and so the PC argument won the day—and truth took a back seat—in fact, it took no seat at all in that school on that day.

Of all the signs of degeneration in our nation, I believe that nothing is more detrimental to our survival than this kind of lockstep, misguided thinking that permeates the American public school system and year after year foists a false narrative about America onto the most vulnerable and gullible among us. We are showing ourselves to be perfectly comfortable with stifling truth, controlling thought, and accepting lies from our leaders—be they in our schools or in the White House. I will point out, as many have before me, that it is not without reason that Satan is called "The Father of Lies." In our courts we place our hands on a Bible, and swear that we "will tell the truth, the whole truth, and nothing but the truth." Our founding fathers knew that a civil society depends upon an ethical electorate interested in seeking the truth. The people who fought for and won our independence from despots knew that if we lie to ourselves, and allow ourselves to be lied to, nothing can save us from ourselves. Our founders knew that truth may at times be elusive, but they knew that truth does exist. And we still know that truth exists—and we know how important it is that truth be told. We know this because of the great lengths that we go to avoid calling someone a liar. Instead of using the word *lying*, today we say that people are "spinning" the truth, which is of course, okay in the politically correct world.

Spinning the truth is exactly what Barack Obama and Hillary Clinton did in the wake of the deaths of four Americans in Benghazi. They knew they had to shield themselves from the truth so they sent U.N. Ambassador Susan Rice, who had little or no involvement with Benghazi, out to the Sunday talk shows to spin for them. When her lies were questioned, President Obama went on the offensive. Instead of admitting the lies, the Obama administration and the media attacked those seeking the truth—calling them racists and woman-haters. That is the danger when truth-telling is not honored—and reveals why our country, at the present time, is so deeply divided.

The need to support liars, and those who obfuscate and mislead, debases discourse, and turns White House press conferences into three-ring circuses of lies, deceptions, and cover-ups. Instead of the administration and the media addressing the issues, and telling the truth, they denigrate the people pointing out their lies. Of what use is that kind of a press to good governance? It certainly isn't what the framers of the Constitution had in mind.

In 1962 when I set out on my first journey in search of America, three quarters of us trusted our government. Today that has been flipped on its head—three quarters of Americans *don't* trust their government. Truth-telling used to be admired and honored, but that which was formerly celebrated is now merely fodder to be manipulated. Words are used not to clarify, but to confuse—all in an effort to hide the truth. And each time someone in the administration tells another lie, parses words, or attempts a cover-up, the Obama *spinmeisters* must hit the airwaves to attack those who are trying to bring the truth to the American people.

As a writer I watched with great interest the reporting on the affair of General David Petraeus with his biographer, not because I was interested in the salacious details of the failings of a great man, but because it seemed to me a great metaphor for a magician's sleight of hand. While most of the press was focused on the sexual dalliances of the disgraced CIA chief, the truth about Benghazi was going unreported. The Obama administration was buying time, hoping the American public would get bored with the story if they stonewalled long enough.

On my sixty-sixth birthday, November 15, 2012, the day the Benghazi hearings began on Capitol Hill I wrote these words: *The affair of General Petraeus was discovered long before he was asked on election day to resign by the Director of National Intelligence, James Clapper. Holder knew about it, Obama knew about it, and they knew that affair would someday be useful to them. Petraeus knew that Obama knew, and he fully expected to keep his job as CIA Chief, and that his affair with Paula Broadwell would be kept quiet, if he helped advance Obama's narrative that four Americans had died because of a protest about a YouTube video lampooning Islam. But Petraeus, as director of the CIA, knew that wasn't true, and when it became evident that he would someday have to testify under oath, he balked. And that is why he got exposed. So now I can think of no reason for Petraeus to do anything other than to tell the truth before Congress. He was double-crossed. What allegiance can he possibly have to Obama now?*

On November 16 I added: *Apparently Obama still has something on Petraeus. Petraeus is continuing to maintain that the timing of his resignation had nothing to do with keeping the affair quiet until after the election. Petraeus is now maintaining that he had said all along that it was a terrorist attack, despite the fact that those who were at the closed-door Congressional meeting say otherwise—they say Petraeus provided cover for Obama and was pushing the administration's narrative about the video. That surely is a matter of fact. (Check the transcript.) Petraeus also noted that Susan Rice wasn't reading from CIA "talking points" when she went out to the Sunday talk shows. Petraeus knew the CIA's original report had been scrubbed. But no one is fessing up and Petraeus isn't willing to say who did it either. Also just learned that the last days of Petraeus were quite contentious. Petraeus will have to admit that he misled Congress and take the consequences. Will he have the character to do that? I believe he will.*

As Steinbeck said, without a belief in God, the concept of right and wrong soon disappears—and truth is replaced by nebulous concepts like fairness and *the ends justify the means.* The secular world that liberal educators have for years been striving toward is almost here. And nowhere is that more clearly seen than in the public schools of America where discipline is all but gone and truth is held in contempt. Lying has many insidious forms, but among the worst is that which goes on in our schools about history, especially American history, and freedom of speech and assembly. God, even the concept of God, and the rock solid foundation of truth, have all but been banished from the American classroom. No longer is the importance of the faith and religious expression of the Founding Fathers and the settlers of this land taught in most American classrooms. I learned it when I was a kid—our teachers taught us why the different colonies were founded in America—but very little, and sometimes none of the story of the faith of the early settlers in America is taught in public schools today, and we as a nation are suffering because our young people don't understand the basics of America's existence—why these courageous people were willing to suffer and die to found a better society.

John Steinbeck was prescient to be worried about the moral degeneration of America. The more secular we have become the more intolerant we have become. And that which we have become most intolerant of is God—and faith in God. America may not survive if we don't put education back in the control of parents, and let them choose what schools their children attend. Only then will the stranglehold that liberals have on young minds be broken.

There are many signposts that will serve future historians as evidence for *the decline and possible fall of America,* but the behind-the-scenes machinations in halls of power regarding the Benghazi cover-up and the effort to curb the free speech of a first grader by public school administrators will remain for me shining beacons proclaiming what was wrong with America in the early part of the twenty-first century. Our educational system has churned out a large voting block of illiterate liberals and secular progressives who no longer understand the need for honesty, and whose ignorance of history as well as their hatred of Christianity is all but complete. I mention Christianity with good reason. Liberals and progressives don't hate all religions—they hate the religion that opposes their agenda—that calls a spade a spade. Only Christianity so clearly opposes the world of the secular progressive. And if liberals/progressives say they don't hate Christianity, the Christianity they don't hate is a Christianity that has been watered down by materialistic thought to the point where it would barely be recognizable as Christianity to the rest of the world—where people are being killed because they won't renounce their Christian faith.

For some reason, which is difficult to understand logically, liberals seem to like Islam, even though it dehumanizes women, despises homosexuals, and considers abortion a grievous sin. That liberals like the religion of atheism is understood, but a liberal's knee-jerk reaction to not call a spade a spade when an Islamic terrorist blows the limbs off dozens of people or when a man murders people while shouting allegiance to Allah is a little more difficult to comprehend. The Obama administration, as of the moment that I am writing this is still calling Major Nidal Hasan's murderous rampage at Fort Hood, during which he killed thirteen people and injured thirty more while shouting "Allahu Akbar", *workplace violence*. It goes along with the penchant of liberals to prefer to call abortion "choice." It obscures truth, and when you are on the wrong side of truth, obscuring reality is the weapon of choice.

I traveled America not knowing whether America would soon have a new President or whether we would be settling in for another four years of President Obama. I wrote the first draft of the book before the election—most of the polishing drafts were crafted post-election, but prior to the inauguration of President Obama for his second term. The Congressional investigations into the attack on our consulate in Benghazi were being held while I worked on the final drafts. At the time this book went to press, the investigation was focused on the lies and the stonewalling of the administration to cover up what happened the night of September 11 in Benghazi. Once those lies are dealt with, attention will shift to the cover-up of what the Obama administration was doing in Benghazi, and the fireworks then, I predict, will really start exploding. Another potential firestorm will be the discovery of what President Obama was doing, or not doing, and who he was in contact with, the night four Americans were dying in Benghazi.

One other significant fact of a historical nature—Europe, during the period in which I wrote this book, was in financial turmoil; America was floundering in a slow economic recovery; and the debate on the "fiscal cliff" facing our country was being vigorously debated. President Obama was wedded to a tax policy of "asking the rich to pay their fair share." Opposing him were those who felt that the job creators of America should be putting their money to use hiring people, starting businesses, or buying equipment rather than sending more of their money to Washington for bureaucrats to waste.

As I've watched these contentious battles, I've come to realize that our political parties are well named. One is for democracy—the right of the majority to govern—what is pejoratively thought of as mob rule. That is precisely the reason that the Arab Spring that President Obama backed with passionate speeches and clandestine money and weapons went so wrong—democratic elections ensure only that the person receiving the most votes gets to hold office. The elite media that waxed so eloquently about the future of Egypt because of the democracy that would soon be taking hold there didn't have the foresight to see the handwriting on the wall that the Muslim Brotherhood would win that democratic election. Democracy does not ensure freedom from despots.

The other political party also harbors government-growing progressives, but Republicans tend to favor the principles of a republic informed by the Constitution—the rule of law based upon telling the truth. Liberals, progressives of all stripes, and Democrats tend to couch their arguments not in terms of what is true, right, or sustainable, but upon their determination of what is *fair*. Independent standards tend not to exist for liberals. It seemed wholly justified to the majority of Democrats to eliminate the mention of God from their platform. God is an impediment to a liberal's concept of fairness. After all, God is not fair. He made women and men different—and right from the beginning he put unfair restrictions on what mankind could do. Why, the liberal/progressive mind demands, should one tree be different from another?

Until this spade is called a spade, I doubt that much progress can be made in restoring America's greatness. At the heart of America's decline is rebelliousness—an unwillingness to accept limits on our behavior. We know how to raise good citizens, but we encourage the behavior that results in children being born out of wedlock, and we do it through our welfare system. Why? Because we've got the wrong-headed idea that it is not fair to discriminate. Where the hell did we get that idea?

When we want a championship football team we discriminate to high heaven. We want the best players, the most committed players, the best team players we can possibly get. That's why we in Wisconsin have been blessed with our beloved Green Bay Packers. Why do we not encourage the best when it comes to raising a team of good citizens?

The alternative is rioting on the streets of America. The people rioting in Greece are those whose livelihood depends on a check from the government. The same will be true in America when the money either runs out or is severely cut back. Government-dependent people will be the rioters. They will demand to be treated *fairly*. Independent folks who have had to take care of themselves will be seeking ways to cut back and absorb the punches for the betterment of their country. But those who have not started their own business, or struggled to help an entrepreneur grow a business will not understand the concept that there is no money available—so they will throw a tantrum to try to get their way—they will resort to mob rule.

Fairness is the mantra that drives the liberal/progressive view of the world. So pervasive is this thinking that as a society we have come to accept the politically correct notion that financial inequality is the main driver of society's ills—and not the evil that is among us. We love to blame the failures of our society on a lack of money. The problem is not poverty. Many of America's best and most productive citizens were raised in poverty. The reason kids are not receiving a good education is not because their family is poor—it is because they or their classmates have not learned the value of discipline, respect for authority, and hard work. Or it may be that they are going to a school where the administrators, who have themselves been educated to be politically correct, do not demand discipline, respect for authority, and hard work. The result is the same.

I have taught kids who have been bussed from their inner city, low-income neighborhoods to the suburbs to be taught in the best schools in the area. And it matters not a hoot how poor or rich is the kid I'm teaching, what matters is the attitude that child brings to class. The best instruction in the world will fall like water off a duck's back if that child is rebellious or uninterested. Often, the best students are the poorest financially, if they bring to the classroom the desire and discipline to learn. The drive to learn can be instilled in children by poor parents, rich parents, and middle-income parents—it's not the money, it's the parenting.

It also doesn't matter if someone's ancestor originally lived in Africa or was at one time a slave. What matters is the behavior or the lifestyle—how the person chooses to live. Despite the claims of muddle-minded politicians who see only skin color or the size of a person's wallet, Americans should return to the practice of judging people on what they do and what they say. Obama is not deplored because his father was from Kenya. He is despised by a large and growing percentage of Americans because he is a terrible President who is destroying the very institutions and economy that made America great. The fact that he resorts to lying, misrepresentation, and the pitting of Americans against each other to advance his agenda, and never leads or takes responsibility are also high on the list of reasons he is so thoroughly despised by such a large number of people. No President in my lifetime has so thoroughly disgusted people.

Even Bill Clinton lying to the American people about his affair with his intern, Monica Lewinsky, did not elicit such revulsion. Most Americans felt that he was restricting his lying to his private affairs, even when he said in the lawyerly language of a weasel trying to avoid conviction for perjury, *depends upon what the meaning of the word 'is' is*. The American people trusted him when he said, "The era of big government is over," especially when he balanced the budget.

But there appears to be nothing that is off limits to Barack Obama's *spin*. Eventually Clinton confessed to his lies, at least some of them. As of this moment, there is no indication that Barack Obama has any intention of ever admitting his lies—even with the videotape of those lies rolling before his eyes and those of the American people, he continues to try to spin his way out of the morass his incompetence, detachment, and deceit have created. He tried to tell us that *there is no there there*, but Americans have been subjected to his lies long enough that they no longer trust him or any of the people who try to spin the truth for him. He may feel he is helping himself with his denials, but he is doing great damage to America's prestige and credibility throughout the world—to say nothing of his own.

● ● ●

I met many people on my journey who were adamant in their conviction that America could not survive four more years of Barack Obama. But for all of Barack Obama's faults I don't feel he is the main reason people are so polarized in America. The roots of our division are deeper than

Obama. The rift goes back to 1973. Obama was not yet a teenager. He was living with his grandparents in Hawaii when *Roe v. Wade* was decided in the Supreme Court. The divide in America was started with that decision and has widened and deepened because one of the two major political parties endorsed what was, until a couple of generations ago, considered a crime, or at the very least a very grievous sin. Compromising on murder is a difficult thing for a country. And if you are a person who does not see abortion as murder, it is easy to find grievous fault with those who vociferously oppose abortion—and once again it is primarily Christians who are the source of opposition to the liberal vision for America.

Liberals counter the Christian argument by saying that America is progressing—evolving toward a better, fairer country—a country where the federal government redistributes Joe the Plumber's money to his neighbor, there are no restrictions on abortion, and even the word "marriage" is redefined. Liberals want to dictate their own morality and their own view of the world, and they are less interested in economic freedoms, or freedoms of conscience and religion. We shall see in the next four years, and possibly sooner, whether this grand experiment in the liberal agenda of Barack Obama is a recipe for the ascendency of America into that *fundamentally transformed America* that Obama promised or whether America is on the precipice of decline and destruction. We have canaries in the coalmine throughout Europe warning us of the dangers of degenerating toward socialism, and we have the examples of numerous governments over the centuries that have collapsed from within because of moral degeneracy and economic malpractice, but President Obama feels that what he is doing to America will not result in its total collapse as it has for numerous other great powers. We're smarter than that seems to be his argument. That may be left for history to decide.

Rome fell.

Fascist Italy failed.

Nazi Germany collapsed.

The USSR imploded and disbanded.

What are the parallels and what lies ahead for America?

How did the Germans end up persecuting the Jews? The better question is how did they begin singling the Jews out? And why? Once you have answered those questions, ask if Christians are being discriminated against in America. And why?

Christians have been persecuted and killed before. In the years of Rome's decline, the emperors made a sport of watching Christians fight lions in the Coliseum. And there is no reason to believe that such things won't happen again. In fact it *is* happening. There's just a good chance you haven't heard about it if you get your news from the mainstream media. Christians are being killed and persecuted in Muslim countries all over the world.

Jews too, of course, have been persecuted and killed throughout history. And there is no reason to believe that it can't happen again. In fact, there are whole nations of people who desire nothing so fervently as to kill every Jew on Earth.

The persecution of the Jews did not begin with gas chambers in Auschwitz. The murder of millions began much more innocuously, as it always does. It began with lies. In the same way persecution begins with a national health care bill that attacks religious beliefs. And it continues with *spinmeisters* who try to conceal that fact. Or it begins with thought police who demand that a former candidate for the President of the United States not be allowed to speak at a high school. And that curtailment of freedom of speech and assembly was thought to be okay until Bill O'Reilly cast light on the situation.

To counter the negative reaction, Grosse Pointe South High School re-invited Rick Santorum. However to appease the thought police, the administrators of lockstep thinking decreed that only students with permission slips from their parents would be allowed to be hear what Senator Santorum had to say. That is a clear example of how it begins. That is how we will become a speck of our former selves—when a man—a Christian, a Roman Catholic—who defends the word "marriage," and is adamantly opposed to abortion, is told that he is not allowed to speak to the students at a school in the United States of America. This is the kind of divisiveness that now defines America.

Despite all this, I remain optimistic because of the sheer number of principled people I met on my journey across America. Independent self-reliant people who treasure the freedoms America once stood for are apparently not now in the majority, at least of those who voted in 2012. But the yeast of their conservatism and the bedrock principles of telling the truth, the whole truth, and nothing but the truth are still alive in the heartland of America. And it can grow if Americans come to understand the institutions, the philosophies, and the fearful thought processes that are stifling the growth of truth, freedom, and free expression in America.

I am trying to reflect the consensus of what I discovered in my journey across America by pointing out what I see as the most egregious examples of wrong-headed thinking in America. This does not mean that no one talked to me of the benefits of four more years of President Obama. It is just that the arguments for Obama were visceral and less reasoned, and need not paragraphs or chapters to convey, but merely short sentences or phrases: "I like him," "He will take care of me," "I like what he says," "He makes great speeches." The people who voiced approval for Obama were typically in their twenties and their comments had the sound of talking points or groupthink jokes told by late-night comics like Jon Stewart. They tended to be felt responses: "He's one of us." The endorsement of Obama never seemed to be tied to higher ideals—to goodness, to rightness, to freedom—only to that elusive concept of "fairness," or to ridicule and condescension for people in opposition to Obama's vision.

That is not to say that all the young people who shared their opinions with me were in favor of Obama. Many young people were adamantly opposed to President Obama. But the most striking takeaway from my weeks on the road was that very few adults spoke out in favor of Obama. People who have been through the maturing process of raising a family or making a living were more likely to want Governor Romney to be their President. But that was not exclusively true.

I was at my Aunt Lillian's house on the Monday night that replacement referees took a victory away from my beloved Packers and gave it to the Seattle Seahawks. In tuning into Monday Night Football we also found ourselves tuning out a whole bunch of political attack ads. During one of those respites Aunt Lillian asked me who was going to win the election.

"If the mood of people I met crossing Wisconsin, Iowa, and Nebraska is any indication, the winner will be Romney," I told her.

She shot back, "I hope not. I'm a Democrat and Romney is too rich."

I've always admired Lillian's spunk. The tone of her voice when she said the word "rich" left no doubt who she was going to vote for. Even though I had never before talked politics with her, or even thought about her political views, I wasn't surprised when she mentioned she was a Democrat. My mom was a Democrat. And Lillian's husband, my Uncle Court, had been a Democrat. But it did, at that moment, occur to me that she might be against abortion, and therefore may feel some conflict, so I asked her if Obama's support of abortion bothered her. Her answer surprised me. "I heard a nun say she supported Obama, so he must be okay."

With that very brief conversation in the midst of a Packers football game I came to understand the importance of attack ads and political alliances. Aunt Lillian was obviously conflicted, but the opinion of a nun had comforted her. Was I less than candid for not pointing out that the nun's opinion was not universally shared in the Catholic Church? You bet I was. But my love for Aunt Lillian and regard for her feelings prevailed. I just said, "Oh," and we went right back to watching the game—enjoying our time together.

In thinking about it now, I see that in addition to not being candid, I could also be accused of cowardice for not mentioning to Aunt Lillian that most nuns feel very differently about Obama's view on abortion. But in my defense I will point out that I was journeying across the heartland to learn what Americans were thinking and feeling. And the best way to do that is to just listen—that was what I had done with everyone else I had met and it didn't occur to me to do otherwise with Aunt Lillian.

I have written this epilogue to give emphasis to what I learned in my journey across America and to clearly delineate my conviction that

America is in trouble if it doesn't change course. I am not pulling any punches. A *lie* is not telling the truth, and a *liar* is one who knowingly presents a false narrative. Calling lies by the more pleasant-sounding word *spin* does not change the fact that the truth is being concealed—and truth is exactly what Abraham Lincoln warned us we could not long survive without.

Political correctness—i.e. political coercion—and groupthink are our enemies no matter whether it is being put out by liberals, conservatives, Democrats, Republicans, Independents, or Libertarians. Readers will soon be able to judge whether my words are those of a prophet or the ramblings of a misguided alarmist. I agree with Obama that we can survive financially as long as we keep using a credit card that someone else will have to pay. I, and millions of other baby boomers, did the same thing when we were young, foolish, and thought we knew it all. But eventually the interest on the debt becomes so high that the lifestyle to which we have grown accustomed becomes unsustainable. We, as a nation, are nearing that point. As Margaret Thatcher, the former Prime Minister of the United Kingdom, eloquently and succinctly put it, *"The problem with socialism is that you eventually run out of other people's money."*

Almost five dollars of every ten we spend is used just to pay our debt. And if interest rates rise, America will be paying six, seven, and eight dollars of every ten to keep from defaulting. *Katie, you'd better bar the door then.* Actually, there may be no bar or even a door to bar—the whole thing might just implode.

If the debt clock could be stopped before it hits seventeen trillion, and begin dropping, America might have a chance. The House of Representatives needs to start exercising the power over the checkbook that it holds. But that will be a contentious battle—few who are now collecting a government check from an entitlement or a job will want to see it end or even reduced. That debate will test the mettle of America. And this debate will cross all party lines—big-government progressives are as likely to be Republicans as they are Democrats. Only among Libertarians are you unlikely to find favor for big government.

Libertarians tend to want the smallest government possible that is still capable of defending our God-given liberties.

But no matter what stripes we wear, if we have an ounce of pragmatism within us, we will soon be forced to concede that America needs a government that spends less than it takes in, every day, every week, every year. We are slowly learning that only in a World War II-like emergency does it make sense to spend more than we make. I was born just as that war ended—at that moment when we stopped the rising debt, reversed course, and became the strongest economy in the world. If we're going to lead the world again, we're going to have to find a different way to bring in that money we need every day to operate. We're most likely going to have to gut or dismantle the IRS, and begin again with a consumption tax—a tax that doesn't play favorites, that takes away from corrupt bureaucrats, lobbyists, and government employees the power they have over the American people, and lets the free market raise our revenue unencumbered by special interests.

But that will not happen until we have an informed and engaged electorate that will demand that our elected officials begin representing us responsibly—there is too much entrenched power in the old system— taking it down will require the concerted effort of millions of motivated citizens who recognize what we are about to lose. Before this trip I assumed that the changes that have come over our country had to do with a generational change in attitudes—that we had lost the will to do the right thing. But this trip into America's heartland exposed me once again to the foundational attitudes that led to the dubbing of the people who sacrificed in World War II as "The Greatest Generation." On this journey across America I came once again into contact with people like Rose who are demanding integrity, truthfulness, sincerity, and sacrifice in interpersonal relationships, and they want no less from those who are governing their country. As I reflected on my journey, I realized that I had seen the foundational, sacrificial attitudes of the Greatest Generation not just in people who lived through the Great Depression and World War II, but also in the hearts of Americans of all ages .

In the months since I completed my journey I have been contemplating the implications of that realization, and I want to pose this question: *Are those foundational attitudes of the Greatest Generation a function of geography, or, more precisely, are they a function of the self-reliant people who typically populate the least populous, least affluent, most independent parts of America? And if that is true, might we once again see a resurgence of those attitudes in America? In other words, might the "starter dough" of integrity that created this great country still be preserved in the heartland of America? And might this America rise again.*

Afterword

*"It's so much darker when a light goes out
than it would have been if it had never shone."*
JOHN STEINBECK, *The Winter of Our Discontent*

A Broken Heart—A Battle Cry

In the seven months since my American journey seven "events" were
visited upon Americans that will either be clarion calls to battle or they
will go down in history as significant signs that Barack Obama was
successful in his promise to voters in Missouri when he emphatically
proclaimed in early November 2008 that "We are five days away from
fundamentally transforming the United States of America."

Those events and/or America's reaction are:

1. The murders of teachers and children at Sandy Hook Elementary School.
2. The Gosnell abortion/murder trial and the blackout by the media of the grisly brutality.
3. The Boston Marathon bombing by Islamic jihadists that killed three and maimed hundreds.
4. The racism of "Let's Hope the Boston Marathon bomber is a white American".
5. The continuing attempts to cover up the Benghazi attack that killed four Americans.
6. The targeting of Constitutional conservatives, Christian groups, and Romney supporters for invasive levels of scrutiny by the IRS, FBI, and ATF.
7. The attacks on the freedom of the press—UPI, James Rosen of Fox News, and Sharyl Attkisson of CBS News— and warrantless recordings of the conversations of billions of phone customers, by the National Security Administration.

In the days following the carnage of December 14, 2012 at the Sandy Hook Elementary School in Newtown, Connecticut, we once again as a nation turned to God and asked, *Why did He not prevent this slaughter of the innocents?* I end this book with a broken heart; my eyes cannot fall upon a young child without my throat constricting and tears welling up in my eyes. I am sending this book, my baby of a year's gestation, into the world with one last question. And it is not about God's goodness and omnipotence in the presence of evil. I do not want to end this book with a discussion of theodicy.

Instead I want to end with one last question for the reader to ponder. No matter what your views are of God—of religion—of faith— might it be useful to ask one essential question about God in the wake of Newtown? *Might He be just as heartbroken about the millions of babies slaughtered in the wombs of mothers every year?* Mothers who have miscarried babies experience grief—surely God does as well.

I don't have the answer to the question I am posing. I only know that in my grief for the mothers and fathers, grandmothers and grandfathers of those twenty babies who were killed in Sandy Hook, for that is what they are only a few years removed from being, I am heartbroken. And now that I have written those words I see there is no logical reason to stop the analogy there. Once you begin that continuum you see that these six- and seven-year-old children, only a few years removed from being babies, were also only a few more months removed from being fetuses—babies in the womb. Life is a continuum, a journey—and this life is a journey to the next.

If I learned anything on my journey, and in the following months, as I considered the fate of America, it is that the tide may be turning on the lie we have as a nation been telling ourselves for the past forty years. Gallup polls reveal that abortion has been sold to Americans by the media with manipulative language like *war on women*. The public perception is skewed. When people are asked whether they think most Americans are pro-choice or pro-life, the percentage breakdown was fifty-one to thirty-five with pro-choice "winning." But the actual percentage breakdown was that forty-eight percent of Americans are pro-life, and only forty-five percent of Americans are pro-choice. In other words the perception that the media puts out is that America is overwhelmingly pro-choice—but it is not. The majority of Americans are pro-life.

The poll reveals a shift in attitude about abortion. Over the past few years America has become more and more pro-life. Americans are demanding that the truth of abortion be confronted. It is easy to avert our eyes, but those simple, heartfelt signs I saw in every state, almost every county, as I bicycled across America are proclaiming that if you believe that Americans should have the right to kill their offspring—then tell yourself, and America, and the world that truth. Those homemade signs say that if you believe that there are no responsibilities, no consequences of having sex—of joining your body with that of another person—then be honest—tell everyone that you don't like the world God created. If you are pro-choice, these signs are reminding you that you are not really for "choice"—you are instead for killing what would, within a few months, be your baby. Those "in your face happy face" signs tell us that if you are wedded to the euphemism of "choice" then let yourself and the world know that you are giving your child *no choice*. The signs I saw as I crossed the heartland of America proclaimed all those sentiments, and more, but they all boiled down to one startling and all-encompassing truth: *Your mother chose life*. The unspoken, but clear message that all those farmers in Wisconsin, Iowa, Nebraska, and Colorado wanted to convey is that the mothers of America should have the heart and the courage to give their babies that same choice—Life.

The Newtown tragedy has forced us to ask ourselves a tough question: *How did we raise a young boy who so devalued life that he was willing to mow little children down as though they were merely targets on the screen of a video game?* And once we have paused to ask that question, we do not have to travel far to ask whether we as a nation are any less offensive to God. Are we not just as guilty of wiping out the lives of hundreds, thousands, even millions of God's children for no other reason than we feel we somehow have the right to do it? *Where in the world did that "right" come from*, the sincere, probing person must surely ask.

As a nation we were founded upon the premise that our rights come from God. Did God give us the right to choose death for our offspring— or is God now irrelevant in this politically correct world that *we* have created. Has "In God We Trust" become just a motto on a coin rather than the guiding principle by which Americans live? In America we have always had people who do not depend upon God, do not worship God, and in fact deny God's existence—who believe that matter created life. But those people were not in the majority in United States of America. But now we are reaching a critical mass of people who not only deny God, but also are antagonistic toward a Godly view of life. There is a reason that among those with no religious affiliation, fully eighty percent favor abortion. Among those who identify themselves as liberals, seventy-three percent is for abortion according to a recent Gallup poll. And among those who identify themselves as Democrats, the percentage that favors abortion is sixty-two percent. Materialism, humanism, and its attendant selfishness have been increasing in America and the world for one hundred fifty years—the "what's in it for me" attitude now dominates, but it wasn't always that way.

The American idea and ideal is based on sacrifice for others. Without sacrifice and an awareness of our responsibility to future generations, it is not unreasonable to believe that we may survive only one generation, or at the most two. The end of America, I think, could come surprisingly fast. And if it does it will most likely come from within—like an overextended business or a family in deep debt, a series of blows that could be withstood if finances were plentiful will overwhelm us and we will sink into a morass of debt—in a world where too many of us are taking—a world where the sustainers and givers can no longer function.

We can still reverse the trend toward insolvency, and moral collapse, but it must be done soon. I would like to be optimistic, but we need a sea change in attitude to reverse course. At the moment those who would save us are being vilified in the press and until that changes, we are not likely to save ourselves. We are now in that terrible time spoken of in the New Testament book of Matthew—that time *when good is spoken of as evil and the evil that men do is spoken of as good.* When I read that sentence when I was a boy, I could not get my mind around how something like that could ever be—*surely we will always know right from wrong*—but now, just fifty years later, we are living in those times.

There are a lot of errors that man can overcome, but losing the ability to know what is right and what is wrong is a burden that is hard to carry. In his masterpiece of a book on morality, *East of Eden,* John Steinbeck wrote: *An unbelieved truth can hurt a man much more than a lie.* The warnings also come from the Old Testament book of Isaiah: *Woe unto them that call evil good, and good evil; that put darkness for light, and light for darkness; that put bitter for sweet, and sweet for bitter!*

Fifty years ago John Steinbeck could get away with Biblical themes in his books, but even back then the New York Times castigated him. That criticism deeply wounded Steinbeck. I think he thought it was because the editors didn't recognize his artistic talent. I don't think he ever figured out that the editors of the *New York Times* just didn't like the America and Americans that Steinbeck wrote about—their stories didn't fit the *Time's* liberal agenda then and they do not fit its liberal agenda now.

You have wearied the LORD with your words. "How have we wearied him?" you ask. By saying, "All who do evil are good in the eyes of the LORD, and he is pleased with them" or "Where is the God of justice" Even the words of the Old Testament prophet Malachi seem to speak of the press of America today and hurt our ears just as much as they hurt the ears of the people in Malachi's days.

I have sworn off the lockstep thinking of political correctness promulgated by the media of America because I saw on the eleventh of September 2012 something about our country that deeply concerned me. I realized that night as I soaked in that hot tub in West Bend, Iowa, that Americans are vulnerable—they can be lied to, just as Germans allowed themselves to be lied to. I saw that a lot of Americans preferred to turn their attention from what they knew to be true to something they wanted to be true. Libya's President informed us immediately that Islamic extremists had attacked our consulate, and he even named them, but too many Americans allowed the elite, in-the-tank-for-Obama media to divert their attention from the four murdered Americans to an unseen video and a nonexistent protest. The liberal media even used Obama's lies about Benghazi and apology to the Muslim world to attack Mitt Romney. Romney was right. Obama was wrong. Yet the American press castigated Romney, even though what Obama did, as Commander in Chief of our armed forces, was despicable.

John Steinbeck realized the dangers that can befall a nation that isn't vigilant. If you're interested read or re-read some of his books. Start with the well-known, but don't overlook books like *The Moon Is Down* that explore the corrupting influence of Nazi (National Socialist Party) thought and influence. The responsibility for what this nation, or any nation becomes, falls ultimately to the people, to the artists of a nation, to those willing to think outside the box—not to those in power. It is up to the people to hold those in power accountable.

Of all the people that I met on my American journey, one stands out as being the key to understanding America in the early part of the twenty-first-century—and that man is Harold, the unemployed father and grandfather who stopped to ask if I needed help the morning I had a flat along the beautiful Cedar River just east of Osage, Iowa. Harold talked for almost an hour about what was good and bad about America. He deplored the state of the family in America, the rising levels of children born out of wedlock, the kids being raised without a father's influence. He also was disgusted that one of our major political parties chose via a voice vote to cast God out of its platform. Harold was aware that God was still in the Democratic platform because the chair overruled the vote of the members, but that did nothing to lessen Harold's contempt for the vote and the cheering that he heard from the audience for the removal of God from the platform.

The lesson from Harold is not the conservative principles that he voiced—it is that despite his core beliefs, he was willing to cast them aside to vote for "one of mine." He thought it was more important to stand not with the person who represented his beliefs in family, country, and God, but rather to stand with the man who had an ancestor who had dark skin—not necessarily a man who had once been a slave, but a man who had come from Africa. Harold didn't say where his ancestors were from, or whether any of them had been slaves—he only said that Obama was "one of mine." I didn't, but I could have told Harold that Obama was also "one of mine," for his mother was "white as milk" according to Obama's autobiography—her ancestors came from the same part of the world as did mine, and she herself was from Kansas, a neighboring state in my Cornhusker days. But it was the black half of Obama that motivated Harold.

And it is the liberal "half" of Obama that motivates the elite media to cover for Obama. And that leads to this question: *How is it that America has been so transformed that a man who champions abortion, does not defend traditional marriage, lies to the American public, lies about his lies, ignores our increasing debt, claims ignorance about all the misdeeds uncovered in his administration, who pits Americans against Americans, and refuses to name our enemy, is the man who is apparently favored by a majority of the people who voted in 2012.* I could not have foreseen in 1962 that such a man would ever be considered for any high office or position of responsibility, let alone the presidency of the United States.

So the question must be asked—*What do those who voted for Barack Obama fear so much from the opposition that they will vote for a man so lacking in character and integrity? Why do they vote for a man who so blatantly lies to them?* Those are questions I find hard to answer, unless you accept an answer that doesn't make any sense. For a good part of the hour I visited with Harold that morning by the Cedar River, he talked of family, of the breakdown of the family, of responsibility, of kids who have none, of people working for what they receive. He sounded like a man who believed what Romney believed, yet he told me he was going to vote for Obama. If that is not racism, I don't know what racism might be. I'm sure Harold doesn't think of himself as a racist, but his vote was entirely based on Obama's heritage—and Harold's perception that Obama would therefore take care of him.

If you want to understand how it is that Barack Obama received ninety-three percent of the black vote—there it is. Despite the fact that statistically blacks in America are faring much worse economically and socially under the policies of Barack Obama than they were under those of George Bush, blacks still voted almost exclusively for Obama. That fact will someday come under scrutiny, and history will not judge Obama, or the voters well—or the press either for that matter. But that is not the immediate concern. Right now I want to understand America and Americans better. I find it interesting that we as a nation are so predictable—that the majority of us who live in the heartland are conservative and favor Mitt Romney for President. And the majority of us who live in large cities, on the east and west coasts, and in the New England states want to live under the policies of a President like Barack Obama. I sometimes wonder if it is because big government tends to reside in big cities.

You can posit that had Romney been a stronger candidate, a man willing to confront Obama on his lies about Benghazi, his weak and confusing foreign policy, his abysmal economic policies, and the fact that his party made no attempt to pass a budget in four years—then Romney would have won. Statistics bear that out. But Romney took on neither Obama nor the press, and he received fewer votes than John McCain did four years earlier against Obama. In fact, if Romney had gotten as many votes as McCain, Romney would have been elected President. Obama received significantly fewer votes in 2012 than he did in 2008.

But Obama *was* elected in 2012, in what many, on both sides, said was the most important election of their lifetime. So, what will this election mean for America? Will it be that watershed moment many have predicted? Finding an answer to that question is one of the reasons I set out on my journey across America. It coincided with the fifty-year anniversary of *Travels with Charley*, but would I have gone on this adventure if I had not felt that America was at a crossroads, a tipping point? It seems unlikely.

A couple of years ago, while writing *An Italian Journey*, I became interested in the life of Dietrich Bonhoeffer, one of the first, and almost only German to oppose Hitler. One of the farmers I had stayed with in Italy told me story after story of the devastating effects of the Nazi invasion of Italy—of what had happened in Germany and Italy during World War II. I wanted to understand how Hitler became ruler of Germany. I had naively thought that Hitler seized power. I didn't understand that Germans had elected him—they voted him into office and they kept doing it. I can't fully relate what I learned about Germany in the almost two thousand pages I read about the life of Dietrich Bonhoeffer, and those critical years in Germany's history, but I do now understand that the people of Germany weren't overthrown in one fell swoop by a monstrous dictator. It was like the story of the frog in the water that was slowly brought to a boil. At first it just felt warm. At first what Hitler was giving to Germans felt good, just like what Obama is promising to Americans now. In fact, America's stock market seems to be doing well because of the billions of dollars the Federal Reserve is flooding our economy with every month. But Obama's policy of monetizing the debt could easily lead to the same situation that created the hyperinflation of Germany's currency, that became so bad that people had to be paid daily in huge amounts of cash, so much that it took a wheelbarrow full of cash to pay for a week's worth of groceries.

I fully believe the observation by George Santayana that has become another misquoted cliché: *Those who cannot remember the past are condemned to repeat it.* "History" is usually substituted for "past," but both sentiments are powerful reminders of the dangers of overlooking the wisdom imparted by past mistakes. Powerful nations have fallen before. Powerful nations have become soft in the past. We can catch ourselves—we just need a few more million people to see the dangers of living beyond our means. The other possibility is for the national press—the elite media—to begin to recognize the dangers represented by a government gorged on political favors and paybacks like the failed Solyndra green energy fiasco that cost American taxpayers four hundred million dollars—or the dangers of the Chicago-style politics that are now found throughout Washington—or for the press to realize that *their* liberties are being eroded by an increasingly overreaching government. Rhetoric like Obama's pledge—"We're going to punish our enemies and we're going to reward our friends"—sounds good to union thugs, and liberals who don't like the politics of conservatives, but it doesn't play so well in the heartland of America. It's a terrible way to run a country, but the evidence is growing that the community-organizer-Saul-Alinsky disciple knows of no other way to govern. The IRS shakedown of conservatives reads like a page from Alinsky's playbook, *Rules for Radicals.*

Because of Romney's misplaced confidence America must now endure four more years of policies that will most likely increase our debt into the neighborhood of twenty trillion dollars. The rich will be protected by Obama's policies, but the burden of this looming financial crisis will fall on the middle class and the poor. It is always that way when the governments of the world collapse, as they inevitably do when the people in power, like Obama supporter multi-billionaire George Soros, one of the richest men in the world, get drunk on that power and overlook the responsibilities of their positions. Many argue that Obama means well. But whether he knows what he is doing or not I suspect that he is fully aware of what he and the people under him are doing;

otherwise he would be firing an awful lot of people, not promoting them. A life of irresponsibility seems to have no end. And were it not for the riots in the streets of European capitals, that fantasy might forever be perpetuated, at least until the proverbial excrement hits the fan. Our financial house of cards is getting ever closer to the giant blades of a nation-killing fan. And Obama's speechifying will have no power to save us.

My fears about the possible collapse of America are based upon the changes in America that I have observed over the past fifty years. I hope I am wrong, but I fear our moral and ethical collapse is precipitating, or tracking along with, our financial collapse. We have time to correct our course, but I fear we don't have a lot of time. Our President is acting like a college kid who has just been given a credit card with a balance and credit limit that keep increasing, and because he is making the five percent minimum payment every month he thinks he is a financial genius

But Obama's misplaced financial priorities are not the only policies that may doom America. Obama and his administration also lie to us about Islamic terrorism—for instance, refusing to call the murder of thirteen people at Fort Hood Islamic jihad—the killing of infidels while shouting "God is Great." The Tsarnaev brothers didn't shout "Allahu Akbar" as they set off their bombs in Boston that blew the legs off a dozen people, but their Facebook page proclaimed it. The leaders these young boys followed want to impose an Islamic Caliphate on this world, and the means to that end is unleashing horrific terror by blowing up people—women, children, men, babies—it does not matter. These deranged people think that the way to covert pagans to their religion is murder and mayhem. That truth must be realized.

We cannot allow political correctness and cowardice to blunt our resolve. We must demand that words carry integrity. Words have meaning and those meanings must not be lost. We must say what we mean and mean what we say. Islamic jihadist terrorists are committed to killing infidels (anyone who is not a Muslim) all over the world. To combat that threat, President George W. Bush launched a "Global War on Terror."

Even that phrase fails to fully address the perpetrators of the terrorism. But in an effort to keep words from having any meaning or reference to consequences, the phrase the Obama administration adopted for the fight against Islamic terrorists, and any other people who want to annihilate us, was "Overseas Contingency Operation." Those weasel words are misleading in at least two very important areas—they do not name the enemy, and those words ignore the fact our enemies are killing us in our own cities. Among those who wish to murder and maim us are United States citizens who are more committed to an Islamic jihad than they are to our American way of life.

It is difficult to understand why liberals don't want to admit that murderous jihad exists. Or why a liberal writing for *Salon* penned the infamous headline, "Let's hope the bomber is a white American male." That headline was refreshing in one sense; it exposed the fixation of the liberal media for blaming America. But alas, even though the murders and maiming were caused by Islamic jihadists, the mainstream media still tried to circle the wagons and proclaim that the boys were just misguided, unloved Muslims who didn't fit in with other Americans. The old "*West Side Story*—Gee Officer Krupke" defense, "I'm misunderstood." It was a new defense in 1961 when Leonard Bernstein brought the musical *West Side Story* to the big screen. *I'm a misfit, so society is to blame.* But it caught on and is an old defense now. And it is devastating society. Liberals don't like blaming individuals; they prefer to blame the collective, the American society. For some reason, blaming Americans is more palatable than blaming the collective of Islamic jihadism. In the immediate aftermath of the Boston Massacre, both Obama and Holder spent more time talking about unfair attacks on Muslims that never happened than about the Islamic jihad that had just killed or maimed over two hundred Americans.

The Boston Marathon massacre was a clarion call to begin telling the truth about the enemies that America faces. Jihad means struggle, but to the radical Islamist it becomes a Holy War seeking the imposition of a Caliphate by the killing of infidels—and it is a threat to peace-loving people all over the world. A President who lies to the American people about Islamic jihad is a threat not just to America, but also to the world. If American opposition to a Caliphate can be eliminated, imagine how fast the rest of the world will fall.

I went on the road to discover America. I spent time with strangers and old friends, and with almost every encounter I was given a reason to place my hope in the American people. The cynicism and snobbery of Washington politics, where corruption is rampant and perjury is almost never prosecuted, and the *anything goes* attitude of network television, are not the sentiments that lie in the heart of Main Street America. Good people, with a heart for helping their neighbors, are spread across this land. True, America has cancers growing, but the whole body is not diseased—only those parts of the body where power is concentrated.

I rode more than a thousand miles across America and came into contact with hundreds of Americans, and my takeaway from the journey is that America is a grand, noble, and enduring idea if we will but return to a principle that we learned soon after we learned to talk—that it is important to tell the truth. We can disagree about whether the liberal vision is better, or whether the conservative or libertarian vision is better, but we have to insist that on one thing we will not compromise—we must tell each other the truth. Only if we know the truth can we rightly govern ourselves. That is the bedrock foundation of our society. When belief in truth dies, society dies. And evil thrives.

America is showing signs of a healthy evil. We are becoming a country in moral free fall, where religious suppression is tolerance, and atheism is the de facto official religion of the state. People ask, *How does it happen that a people, a whole nation, can perpetuate evil?* Hitler did not just begin one day killing Jews. He began first by telling Jews that he was putting them in cattle cars and moving them for their own protection. And how did a whole nation fall for Hitler's lies? It happened because the press was not doing its job. Evil was covered up. Do you suppose the newspapers of Germany were writing about what awaited the Jews at the end of their train ride in cattle cars? Was the press in the 1940s writing about the murders of the Jews in gas chambers, of the lining up of Jews in front of trenches and firing at them with machine guns?

Do you suppose in America during Obama's second term that NBC, ABC, CBS, and PBS were telling the story of the abortionist in Philadelphia who severed the spinal cords of babies, pierced their brains with knives, and left them to die on cold tables? No, they didn't. It did not benefit their agenda to show abortion for what it really is—the murdering of babies. The images of all those mutilated babies discovered in the raid on that abortion clinic are hard to get out of your mind once you've seen them. Therefore those gruesome photos did not make the pages of the newspapers, nor were they shown on the evening broadcasts.

The murder trial of Kermit Gosnell has not just been buried—it has not even been mentioned by the major networks. In case you didn't hear about it, Gosnell was charged with killing one woman and four babies, although the actual number was much higher. Photographs of the dead babies and testimony of eyewitnesses revealed that Gosnell's procedure for dealing with babies who survived abortion was to sever their spinal cords at the base of the neck. The abortionist's lawyer mounted two defenses. One—the babies weren't really alive, but only appeared to be. The response of any clear-thinking person should be—*why then did this man feel the need, time and time again, to jab scissors into the neck of each baby to cut its spinal cord, if all those babies were already dead.* The heart-wrenching photographs of babies with gaping wounds in the backs of their necks tell a different, more truthful, more painful, more tear-filled story.

The second defense of the abortionist's lawyer was: *What is the difference whether the baby is killed inside the mother's womb or outside?* To which a logical person might say, *Right on counselor! Why indeed has our society deemed that we are going to allow the mothers of America, with the aid of doctors to kill their babies?* Planned Parenthood lobbyist Alisa LaPolt Snow was recently asked, "If a baby is born on a table as a result of a botched abortion, what would Planned Parenthood want to have happen to that child that is struggling for life?" She replied: "We believe that any decision that's made should be left up to the woman, her family, and the physician."

And truly, *what is the difference* whether those babies are inside the mother's womb, or lying on a cold table? Her shocking answer revealed the philosophy of Planned Parenthood unvarnished and closely followed the Obama mantra, which he delivered to a Planned Parenthood convention a few weeks later. President Obama's speech was broken up by dozens of applause lines, and the audience was more than willing to accommodate him: "The only person who should make decisions about your health is you." (Applause)."So the fact is, after decades of progress, there's still those who want to turn back the clock to policies more suited to the 1950s than the twenty-first century." (Applause) "And they've been involved in an orchestrated and historic effort to roll back rights when it comes to women's health. Forty two states have introduced laws that would ban or severely limit a woman's right to choose. (Applause) When you read about some of these laws, you want to check your calendar; you want to make sure you're still living in 2013." (Laughter and applause)

Few in the audience apparently noted that the speech was littered with misstatements, misrepresentations, and euphemisms; not once was the word "abortion" uttered, not once was the reality of mothers killing their offspring addressed. And of course it needs to be noted that even the word "abortion" is a euphemism for the cold hard fact that a future human being is killed during an abortion. Also, not one word was uttered that night nor has one since been uttered publicly by President Obama about the murders of babies by abortionist Kermit Gosnell.

The parallel between Gosnell, the Nazis, and the reaction of the press and much of the public is striking. The murder case brings to mind the Nazi doctor Josef Mengele, whose nickname was "Angel of Death." His job at Auschwitz was to determine who lived and who died, who was experimented on, and who was sent to work in labor camps. Mengele drew a line on the wall of the children's cellblock one hundred-fifty centimeters (about five feet) from the floor and children whose heads did not reach the line were sent to the gas chambers to be killed. Mengele also performed operations without anesthetic; he did such things as removing parts of the stomachs of his "patients," and at least once he even removed the heart of a Jew without anesthesia. Another striking thing about Mengele was that he showed no remorse for the gruesome experiments he performed on the Jewish people. The same seems true of Doctor Gosnell. He kept trophies in his office—of the babies he killed.

When Gosnell's abortion clinic was raided, investigators found five jars filled with formaldehyde containing the severed feet of babies in Doctor Gosnell's office. Gosnell joked to his staff about one baby as he was killing it, "This one is so big he could have walked me to the bus stop." Another baby was born into a toilet, and the "nurse" who had been assisting the pregnant woman reported that the baby began swimming motions in an effort to escape its watery death.

As I've followed this trial in which Gosnell is charged with killing fetuses more than twenty-four weeks after conception, and some as many as twenty-eight weeks, the thought hit me that those fetuses are at six and seven months—close to full term. And that thought takes me back to the story of four-year-old Colton Burpo meeting his never-been-born sister. The sister who welcomed Colton to Heaven was in her mother's womb for only eight weeks before she was miscarried—a total of two months. Who in this society of ours, besides God and mothers who miscarry, take notice of two-month-old fetuses?

The Gosnell murder trial began in March 2013, but during the first two months ABC, CBS, NBC, and PBS ignored it. But some light may finally be shining on this story now that spring has come. Fox News covered it from the beginning. A couple of liberal commentators, most notably Kirsten Powers, noticed the blackout by the elite media and called out her liberal colleagues. The mainstream media can ignore everyone except one of their own, so they are now repackaging the truth to come up with excuses for the reasons for the blackout. But Powers called it what it was—a trial that showed the gruesome reality of "choice" to the world. The light she cast on the grisly facts of the trial exposed the liberal bias of the mainstream press. She shamed the New York Times and the major networks. And now the people who get their news only from NFM (the non-Fox media) are slowly becoming aware of the atrocities being committed in Philadelphia in the name of "a woman's right to choose."

Abraham Lincoln declared his faith in the American people and in the power of truth—proclaiming that Americans have the strength of character to handle the truth. Truth, he insisted, was essential to a free and open society. I doubt that he could have foreseen today's politically charged climate in which the truth of a statement is determined not by whether the statement is in fact true, but whether someone from your political party has said it. Lincoln was confident that we could survive as a nation as long as we remained vigilant and demanded that our leaders have the courage to tell Americans the truth.

Many of the people I met on my American journey believe that Barack Obama is the enemy. But I don't see it that way. President Obama is just the poster child for liberalism and political correctness run amok. He reminds me of that great icon of the mid-twentieth century America that has been with us these past fifty plus years—the philosophy of Alfred E. "What, Me Worry?" Neuman. Obama is like a *Mad Magazine* parody of a President. In fact, he and Neuman bear an eerily striking resemblance—Alfred Edsel Neuman and Barack Hussein Obama—both in appearance and attitude.

Consequences? What consequences? Sixteen trillion—twenty-one trillion dollars of debt? What, me worry? No problem—we'll just keep printing money! The IRS targeting conservative groups? "I knew nothing. I first learned about it when you did, in the same news reports." "If Sasha and Malia get themselves pregnant? Why would I want to punish them with a baby?" I'll get them an abortion. Consequences are for people living in the dark ages of the mid-twentieth century. "Check your calendar." It's time for a new morality—for "a fundamental transformation of America!"

If America fails, falls, or falters, the fault will lie with the willingness of the American people to lie to themselves and their willingness to accept the lies of others, and not with what one person has done to America. We have done it to ourselves. We have allowed too many people to feed us false narratives—that it is okay to kill our offspring in the womb, even outside of it, and that Islamic jihadists are not our enemy. But if we tell ourselves the truth about these grave matters and everything else, and act on that truth, America will not only survive, it will thrive. And we can take comfort in knowing that we thrive because we had the courage and conviction to heed the warnings of Pogo: *We have met the enemy, and he is us.*

Winston Churchill, that great leader of wartime England, noted, "The truth is incontrovertible. Malice may attack it, ignorance may deride it, but in the end, there it is."

John Steinbeck also knew the importance of our nation holding onto truth. His search for a title for his book about the plight of America in the Dust Bowl of the 1930s led him to *The Battle Hymn of the Republic* by Julia Ward Howe. In fact it was his wife who gave him the idea, which he felt turned out to be the best title of any of his books. But Steinbeck knew that the importance of truth in the struggle for freedom would be lost on readers if they didn't understand the context. So he asked that the lyrics be printed on the inside covers of his book to help his readers fully understand his reasons for naming his book about freedom *The Grapes of Wrath.*

The publisher didn't fully understand Steinbeck's reasoning and printed the galley with just the stanza in which the phrase "grapes of wrath" appeared. Despite staunch resistance from Viking, his New York publisher, Steinbeck insisted that the words from every stanza be printed in the front and back of his book. He wanted none of his readers to miss the fact that the title for his definitive book about the struggle of America to survive had come from the popular American song that had helped preserve the United States of America during the Civil War. For the same reasons I am also including all of the stanzas as I conclude my story about my journey *in search of America and Americans.* I feel these words apply as much to the problems of Julia Ward Howe's time and Tom Joad/John Steinbeck's time, as they do to ours in the twenty-first century. America is unique in the world, and this song captures our nation's essence.

The Battle Hymn of the Republic

Mine eyes have seen the glory of the coming of the Lord:
He is trampling out the vintage where the grapes of wrath are stored;
He hath loosed the fateful lightning of His terrible swift sword:
His truth is marching on.

Glory, glory, hallelujah!
Glory, glory, hallelujah!
Glory, glory, hallelujah!
His truth is marching on.

I have seen Him in the watch-fires of a hundred circling camps,
They have builded Him an altar in the evening dews and damps;
I can read His righteous sentence by the dim and flaring lamps:
His day is marching on.

Glory, glory, hallelujah!
Glory, glory, hallelujah!
Glory, glory, hallelujah!
His day is marching on.

I have read a fiery gospel writ in burnished rows of steel:
"As ye deal with my contemners, so with you my grace shall deal;
Let the Hero, born of woman, crush the serpent with his heel,
Since God is marching on."

Glory, glory, hallelujah!
Glory, glory, hallelujah!
Glory, glory, hallelujah!
His truth is marching on.

He has sounded forth the trumpet that shall never call retreat;
He is sifting out the hearts of men before His judgment-seat:
Oh, be swift, my soul, to answer Him! Be jubilant, my feet!
Our God is marching on.

Glory, glory, hallelujah!
Glory, glory, hallelujah!
Glory, glory, hallelujah!
Our God is marching on.

In the beauty of the lilies Christ was born across the sea,
With a glory in His bosom that transfigures you and me:
As He died to make men holy, let us die to make men free,
While God is marching on.

Glory, glory, hallelujah!
Glory, glory, hallelujah!
Glory, glory, hallelujah!
Our God is marching on.

He is coming like the glory of the morning on the wave,
He is Wisdom to the mighty; He is Succour to the brave,
So the world shall be His footstool, and the soul of Time His slave,
Our God is marching on.

Glory, glory, hallelujah!
Glory, glory, hallelujah!
Glory, glory, hallelujah!
Our God is marching on.

Truth, consequences, and freedom—those concepts are the bedrock principles of *The Battle Hymn of the Republic*. It was one of Sir Winston Churchill's favorite songs and was played at his funeral in St Paul's Cathedral in 1965. It was also sung on September 14, 2001, at the Washington National Cathedral and at St Paul's Cathedral in London during memorial services for the victims of the September 11 attacks. The Marine Corps Band performed it when President George W. Bush greeted Pope Benedict XVI on the South Lawn of the White House on April 16, 2008. Martin Luther King's final sermon, "I've Been to the Mountaintop," delivered on the evening of April 3, 1968, the night before his assassination, ends with the first line of Julia Ward Howe's memorable song: *Mine eyes have seen the glory of the coming of the Lord*. The words of *The Battle Hymn of the Republic* are often sung at Presidential funerals, such as Ronald Reagan's in 2004, and at Presidential inaugurations, including that of President Barack Obama on January 21, 2013—although it is probably significant that the stanzas mentioning consequences were not sung.

The Battle Hymn of the Republic is an American institution. Its words should be neither ignored nor forgotten. We cannot allow history to be rewritten. This song captures the spiritual foundation of America. Tell the truth or face the consequences. When I was young there was a popular television program called *Truth or Consequences*. Do even our game shows tell us who we are? Today we watch *Who Wants to be a Millionaire?* But in my childhood *Truth of Consequences* was a game show and it was also a concept that we clearly understood.

Another game show from my childhood was *To Tell the Truth* in which two of the three contestants were allowed to lie and the third was sworn to tell the truth. The panelists had to determine which contestant was telling the truth. If only we could get our leaders and the people of the media to accept the premise that they must tell the truth and that those who are not telling the truth will be exposed!

Today, those who are sworn to uphold the Constitution, and are under oath to tell the truth, do not in fact tell the truth—to Congress or to the American people—and they are not given any consequences for their lies. At least not yet have those who lied to the American people and to Congress about Benghazi been held accountable. Instead of truth, Congress and the American people were subjected to an indignant, arm-waving, desk-pounding tirade: *We have four dead Americans. Was it because of a protest or because of guys out for a walk one night who decided they'd go kill some Americans? What difference, at this point, does it make, Senator?*

Yes, Madame Secretary Hillary Clinton, *what difference, at this point, does it make* that people tell the truth? You have lied for all these months about Benghazi. You even hugged the next of kin of Christopher Stevens, Sean Smith, Tyrone Woods, and Glen Doherty and whispered in their ears that you will bring to justice the maker of the "non-event" video that you blamed for their deaths. If Dante was right about the hierarchical nature of the next life, there must be a special place in the *Inferno* for the person who knowingly and willfully lies to the grieving widows, mothers, fathers, brothers, sisters, and children of fallen heroes.

So yes, instead of a made-for-TV moment in response to Senator Ron Johnson's probing question, go to the families of those four murdered

Americans and wave your arms and yell, "What difference does it make who killed them?" And they will most likely tell you that indeed it does make a difference who did it and why, and they may well ask, "Could more have been done to protect them?"

Ask the surviving family members of any murder if it makes a difference who killed their loved one and why. There is no statute of limitation on grief. And there is no statute of limitation on truth. Truth is the one thing, above all others, that parents whose sons or daughters have been murdered most desperately seek.

But as this book goes to print the families of those four murdered men have not been told the truth, nor have those "guys" been brought to justice. The truth, with the aid of the mainstream media, was kept from those families and from the American voters during the election of 2012, and the loved ones of those four young men and the American people are still being kept in the dark about that infamous day in American history.

If our enemy is among us, we can only know about it and protect ourselves if we demand that the people who serve us tell the truth. Not only is it incumbent that the members of the media and those serving us in government tell us the truth, they must also actively seek it, whether they are an Independent, a Democrat, or a Republican. The number of major news organizations that were looking for and telling us the truth about Benghazi, was so few that the Obama administration, in classic Saul Alinsky Chicago-style politics, was able to get away with painting those who were telling the truth as liars. President Obama lied about his lies. That is a dangerous minefield for a country to step into, but that is exactly where America found itself following the murder, mutilation, and abandonment of Christopher Stevens, Sean Smith, Tyrone Woods, and Glen Doherty.

The consequences of truth—and the courage to call things what they are—still stands as our greatest ally in the fight to preserve America and its freedoms. To fight our enemy we have to know our enemy.

The title is not "The Battle Hymn of the Democracy" but instead *The Battle Hymn of the Republic*—there is a huge, distinctive difference, one worth fighting for, and as the song says, dying for. Majority does not make right—we are a unique nation of laws and principles. Julia Ward Howe wrote *The Battle Hymn of the Republic* in November 1861, when America was involved in a bloody and contentious battle known as the Civil War. We are in no less of a battle today. A battle in which, just as in the Civil War, legs are blown off, and people are killed. This time the carnage, while not yet as widespread, seems even more brutal. This time a little freckle-faced eight-year-old boy was killed, and the sister of that boy lost a leg. And it is not just happening overseas, it is happening right here on our American streets. And not because that boy and that girl had anything against Muslims, but just because they were enjoying a very American thing—cheering for their father, who was crossing the finish line of that iconic American footrace, the Boston Marathon. That is the named enemy we face—an enemy who would blow to pieces a precious family—and the sooner our President and our press have the courage to name our enemy, the sooner we can protect ourselves from the unfathomable horrors this enemy inflicts.

But to defeat this enemy America needs to become a nation that rebuilds itself on the foundation of truth. We need to not just sing every verse of *The Battle Hymn of the Republic;* we must take to heart every verse of *The Battle Hymn of the Republic.* It can remind us that we are once again engaged in a battle, it can help us know the enemy, it can help us know ourselves, and it can help us know who else is fighting on the side of truth and freedom. Every stanza of that song serves as a reminder of the importance of the bedrock principle of truth-telling in our nation's struggle to remain a free nation.

And that's how this traveler came home from his American journey, with a burdened heart, but also with an expectant heart that within America still exists a courageous core of citizens who once again are going to rise up and insist that yes indeed, it *does* make a difference—*at this point*—that truth be told.

And if for some reason those courageous citizens for whom truth is a battle cry do not prevail—we have history to teach us that lesson as well.

ABOUT THE AUTHOR

James Ernest Shaw lives and writes from small-town America,
along the shore of a spring-fed lake, in the heart of what
John Steinbeck called *the prettiest state I ever saw.*
He and his wife, Mardi, divide their time
among their five children
and eight grandchildren.

www.facebook.com/AmericanJourney
www. facebook.com/ItalianJourney
www.JamesErnestShaw.com

WITHDRAWN

CPSIA information can be obtained at www.ICGtesting.com
Printed in the USA
LVOW07s1633010915

452382LV00003B/529/P